MADNESS MADE ME

This memoir sucks the reader in from the first page. Mary's story, from the psychiatric ward to the United Nations, offers hope to the millions who are told their emotional pain is an irreversible brain disorder.

John Read, Professor of Clinical Psychology,
University of Liverpool, author of *Models of Madness*.

An incredible tour de force. Mary replaces the narrative of psychopathology with the subversive idea that there may be value in madness. Everyone should read this beautifully written, ground-breaking book.

Rachel Perkins, mental health service user and co-author of
Inclusion and Recovery: A Model for Mental Health Practice.

Mary invites us into her life on her fascinating path from serious distress to thriving. A privilege to read with a brilliant ending.

Fran Silvestri, President and CEO, International
Initiative for Mental Health Leadership.

MADNESS MADE ME

MARY O'HAGAN

Published by
Open Box
PO Box 6627, Marion Square, Wellington 6011
New Zealand

This edition published 2014

The right of Mary O'Hagan to be identified
as the author of this work in terms of section 96 of the Copyright Act
1994 is hereby asserted.

Designed, typeset and produced by Mary Egan Publishing
www.maryegan.co.nz
Cover designed by George Connor
Printed in New Zealand

ISBN 978-0-473-27980-6

*In memory of Judi Chamberlin (1944–2010), who
introduced me to the mad movement.*

AUTHOR'S NOTE

Madness Made Me is a patchwork of fragments that I have collected from my own writings and memories, arranged with some creative licence and stitched into a narrative. I chose fragments which best served the big message of this book – madness is a profoundly disruptive and full human experience that deserves respect. This memoir doesn't tell *the* whole story or even *my* whole story; it simply exposes a vein of knowledge based on my lived experience that cuts through the rock of conventional truths about madness.

I use the word 'madness' throughout this book. Readers may wonder why I use a word that carries centuries of prejudice. Why not use the term 'mental illness'? The problem is there are no words that describe us as equal to others, either in ordinary language or in professional discourse. Even if some of the words started off as neutral they have become polluted by pervasive stigma. In response to this, some of us have reclaimed the word 'madness' – we have removed it from the trash can of insults and polished it to reveal a unique pattern of human experiences.

I am highly critical of the mental health system and this may be discomforting to some readers. Most who work in mental health services do their best within the confines of their own mental models and the circumstances they are placed in. I don't know if I would do any better in their shoes. I have no desire to publicly identify the people I encountered and have done my best to preserve their anonymity by altering the details of places and events, by morphing or merging their characters and changing most people's names. The exceptions are my parents, John and Clare; my siblings Sean, Shonagh, Lucy, Dominic and Liam; my cousin Diana; my uncle Pat; my sister-in-law Asi; my niece Siobhan; and my children, Ruby, Felix and Rupert. In Chaper 9, I use the real names of Peter McGeorge, Titewhai Harawira and Carrington Hospital because the events surrounding them are in the public domain. In Chapter 10, I mention psychiatrist Nancy Andreasen by her real name because the title of her book is featured in a public discussion I write about. In Chapter 11, I name newspaper columnist Michael Bassett. I also use the real names of some of my colleagues in the mad movement whose words I quote: they are Judi Chamberlin, Debbie Noble, Rod Davis, Corinne, Mari Yamamoto, Kate Millet, Howie the Harp, Flick Grey and Tina Minkowitz. All other names that appear in this book have been changed.

CONTENTS

PROLOGUE:

THE WAY IT WAS

I'm locked inside a black box.

I've hidden the blackness all my life hoping there is a purpose to everything. I've painted the walls with false windows and a view of a grand universe. I've drawn fake pictures of a life worth living. I've built a pretend door that leads into a promising future.

Now all the decorations are gone. The bare boards have closed in on me with the terrible truth that life is a sham. It started when I couldn't see the point in going to my university lectures. Then I couldn't bring myself to see my friends. Now I don't see the point in being alive.

I've been in bed for days with my door shut and the curtains drawn. My whole being is screaming at my discovery that life is a sham. I struggle to put a thought or a sentence together. I can't talk. I can barely move. My chest burns and I rasp with shallow breathing. Sleep comes in broken snatches.

I wake. It must be daytime because light is seeping through the gap in the curtains. I stare at the clock and slowly realise the day and the time. With enormous effort I leave my bed and crawl down the road to my next appointment with Dr L'Estrange. I crouch in front of him like a snapped stem. After a long silence, he says, 'You need to go into hospital.'

←———※

I'd been seeing Dr L'Estrange on and off for two years before the black box completely closed its lid on me. I met him first in the winter during my second year at university. I felt zoned out, slowed down and desolate. I couldn't eat. My friends told me I was getting too thin, so I tried to force two bowls of porridge down my throat every morning. I sat there, gagging as I pushed the paste into my mouth. I told my friends I thought I had a fatal wasting disease. They looked concerned and told me to go to the doctor.

Student Health was in an old wooden building near the campus. I sat in the waiting room wondering what to say to Dr Beecham so she didn't think I was wasting her time, when a middle-aged woman in an out-of-shape knitted beige suit called my name. She sat behind a big old desk and looked at me with bloodhound eyes.

'I've lost my appetite,' I told her, cringing at my pettiness, as if I'd come to moan about a broken finger nail or a sandfly bite. I waited for her to raise her eyes to the ceiling and tell me to stop bothering her, but she started probing me about how I'd been feeling. I wasn't sure what this had to do with my fatal wasting disease.

'I feel gloomy and slowed down.'

'Have you felt like this before?'

'Yeah, last year when I thought I was being possessed by a spirit that was telling me to kill myself and other people as well.'

The doctor looked at me as though I'd said something of great significance. I could see I'd just talked my way into a trap labelled 'psychiatric'.

'You can't eat because you're depressed. Normally I would just prescribe you anti-depressants but your case is complex. I'd like you to see the psychiatrist here, Dr L'Estrange. Today if possible.'

That afternoon I walked up the stairs at Student Health into Dr L'Estrange's office. It was a big room with a boarded-up fireplace, two leather chairs and a desk in the corner. Dr L'Estrange sat holding my file. He was a small serious man with a beard and glasses, smoking a pipe. He looked like Sigmund Freud. He motioned me to sit down and peered at me with intense blue eyes.

Dr L'Estrange asked me about my appetite, sleep, mood and any weird experiences I'd had. He asked me about the spirit that wanted me to kill. Then he got onto my mother and father, siblings, friends, kindergarten, school, university, sex, drugs and religion.

Dr L'Estrange leant forward and made a circular gesture with his pipe in his hand. 'Can you tell me, when do you think this all started?'

I sat in silence, wondering where to begin.

1.

BECOMING ME

There are many stories that tell of where madness comes from. Some of the stories are as ancient as madness itself while others were not told until my generation came of age. A few of the stories are as well known as nursery rhymes but some are unique to the teller. There are the official stories and the subversive ones, the stigmatising stories and the heroic ones. There are my stories and other people's stories. So many stories, because no one really knows where madness comes from.

There are far fewer stories about sanity because it gets less attention than madness. Sanity is hardly ever described – it is too pervasive, too ordinary to get noticed much. Sanity is the dominant culture of the mind. Like the dominant culture of a country, sanity is usually blind to itself, until it notices a different culture in its midst. Sanity only starts to have meaning when it is breached through madness, just as day only has meaning because there is night.

The return to sanity, sometimes called recovery, also gets less attention than madness. Most mad people who tell or write their stories say much more about their madness than their return from it. And the psychiatric story, in its creation of madness as a chronic condition, does not seriously seek answers to the origins of sanity or recovery, which is why mental health professionals like Dr L'Estrange do not ask about them. Add to this the architecture of human story-making: how stories built on a blueprint of loss, hardship or a fall from grace are more compelling than stories that spring from good fortune or well-being.

But sanity, madness and the return to sanity all deserve the same amount of attention because they cannot exist without each other. The conventional wisdom says madness and sanity can never meet over the wall that divides them. But I cannot see the origins of my madness and my sanity as two parallel stories; they are one story in two dimensions. Madness and sanity are not two different garments; they are the warp and weft of the same fabric.

Maybe it all started on a frosty night during the winter of 1957 in a garage bed-sit in Dunedin on the south-east coast of New Zealand.

My young parents, Clare and John, tucked my older brother Sean into his cot for the night. 'Oh, he's been lovely today,' said Clare.

They huddled in front of a one-bar heater for the evening, while Clare folded the washing and John read a medical text book.

'Time for bed,' Clare called holding the hottie.

They got into bed, under a portrait of the Virgin Mary, and held each other shivering, laughing, fighting for the hottie. Then they looked into each other's eyes, their pulse quickened, they ached with desire, and the gate to the great lottery of human creation was opened.

While they slept, millions of my father's sperm thrashed through the dark landscape of my mother's womb, into the long narrow passage where my mother's egg waited to let one of them in.

But the story of me didn't just begin that night, with the fusion of my parent's genes. The story of me, and the story of everyone, started millions of years ago in a cave in Africa where the first humans lived. They passed on their genes like microscopic batons through thousands of generations. Until they made me.

Among the genes I inherited were ones that give me the capacity to imagine unseen worlds, experience existential terror, hibernate, go into overdrive and make rogue leaps of creativity. These are the genes that gave me the capacity for the state of being now called madness. They could have been useful to my ancestors in the caves, but these genes are now considered surplus to requirements.

Days after the fusion of my genes, I bedded myself into my mother's womb, ready to take her blood. With every pulse she made me more human. In the red-tinted darkness, she planted the seeds of my sanity and madness, when she drenched my cells with her blood, thick with nutrients, laced with nicotine and early-evening gin.

'I'm pregnant,' my mother whispered to my father.

He kissed her on the cheek. 'A little playmate for Sean.'

By the time I was expelled from my mother's womb into the harsh bright world, my parents and Sean had left their garage bed-sit in Dunedin to live in a roughcast bungalow close to the bottom of the world in a rural town called Winton.

My mother held me, and my father came into the delivery room as they gazed at me for the first time. Two weeks later she wrapped me up and took me home. She stayed at home most of the time with me and Sean, while my father drove to work in his pale-green Volkswagen with a brown leather case full of bandages, bottles and syringes. Over the next few years she gave birth to my sisters Shonagh and Lucy.

⟷

Maybe it started when my parents abandoned me to the care of others.

Every Tuesday and Friday morning my mother walked two blocks to kindergarten while I rode my tricycle. As we got inside the gate, Miss Castle took my hand and my mother turned to go home.

'Don't go,' I whined tugging at her coat.

'Darling, I've got to go. I'll see you at lunchtime.'

She released her coat from my fingers and retreated from me while I sank with desolation. Miss Castle told me to play with the kids. I played alone in the sandpit.

One day I saw a boy leave early with his mother. Leaving looked easy. I could do it too. The kids were flying around me and Miss Castle was busy inside. I ran to the other side of the building, seized my tricycle, opened the gate, and pedalled as fast as I could down the footpath towards home. My thin legs whizzed. My heart galloped. For a moment I was exhilarated at my power to escape and terrified that Miss Castle would come and catch me.

Then it happened.

My tricycle and I lurched off the footpath into the gutter. I lay there with a skinned knee, crying in pain and humiliation. Miss Castle came running towards me, yelling, 'Come back here!' She told me I was a naughty girl and locked me in her office with a book about firemen. I sat with the book on my knee and cried until my mother arrived at lunchtime.

Then, when I was five, my parents left me at the hospital to have my tonsils taken out. Under the bright lights I lay on my back. All I could see were gowns and masks, eyes that belonged to no one, dials, steel and a little oval cup-like thing coming towards my face. 'Count to ten,' a voice said. I got to two. Through the blackness I heard the cold snipping of scissors.

I woke in a strange bed in a room I'd never seen before. Brisk nurses walked past me, too busy to see my anguish.

'Where's my mummy?' I squeaked.

'She's busy. They'll be in later to see you. Now be a good girl and lie down, please.'

I vomited red stuff onto the floral carpet. It landed tidily on a burgundy rose where the nurses couldn't see it.

All afternoon my throat burned and I cried unnoticed, until I saw my parents at the door.

←——————→

Maybe it started when my parents tried to protect me from the hardness of the world.

It was my first year at primary school on a cold Saturday afternoon. Sean and I put our coats and gumboots on, while my parents coaxed Shonagh into the pushchair and laid Lucy in the pram. We both ran ahead, down the new concrete footpath, round the corner to the

Centennial Park and straight to the red and yellow merry-go-round.

We grabbed the bars and pushed. A big boy with blond hair came over and started pushing with us, until we were running so fast my legs couldn't keep up. I jumped on. The boys kept pushing. The wind lashed my face and everything looked streaky. I yelled with delight.

I heard my father shouting at us to be careful. I felt the thud as the boys jumped on. I felt the blond boy crash into me. I felt my face smash onto the bar. My delight flipped into terror. Screaming, I jumped off without letting go of the bar, and the spinning ground upended my feet. As I was falling, an arm grabbed me round the middle, and a large hand grabbed the bar and slowed the merry-go-round to a stop. My father picked me and held me but I kicked and screamed so much he had to let me go. He and my mother crouched around me with their arms out, as I stamped on the spot, and ran around bellowing in crazed circles. For a few moments nothing existed but the pain in my face. Then the world came into view, and I collapsed into my parents' arms.

Some years later my mother sheltered me from Mrs Glower the discipline mistress at my high school. Mrs Glower was a tall woman who swooped around the quad in her black cloak like a hawk. Once or twice every week my name was called out to go and see Mrs Glower after morning break. I lined up behind all the other naughty kids outside her office, trying to look defiant, but my knees shook and sweat poured down the insides of my arms.

Mrs Glower loomed over me. 'Where were you on Friday afternoon?'

'I went to Dunedin with my father to see my grandmother. She's had a stroke.'

'You had no right to do that, and your parents should know better,' she spat at me. 'I'm giving you detention.'

She locked me in a classroom at lunchtime and told me to iron dozens of grey school rompers. In my fury I nearly hurled the iron through the window. I did the worst ironing job I could without having to repeat my detention. I tossed the rompers in the basket, all crinkled around the edges with a grudging small smooth patch in the middle of each one.

I hated Mrs Glower for the way she ripped into me and my family, for taking my freedom away, and for insisting that her petty heartless commands were more important than looking after my grandmother. I went home in tears and my mother hugged me saying Mrs Glower had gone too far and I had done nothing wrong.

←———→

Maybe it started when my parents took us from our homeland to a cold crowded country I didn't know.

We docked at Southampton on a foggy morning and caught the train to Edinburgh. Hours later we stood outside a grim row of terraced houses.

'This isn't a proper house,' I wailed.

The building was made of thick brown stone blocks dusted with soot. It was joined up with all the other houses and it was so tall I could hardly see the top of it. For a moment, as the clouds moved behind the big building, it looked like it was swaying, about to fall on top of us. We climbed four flights of grey stone stairs to the top flat. When my mother opened the door I saw a small empty space. I opened my mouth and wailed again. I wanted to go back to our roughcast bungalow with the big lawn and the sun. I wanted to go back to my real home.

A few days later, my mother walked Sean and I to the local school, a severe, cold-looking place with no grass and a black iron fence with spikes. My teacher was severe and cold-looking too, with a red nose and a pinched old face. I gagged on my pallid school lunches of fish fingers, boiled potatoes and translucent cabbage. Pale children with strange accents ran around the playground in the weak sun, while I stood in the shadows longing for the big school paddock and the places I knew.

I wrote postcards to my grandparents telling them I couldn't wait to get home. Somehow the memory of my grandmother with her big bottom and her walking stick, and of my grandfather tickling us with his two-fingered hand, kept calling me back.

One night in the flat, while he was drying the dishes, my father said, 'Lead can make people really sick – especially young children because they go around sucking things and exploring with their mouths.'

'It's frightening,' said my mother.

They looked serious and nodded at each other.

This was my opportunity to get sick again, so that people would notice all was not right with me.

I found a pencil and lay on my bed sucking the end of it for hours. I imagined my parents coming into my room in the morning, finding me groaning in pain, calling the ambulance, holding my hand as I was rushed to the hospital, standing by my bed while the doctors inspected me, and fussing over me when I got home.

But I woke feeling fine the next morning. I lost faith in my pencil and I couldn't understand why sucking on so much lead hadn't made me sick, until I learnt several years later that my parents were talking about lead in old house paint.

After several months in Edinburgh, we went to live in Hertfordshire. Sean and I didn't want to be English. We didn't want to be pale, polite children who spoke in la-de-da voices and played nothing rougher than conkers. But it would be another two years until I saw Mount Taranaki on the west coast of New Zealand rising out of the sea on my eighth birthday.

'We're home!' I yelled. My family joined me on the deck.

I stood there, full of wonder at the gleaming white mountain, at the deep green paddocks and the bright sun; full of joy and pride that this was my land and I would soon return to my grandparents and our roughcast bungalow with the big lawn.

←——————×

Maybe it started back in the school with the big paddock when the rigours of the confessional burdened my conscience.

Sister Mary Aloysius marched our class in rows of two down the path by the paddock, across the main road to the old brick church. The winter sun flickered between the clouds. As we filed in, patches of coloured light wavered in the gloom. We dipped our fingers into the moulded plaster shell of holy water and made the sign of the cross. We walked down the centre aisle, genuflected and sat in the front left-hand pews. Father Dempsey ambled into a wooden box to the side of the altar and a kid went into the box through another door.

I started to recite my list of sins in preparation. 'I didn't do the dishes. I stole a rubber. I swore.' It was the same list every time. But recently there had been another sin I was too scared to confess.

I had committed this sin when Sean and I were at the creek eeling after school one day. He was downstream when I saw an eel lying on the opposite bank. I waded over to get it, eager to impress my brother. Three boys from school got to the eel while I was still knee deep in water.

'Hey, I found that eel before you,' I said. 'Give it to me.'

Terry Laverty held the eel up and grinned at me. 'Only if you pull down your pants first.'

I wanted the eel so much I pulled down my pants. The boys laughed and whistled. I was starting to enjoy this.

'Hey, I'll even do a wee for you.' I giggled so much the wee splashed the inside of my thighs, and on my pants and shorts which I was forcing forward with my hands. The boys rocked and whooped as my wee disappeared down the creek.

I pulled up my pants and shorts and waded towards them.

'Now give me my eel please.' Terry dropped it in the mud and ran away.

I washed my trophy and ran with it to show Sean.

'Hey Sean, I got you an eel,' I yelled.

He took it. 'Yuk, it's rotten,' and he threw it into the creek.

The next day Terry Laverty and his friends told the kids at school that I'd pulled down my pants and done a wee. Everyone laughed at me and called me rude. I felt ashamed and wondered if I had committed a mortal sin.

My mother found out. 'I don't think it was a good idea to do that. You must have really wanted that eel,' she said, looking up from her book.

'Is it a mortal sin?'

'Not at all,' she laughed, squeezing me with her free arm.

But I still felt humiliated.

It took me two years to work out how to confess my big sin without subjecting myself to the shame again. In the darkness of the confessional I added as casually as I could to my usual list that I had been rude. Thankfully, Father Dempsey didn't seem to notice the gravity of my admission and gave me the same penance as usual – three Hail Marys at each station of the cross.

←——————→

Maybe it started when, at ten, I experienced my first big loss. The kind of loss that carves trenches of despair into neural memory.

My mother and I were bathing my baby cousin Diana. We both cooed at the baby and gently lapped the water up to her chin. 'You know, Mum, I really like babies.'

'Well, I've got some news for you darling. I'm having a baby in the winter.'

I was overjoyed. The summer and autumn dragged on and I waited and waited and waited. My mother's due date came and went and still I waited. Then on a frosty morning she got up and told us the baby was coming. My father took her to the maternity home.

'Please come and tell us at school when it's born,' I pleaded with my father.

I was so excited I couldn't concentrate on my school work. The bell went for morning break and as I went outside into the playground I saw my father walking towards the school. He smiled and said, 'You have a new brother. His name is Dominic.'

He took the four of us to see our new brother at the maternity home – Sean, me, Shonagh and Lucy. The baby was small and pink with black hair and I loved him immediately. That evening I played on the street and boasted about the baby while my father celebrated inside with gin and friends.

The next evening the celebrating continued, as Sean and I snuggled on the vinyl sofa with my father and a big bag of pineapple lumps, to watch a black-and-white war movie on TV. A big tall general called Montgomery was saluting a whole lot of tanks crawling through the desert.

'Monty was a great general,' said my father.

'Did Uncle Pat know Monty when he was in the war?' Sean asked.

My father laughed. 'It was a big war. Pat was one of the little fellas. Anyway he was flying planes over Europe.' Then he tickled us to distract us, so we wouldn't see him take the last two pineapple lumps out of the bag.

Sean spotted him. 'Hey, they're not yours.' And we both started to wrestle him on the sofa.

We were all laughing and yahooing when the phone rang. My father untangled himself to answer it and gave us a pineapple lump each.

Monty's tanks were getting blown up in the desert by the Germans. Bodies were lying everywhere. Monty looked grim. 'We will win this battle, chum, we will win it,' he said to another soldier.

Then I heard my father say, 'Has he gone blue? I'll be down right away.'

My father turned towards us and looked grim, like Monty. He called a babysitter, tucked us into bed and drove to the maternity home. I was too scared to ask him what was wrong.

The next morning my father woke me. 'The baby's gone to hospital in town because he needs to be in an incubator. There is something wrong with his heart.'

'Will he be OK?' I asked.

'I don't know,' he said, turning away.

I sat in front of the heater, where I always got dressed in the winter, and cried with a sadness I had never known before. My father was busy with the other children, and kept telling me to hurry up and get dressed.

Three days later my father came home and held me. He told me that Dominic had gone to heaven. He took all the baby things out of the house so my mother wouldn't get too upset.

The house started to fill up. My mother arrived first and we had a cry together. Then a procession of sad-looking people came to our door with soup and flowers. In the afternoon my grandparents arrived with a car full of food and drink. We rushed outside as my grandmother inched herself and her walking stick from the loaded car. When she saw my mother walking down the driveway her chin wobbled; my grandfather stood behind her with a tear in his eye and a bottle of gin in his two-fingered hand.

Somehow I felt light, almost elated. I didn't have to go to school and I had fun drawing pictures of medieval kings in armour. The house was full of people, talking, laughing, crying, patting our arms. I was in the middle of a big occasion.

The next day the church filled up for Dominic's funeral. As we walked in I saw his tiny white coffin lying on a stand in front of the altar. It almost seemed to float in the gloom. I was still in one piece until his coffin disappeared into the ground. That's when I started screaming inside.

I cried a lot. Sometimes I cried alone in my bed. Sometimes I cried with my mother. At school I stood my textbooks up on my desk so that no one could see me crying. I hated the other children in my class who had babies in their families. From time to time Dominic kept filling my head with desolate, bereft feelings, through my teenage years and into early adulthood.

←———→

Maybe it started with the knowledge that tragedy and loss do not have to destroy people.

I saw wives who were still able to chat and go shopping after their husbands died, children with 'mental' fathers at home who whooped around the playground. I saw that life went on after Dominic died. I saw my mother cry and share a joke with someone half an hour later. I saw her produce another baby called Liam who was healthy and came home to us. I saw recovery all around me.

I also saw that the return from affliction was not always easy or possible. The couple down the road who were killed when they thought the light of an oncoming train was the full moon. The girl in my class who died of a brain tumour. My school burning to the ground. These tragedies frightened me but they also aroused the hero in me.

Some days after school we played Germans and goodies in the garden with broomsticks and wooden clothes pegs fitted together to look like guns. Sometimes I preferred being a German: performing with an evil accent and staging a gruesome death had more dramatic scope than being a goodie. But sometimes I liked being a goodie because I could be a hero.

Sean yelled, 'It's five o'clock.' We scattered our weapons all over the lawn and ran inside into the beige-and-brown living room. The television had an imitation-wood casing and a beige panel down the side with switches on it. It flickered on. A handsome man in a white cowboy hat reared up on his white horse. 'Hi-yo, Silver! Away!' The Lone Ranger was off to fight the baddies with Tonto.

The Lone Ranger faced adversity, conquered evil and saved the innocent. So did the people we read about in Ladybird books, like Boadicea and Joan of Arc, brave kings and fearless missionaries. I read the Narnia series about the kind lion in a holy war with the White Witch. I devoured stories of lost children ducking the Nazis while they wandered through Europe looking for their parents. As well as *The Lone Ranger* I watched Hogan in *Hogan's Heroes* and Jim the good spy in *Mission Impossible* and longed to be a hero like them. When I closed my eyes at night I made up stories about saving my classmates from my burning school, running through the flames, dragging them out into the sun choking, while the nuns cheered me on. I made up other stories of saving people, like kind old Father Connor collapsing on the far side of the school paddock with a heart attack. I would run over to him and breathe air into his mouth until he woke spluttering and full of wonder that I had saved his life. Then I imagined I would get a special award for saving Father Connor at the school prize-giving.

Gradually I understood that much of the adversity in the real world was created by the people in it. I hated injustice and I wanted to fight it like a hero.

One day at school, my six-year-old sister Shonagh started to cry on the bench outside her classroom. None of her other classmates were taking any notice of her, so I ran over to her.

'I've forgotten my lunch,' she wailed.

Standing right in front of her classmates I yelled, 'Hey, you kids, my sister's starving. She needs some food.'

The kids started laughing and pointing their fingers at Shonagh. I got angry.

'Listen, you kids,' I yelled again looking fierce, 'you're supposed to share things. She's got no lunch. So just give her some food or I'll tell on you all for being mean.'

The children went silent. I found an empty lunchbox and took it around her classmates until there was enough for her to eat.

By the time I was twelve, the world I could be a hero in had become larger. My mother gave me a Unicef poster of the world which I hung on my bedroom wall. The countries in pale yellow had more than enough food for everyone, there were some in-between countries, then in mustard there was Africa and large parts of Asia – the places where people starved. I looked at Africa and saw myself in a grass hut in a dusty village, giving out food I had brought from my country to black children with bulging stomachs, their grateful mothers telling me I had saved their lives.

As a teenager I discovered even more ways to be heroic. Sometimes it was saying no to my teachers when I thought their rules were stupid. Or it was running faster than anyone else. Or it was knowing how to act the scariest pirate in the local production of *Peter Pan*. Or it was illegally putting up posters to help save a lake that was going to be flooded to make electricity. Sometimes it was simply telling my truth to people who didn't want to hear it.

I learnt that the heroic comes from knowing my truth and slaying the dragons that try to destroy it. Somehow I was far better at slaying the dragons outside me than the ones inside me. Even so, my sense of the heroic gave me a template for my struggle with madness, my return from it, and my advocacy in the mad movement.

Maybe it started with my discovery that others did not always approve of my mother.

I was at the parish picnic, puffed from running. So I lay on my back with my knees up, behind my aunt and her friend who were squatting on a green tartan rug. As they smoked cigarettes and drank tea from a thermos, they talked about a teenage girl who got into some kind of trouble and left town, and Father Dempsey's new housekeeper. Then one of them started to talk about my mother.

'Have you noticed how she's changed since she got back from Britain?'

'She's got some gorgeous clothes.'

'But did you see her lacy black stockings?'

'Truly?' They both giggled.

'Not only that, she smokes cigars, you know those long thin ones.'
More giggles.

'Patricia told me she's been going around saying priests should get married.'

'You're kidding. I wonder what Father Dempsey thinks of that.'

'Not much, I hear.' They both laughed again.

'You know she's so modern, she'll probably get divorced next.'

'Goodness me. It's getting more like Hollywood every day.'

I moved away in silence. My eyes stung as I imagined the scene, my parents telling us kids my father was moving away. Then the next scene, where we were all crying as he was packing his suitcase. . . but I was jolted out of my dark imaginings by Father Dempsey's voice over the megaphone, calling for the kids to line up for the sack race.

A year or so later I told Sister Aloysius in a catechism class I didn't believe in miracles or the Resurrection. She looked at me with concern, as though I had a serious disease, and told me to stay after class. Father Dempsey walked in after all the other kids had left. He had red hair and a wide Irish face, and he looked like everyone's friend, until he opened his mouth.

He stood over me. 'Sister has been telling me you've been saying some ungodly things in class. Where did you get these ideas from, young lady?'

'I don't know. From my mother, I suppose.'

'Well, it's your mother who's cracked then.' Father Dempsey looked like he'd just said 'Checkmate.'

I was stunned and lowered my head with embarrassment, though deep down I knew Father Dempsey was wrong about my mother.

A few days later Father Dempsey went to see my mother.

'We're bringing up our children to work things out in their own way,' she explained to him.

Father Dempsey went away praying even harder for our salvation.

✦———✦

Maybe it all started with the love and luck of my family.

My parents, my aunts and uncles and my grandparents were my adult role models. None of them were conquered people. They all had a secure place in the world. No one in living memory had robbed them of their culture, language or other treasures. None of them had ever gone without a meal. They all lived in their own houses and could afford to buy presents, shoot ducks, play tennis and go on holidays. None of them were bitter, ashamed or angry at their lot in life. Those whose personalities were edged with eccentricity, humour or questioning minds carried themselves with confidence.

My family knew they had a right to be in the world and that they mattered. They had the right skills, connections and language to get around that world with ease. All this fed my self-esteem. If they mattered, I mattered. If their views counted, my views counted. If they could make a contribution to society, so could I.

My parents, for all their inconsistencies, always looked pleased to see me and were interested in what I had to say. They made sure I had enough food, clothing and sleep. They usually comforted me when I cried. They held me close and read me stories. They let me play without interfering. They encouraged me to question others' truths and to develop my talents without pressuring me. I never doubted their love for me.

There was also a long memory in my family, like a backdrop in a darkened theatre, of where they came from, before they made good in the new country – centuries of poverty, famines, 'galloping consumption', and colonisation by the English and the Catholic Church. Most of my forebears and their communities were the underdogs of Europe. Privilege was recent in the story of my family; they knew it was a consequence of favourable circumstances rather than innate superiority.

But my family gave me more than love and luck. My parents showed me a world of diversity and new ideas. They were well-read people who thought for themselves. The world opened up for them when we lived in Britain in the mid-1960s. It was the time of Twiggy and the Beatles, and of reform in the Catholic Church. The world opened for me there too, much wider than it ever could have in our conservative rural town.

I saw crumbling old castles, the biggest toy shop in the world, the Eiffel Tower, camels in Egypt, people of all colours, and real Daleks in a Dr Who pantomime.

When we returned to Winton, the small town near the bottom of the world, my parents were changed people. They were poised between being outsiders and insiders. Their friends spanned the spectrum from farmers with huge red hands and old-fashioned hats, to middle-aged drop-outs with long hair and Roman sandals. They knew the art of shunning convention but also of tolerating it. Others, like Father Dempsey and the women on the tartan rug, were not always so tolerant of them.

←——→

Maybe it started when I first felt burnt by failure as an underperforming Brownie.

Every Monday after school I went to Brownies in the memorial hall in my pseudo-military uniform. We stood stiffly in lines in front of Brown Owl and chanted something about God and the Queen and doing a good turn every day. Then we played Port and Starboard. At the end of the sessions we sang, 'Rock My Soul'. We did girl stuff at Brownies like selling Girl Guide biscuits and learning how to make a bed like a nurse, instead of like my mother. We tucked the sides of the sheets at the foot of the bed under the mattress at a forty-five degree angle so all you could see was neat diagonal line. I got a badge for bed-making to put on the arm of my uniform. I didn't get a badge for anything else. Some of the girls had badges up and down both their arms.

One day Brown Owl came over to me. 'Mary, did you know you're getting too old to be a Brownie?'

'Does that mean I can become a Girl Guide?'

'Well, dear, you can but you haven't earned enough badges, so we can't fly you up with all the others.' Her mouth did a disappointed twist.

On 'fly up' day I stood aside while the other Brownies ran between two welcoming rows of Girl Guides under the arch made with their arms. Everyone cheered and whooped. Then Brown Owl walked me up in silence, outside the arches, as my eyes filled with tears.

My knack for underperforming continued into high school. Twice a year I came home with reports that put me near the bottom of the class in most subjects. My teachers wrote in a chorus that I didn't do enough work. My Latin teacher, whom we called Choir Boy, gave me a mark of one and a half per cent at the end of the year. He wrote, 'A self-evident waste of time – I hope other subjects are her salvation.' I was surprised to get such a low mark since I did a whole page of translation for the exam. But I couldn't blame Choir Boy for being annoyed with me.

We could tell Choir Boy was a pushover in the first minute of the first day of the year. Through the gauntlet of kids, he trotted to the front of the class as though the floor was burning his feet. He was balancing a tower of textbooks that toppled into forty pieces just as he was about to put them on his table. We all lashed him with laughter and he blushed all the way down to his huge Adam's apple. He was skinny and blond with spindly legs and badly shaved sideburns. He spoke in a high-pitched posh English accent. Yes, we knew he was ours to play with.

I perfected the art of scholarly diversion in Choir Boy's class. While he wrote long Latin phrases on the blackboard I led the charge with my fountain pen. I showed the others how to flick their pens with their wrists so that droplets of ink flew though the air towards their target. We covered the walls first. Then one day I sneaked up behind Choir Boy and flicked my pen at the back of his shirt, smattering the clean white fabric with a curved row of bright blue droplets. The kids sniggered while I returned in a flash to my seat. Choir Boy turned around, looking suspicious.

The next day he came into class looking flustered. 'Someone ruined my shirt yesterday and I've had to buy a new one.'

The kids looked embarrassed and started sniggering. Choir Boy went red and raised his voice. 'If I ever find out who did it, that person will live to regret it.' And he threw his piece of chalk to the ground with such force we were silenced. Choir Boy knew he was beaten, and though I had fun doing it, I felt for him when the chalk ricocheted around his feet.

My parents showed mild disapproval at my school reports and the antics they got to know about. Part of me wanted to work and succeed in my subjects. Part of me also wanted to rebel and succeed at failure.

31

I was full of anger at the school for being so regimented and for making me learn things that bored me. I was angry at myself too for not doing the work. The trouble was I preferred failure to mediocrity. I definitely preferred failure to doing what I was told.

But there was one thing I could win. I despised the girls in my class who were good at everything and never misbehaved. I despised the rewards they got for being so boring and conformist. Part of me also wanted to beat them at something. There was one girl called Margaret who was the best at everything – best at school work, best at music, best at sport. I lined up with her in the final of the 400 metre race in my first year at high school. Everyone said Margaret would win but I was determined to beat her.

'On your marks, get set, go.'

My legs rose and fell like well-oiled pistons. My body sliced through the air. My feet sprang off the grass. I was all speed and grace like a young antelope scampering across the veldt as I passed Margaret along the back straight. Then I started hurting and the power in my running began to drain away. I gulped for air. My heart raced. My legs shook. My skin went hot and damp. My throat ached and tasted of blood. But I kept going, round the final bend running on empty. I crossed the white line and collapsed while my burning chest convulsed for air. Margaret came in second. I was ecstatic.

Running taught me that I could succeed at something. But the most important thing it taught me was how to keep on going when things like oxygen deprivation, madness and other terrors conspired against me.

Maybe it started when I began to say no at thirteen.

I biked to school every morning in the wind, shivering inside my ugly cotton school uniform. A teacher saw me wheeling my bike into the school grounds.

'Where are your hat and gloves?'

'I forgot them.'

'There'll be a detention if I see you without them again.'

At that moment I decided I would never wear my hat and gloves again. I decided to say no to the confinement of my school. Saying no to the stupid things my teachers wanted me to do gave me energy and a sense of purpose. But over the years I discovered some problems with this approach – poor reports and an endless round of detentions for misbehaving or not doing my homework.

Beak supervised us for study periods. One day I was quietly looking out the window. Beak stood in front of my desk with his arms folded.

'Put your head down and do some work please, young lady.'

'I'm not disturbing anyone. I've got a right to look out the window. You can't make me work,' I said back to him.

The other kids in my class giggled as I performed for their gratification. Beak led me by the ear to headmaster Crud's office. Crud said, 'Explain yourself, please.'

'I've got a right to do what I like in class if I'm not disturbing other people.'

Crud looked sceptical.

'He can't make me work. He's really controlling and obsessive. All the kids think he's nuts. I reckon he needs to see a psychologist.'

Crud smiled at my earnest attempt at diagnosis. 'You will not answer back to teachers again. Understood?'

I nodded and he sent me back to class.

———

Maybe it started with lost love.

At high school I hung out with Sean and his friends. Most of them were older than me. We hooned around in old cars looking for parties on Friday and Saturday nights, with beer in the boot and cannabis in our pockets. We danced to Led Zeppelin and Deep Purple. If we were lucky we might find someone to kiss and fondle in a corner all evening. Sometimes we had serious conversations about the state of ourselves and the world – the evils of apartheid, our plans to live in self-sufficient communes when we left home, our rage at teachers and parents, and our depressions. Occasionally we vomited in other people's flower patches.

We hated commercial music. Most of all I hated David Cassidy and

The Partridge Family, a sick American TV show about a sappy family of kids who sang trashy pop songs. David had a shaggy haircut, polyester flares, a low-cut shirt with hearts on it and perfect American teeth. I bought a big poster of David Cassidy and took it with me when we were having a few beers in a park one summer evening. I put the poster behind a bush and peed on it. Everyone else thought it was a huge joke and they all peed on David as well.

At fifteen I fell in love with a thin boy with blond curly hair and a soft unshaven face. I loved him because he was gentle and clever and made me laugh. Tim and I spent the summer holding hands, kissing on the beach, drinking beer and doing pranks. One day, we were walking in the park and we saw a bronze statue of two seals, one nudging up to the other's back as though it was climbing on top of it. 'They look like they're having it away,' laughed Tim.

'In front of all those little kids too.'

'It's disgusting,' said Tim in his best outraged voice.

'Hey, we should write a letter to the paper complaining about it.'

'Yeah, sort of like, "I was strolling through the park the other day when I came across the shocking sight of two seals immortalised in brass while at the height of copulation".'

I whoop with enthusiasm. 'Yeah, signed "Concerned Citizen".'

The letter was published in the paper. Lots of other letters followed, many of them written by us, under different pseudonyms. A few days later a photo of the seals with the whole story featured on the front page of the paper, and a city councillor defended the statue by writing that Concerned Citizen must be a pervert to see the seals in that way. Then the story showed on the national television news. Tim and I had so much fun with it.

But Tim went to live in another town and after a while I dropped him because I was sick of missing him. By the time I realised my mistake he had another girlfriend.

I saw Tim the next time he came to town. I was so heartbroken I stole his boots at a party and started walking home in them down a dark country road. Tim came after me and politely took them back. I went home in my own shoes and cried all night and the next day. I cried

34

because I wanted him back and because I had never been so humiliated by my own behaviour.

←———→

Maybe it started with my refusal to be a pretty little girl.

I grew up when girls were supposed to wear rosebud dresses and play together with their dolls and tea sets. But I wore trousers whenever I could and liked fist-fighting and playing with guns on our big lawn. Guns were such fun. We could terrorise each other with them. We could hide behind the shed and ambush people with them. We could kill people with no more than a mean look, a cackle and the click of a plastic trigger. We could die like cowboys – staggering, clutching our chests, groaning and sinking to the ground.

Unfortunately most of the girls didn't like playing with guns so I hung around with Sean and his friends. They did exciting things like making tree huts, going eeling and chasing pigs. But I was not always welcome and Sean's friends often told me to go away.

I loved guns so much I made my own. At seven I made one out of a short broomstick, with a handle taped to it at one end, and a red knitting needle taped to the other end so that it looked like a bayonet dipped in blood.

Around that time my mother bought me a white lacy dress and veil for my first communion, from an Italian postal order shop. After the anti-climax of eating my first tasteless round wafer, I arrived home from the church and immediately started playing with my gun. My parents laughed and my father took a photo of me in my lacy white dress and veil holding the gun over my shoulder. Later they showed the photo to visitors. Everyone thought it was funny but I was so embarrassed I left the room.

As a teenager I thought tomboys like me were destined to be lesbians. The only lesbians I met were colleagues of my father's, who came to Sunday lunches when I was about twelve. One of them was pretty and gentle; the other one was butch and funny.

'Where is your family, Allie?' my mother asked the butch one.

'I ain't got a family.'

'Why don't you have a family?' I asked her in my innocence.

Allie looked at me with mock menace. 'Because I ate them.'

Everyone laughed and laughed, but later my parents said how sad it was to be a lesbian and not get on with your family.

I grew up thinking that lesbians were unhappy people who hid away because no one liked them. A book my mother gave me on sex education said lesbianism was a phase some teenagers went through but most grew out of it. Those who didn't, developed mental problems. At school other children giggled about lesbians and my friends just went yuk. I definitely didn't want to be a lesbian – it terrified me more than anything. It barged into my consciousness and battered me with its strength and persistence. It hounded me for years.

⋆————⋆

Maybe it started when I discovered the pleasures and perils of self-induced altered realties.

It was after Mass on Easter Sunday. Party time. Us kids ran around the garden shooting each other with pistols we'd made out of wooden clothes pegs. I ran inside to the din of chatter and clinking glasses. A bald grown-up with a red face looked down at me and shouted, 'Haven't you killed all the baddies yet?'

'I've run out of bullets.'

'Here, I've got an arsenal of them.' He raided his suit pocket and held them out in his hand.

We both laughed as I put the pretend bullets in my pretend pocket.

My aunt bent down to me. 'Would you like to do your giddy dance for the grown-ups?'

I put my feet together and twisted myself around, clockwise on the spot. My arms flung wider with every turn. My Sunday dress flared like cupcake paper. My hair went horizontal. As I got faster, my heels floated and my toes became a spinning rudder. The beige-and-brown living room disintegrated into a blur. I heard a high whining in my ears. Faster and faster, the vertical energy holding me as steady as a stake. I was in another world without edges and hard things. I twirled as fast as I could. Then stopped.

Everything dropped – my hair went vertical, my dress drooped, my heels fell, then all of me lay on the floor giggling, as the other world swayed back into view. The grown-ups laughed and clapped. They charged their glasses and I ran outside to load my clothes peg.

At high school I discovered I could use substances to enter another world without edges and hard things. My brother Sean and I drank bottles of beer and cheap sparkling wine in the back seats of our friends' cars. We bought marijuana and smoked it in the trees at the end of the school field, or outside the windows of our bedrooms. We read the *Whole Earth Catalogue*, a Seventies manual for self-sufficiency that had drug recipes using ingredients like rotten broom, morning-glory seeds and nutmeg. We tried all the recipes with great anticipation but none of them worked.

In the winter holidays during my last year at school, my friend Jim came around to my place with a bottle of chloroform he had stolen from his stepfather. We sat alone on the front veranda sniffing it all afternoon. I loved the way it made the world go all faint and grainy, like a bleached old home movie rolling out in slow motion.

Jim took me for a drive to a native bush reserve with a river running through it. Kids went there to do nature trails at school. Other people went there to do drugs or sex or shady deals. Jim turned into the reserve and braked hard when he saw the river right in front of us. My nose was in the bottle and the jolt splashed chloroform into my mouth. In a panic I ran to the river to wash my mouth out and everything went black.

I came to, lying in the bottom of the river, looking up through the water wobbling in the light. Jim giggled hysterically as he helped me out. He put a blanket around me and rubbed me so I didn't shiver too badly. We drove home laughing about our great adventure.

At university, I got into heavy drinking. It started when I felt helpless against the evil spirit. I struggled out of the dark cavern of my bed at midday and got drunk every afternoon with a friend who lived down the corridor at my hostel. Rachel was drinking because her father had died in the summer leaning against the aluminium mast of his boat as it drifted into overhead wires.

If there were any other drugs around I grabbed them. One evening, when the spirit had drained all the life out of me, I drank two cups of boiled datura flowers picked from a nearby garden. The next thing I knew, the floor came alive with writhing creatures that were part-human and part-animal. They had pale, poxy faces and piercing red eyes. Some of them had no limbs; others had thigh bones hanging down with the flesh newly ripped off them. I was petrified but tried to make polite conversation with them.

Just then, two soldiers appeared with guns looking for women to rape. I screamed and ran outside into the night. Footsteps echoed behind me and bullets whizzed past my head. I ran to the safety of a neighbour's house for help, not knowing I was in my underwear and speaking gibberish. For two days I was in the grip of the most terrifying and grotesque hallucinations. They haunted me for many months.

I never took datura again but other drugs were fun. For a year I got stoned a lot of the time, often starting with a joint for breakfast. I enjoyed being stoned. I loved the strangeness of it – the wacky conversations, the giggling, the lovemaking, the munchies, the revelations, and the easy, slowed-down feeling.

Sometimes I took drugs to escape my demons. But usually I took them so I could be a tourist in my own town. Instead of going to another country for a new experience, drugs changed the way I experienced the place I was in. It was usually fun and it didn't cost nearly as much as an overseas trip.

←——→

Maybe it started during my struggle to squeeze out of my cocoon to join the world.

I didn't speak until I was three. At kindergarten I played in the sandpit alone while the other children ran around me as though I was not there. I went home at lunchtime and sat on the chair by the fire. The world around me went hazy. It felt like there was only me in my world and that everything else was a long way away.

Maybe I felt isolated because I had glue ear. Maybe it was because I'm an off-the-chart introvert.

Through my years at school, I struggled to ease my way into circles of children. Many of them ignored me and didn't make a gap to let me in. I often felt awkward and lonely.

There were other kids who couldn't get into the circle either, so I sometimes played with them. If I couldn't always get noticed in the playground, I made sure I got noticed in the classroom. At high school I was the class clown. This usually involved doing something to annoy the teacher. Part of me liked making the kids laugh but the price I paid was being told off and getting lots of detentions.

In my first year at primary school I made friends with Katherine who had ringworm and a mild intellectual disability. Katherine and I didn't say much to each other but we played a lot and got up to mischief in class. Later I made friends with Laura who had glasses and dirty teeth, then it was Ainsley, who lived with her mother in a damp little house by the railway; Aroha, who was Maori; and Brad, whose father was in prison. In some ways I was more comfortable hanging out with these kids. As I got older they started to interest me on another level when I realised they came from different backgrounds to mine.

Though I had friends I often felt lonely and isolated, as though there had always been an invisible wall around me. Parts of me could climb over the wall but they were often the parts I wanted to hide. Sometimes the parts of me I couldn't get over the wall were the parts I wanted to show.

I could see a painful mismatch between my idea of me and other people's idea of me. Take my role as the class clown, for instance. It wasn't a part of me I really wanted to show but it was better than being invisible. Then there was the way I dressed. If I dressed the way I wanted to, like a boy, others thought I was butch or weird. But if I dressed like a girl I didn't feel comfortable. I wanted to be me and to be acceptable to my peers at the same time. Sometimes I couldn't do both. Sometimes I didn't even know who 'me' was any more. I was like a wobbly young sun struggling to spawn planets to adorn its solar system. Parts of myself struggled to find their place in my social system, just like new planets in a solar system spin out in disarray before they even get into orbit.

←———→

Maybe it started when seismic social change kept shifting the ground I stood on.

My parents read Alvin Toffler, Marshall McLuhan and Germaine Greer. 'Change is coming,' they announced in the early Seventies. 'The world will never be the same again.' We had long and lively discussions at the dinner table about poetry and politics, environmentalism and nuclear war, counterculture and the Catholic Church.

Sean grew his hair and frequently got sent home from school to get it cut. My mother got angry at the school and snipped Sean's hair on a kitchen stool in front of a poster with a judge wearing a long wig saying, 'And as for your hair young man. . .'

I decided I wanted to be a hippie and to sew flower-power patches onto my school blazer. When I grew up I wanted to live in a commune, then go to Africa to help the starving millions. I read *The Little Red Schoolbook* and at thirteen I held a placard that said, 'New Zealand troops out of Vietnam now'. But deep down I didn't really know what to believe in, apart from being good to my fellow human beings.

During my childhood the great platform of values that had held people for generations collapsed. I began my childhood learning the Hail Mary and going to Latin Masses; I ended it an atheist. I was born before the contraceptive pill when sex outside marriage was unacceptable, but by the time I was a teenager free love had arrived. As a baby I heard Bing Crosby crooning on my parents' record player; less than twenty years later I danced to the anarchic screams of the Sex Pistols. When my mother held me in her arms she imagined that like her and her mother, I would marry and become a homemaker; she could not possibly have foreseen what I became.

In the middle of such change I had no answers to the big questions like: Why am I here? How was the world created? Are there any universal values? What can human beings know for sure? Timeless questions without any solid answers. My youthful frustration that I didn't know these answers propelled me into a state of 'god envy'. It wasn't fair that I stood on this outlying planet with my puny mind for just a flash of time. I wanted to know everything, to see to the end of the universe, and to travel through time. But I was stuck with being human.

I had no answers to the smaller questions either. I wanted to belong somewhere but the only place I felt I truly belonged was my family. At kindergarten I played alone in the sandpit while the other children rushed around me. I didn't quite belong. I didn't quite belong in Britain or in our small rural town either. I didn't quite belong in the Catholic Church, in Brownies or in my schools or anywhere else.

I wanted to know where I was going with my life, to succeed at something, but I thought I couldn't know who I really was. It was as though there were several movies running through the projector at once and I couldn't sort out one image of me from another. I couldn't tell if there was a real me or not, who knew what I wanted and could make free decisions. Was I a plodder or clever? Was I a good person or a selfish one? Should I do what I wanted or what others wanted? Was I able to express my true feelings or was I condemned to always conceal them? Was I straight or a lesbian? Did I believe in a higher purpose or in a cold and random universe? The ground of my being crumbled in ambivalence.

Later at university I studied philosophy, hoping some of the answers would reveal themselves. But philosophy just added to my burden. One of my lecturers introduced us to the theory of knowledge. He quoted an ancient philosopher who said, 'I cannot know anything for certain, not even that.' That sentence haunted me throughout the years of my madness.

← →

Maybe it started when I tried to recover a heritage that had slipped away from me.

I left school after scraping through my qualification for university. There was no way I wanted to stay for the final year, so I went to England with my family for six months instead. We stopped over in Rome and I was enchanted by its history. The oldest building in my own country was one hundred and thirty years old but here I was looking at the Colosseum which had stood for two thousand years.

I walked astonished through the catacombs where the early Christians worshipped and buried their dead, I felt the 'holy' seep through the old archways and painted rooms of the Vatican, I cowered in awe at Michelangelo's statue of Moses. And it all seemed so much grander than Father Dempsey and his petty doctrines. Maybe I could belong to the Catholic Church after all. In Rome the church was so old, the art was so saturated with beauty and power, the music was so sublime. After some years of abandoning the spiritual, I went in search of it again.

We got a bus up into the hills around Rome to visit a monastery where one of the monks had a stigmata. I started to think maybe miracles could happen and I wanted to see the holes in his hands. But when the monk came out to greet the tourists he was wearing black fingerless gloves. I was disappointed. Maybe the man thought his wounds were too terrible for others to see. Or maybe he was a fraud.

Our next stop was England. One day I was out on a drive with my family and when they stopped the car, I got out and walked into a small pine forest. Suddenly, when I looked up, the sick-looking brown trees and the pale sky were glowing with a white light that was beyond description. I knew I was witnessing a reality that seldom showed itself to people. It was like the universe or God had rolled over onto its back for a few seconds and showed me its sacred underbelly.

In Europe I found my spiritual heritage. I also found my family heritage. I went to places where officials kept dusty old records of births and deaths, and census forms from the nineteenth century in huge books. I was like an archaeologist, except my clues didn't come in the form of ancient rubbish, or bones or pottery; they came from old official pieces of paper. Like an archaeologist, I was trying to create a story out of tiny fragments.

After many hours in musty archives rooms, I started to see the outline of the story of my family going back many generations. I was frustrated that it would always be an outline and never a full story. It was like finding the contents page of a book, knowing that another chapter was destroyed every time one of my ancestors took their story to the grave with them.

Europe showed me its part in my heritage. It helped me to understand where I came from, but it gave me no clues on where I was going in my life.

The next year I started university and I was still giving God a go. I joined a charismatic Catholic prayer group for students. They were wholesome people with wide open faces who read from the Good News Bible. Every meeting they would raise their arms, sing to guitars about how they loved Jesus, and make strange gurgling sounds they called the gift of speaking in tongues. I hardly opened my mouth and I didn't get into any states of rapture. This turned out to be another place I didn't belong.

But I still believed in spirits. I believed in them because they were part of my heritage, because I had experienced them, and they gave life some mystery, a higher purpose. Spirits meant you went on after you died. They meant you could be with the dead people in your family, even if you have never met them. If a spirit caused your problems, that gave the problems some nobility, some importance. You were the chosen one, anointed with their invisible powers.

←———→

Maybe it started when a spirit parked itself in the vacant lot of my being.

Three weeks into my first year at university, my grandmother with the big bottom and the stick died after a large blood clot pulsed up the highways of her body into her lungs. The tallest tree in my family had been felled. The space where she once stood would never be filled again. All my life the other trees in my family had swayed in the wind with laughter, new ideas, anger and tears. In some ways my grandmother had sheltered me more than anyone, because she was solid and wouldn't be moved by any nonsense or whims. We left her in the ground on a big hillside overlooking the ocean.

A few weeks after my grandmother died I was sitting alone in my university hostel room, fretting about my meaningless life, when I felt a strong presence in my room. It was my great-great-grandmother, letting me know how sad and bitter she was that her only child born out of wedlock was removed from her the night she gave birth to him. Her spirit vanished quickly but its presence overwhelmed and exhausted me.

The spirit kept sneaking back to me when no one else was around;

her heavy energy paralysed my body and colonised my mind like an invisible nerve gas. She was like an illegal immigrant from the land of the dead, using me as a vehicle back to the country of the living. I was terrified and enchanted by her power, but over the weeks she slowly sucked the life out of me, until one night she told me I must kill myself.

Usually she came and went like a polar gust passing through a room, but this night she wouldn't leave. As I ran in terror to my friend's flat, everything looked ugly and evil – the trees, people passing by, the rocks in her garden, my own face in her bathroom mirror. The spirit kept telling me to kill people I loved. I asked my friend to tie my hands behind my back so I couldn't do anything bad. She refused. I could hear the spirit moving around the living room, calling my name with a chilling voice.

After a night of terror with no sleep, I rang a priest I knew. He called together some of the other people I knew from the Catholic prayer group. They put their hands on me and they said a prayer of deliverance over me: 'God, Father Almighty, in the name of Jesus we ask you to win this battle for Mary's salvation. Deliver us, Lord, stop once and for all the oppression of the evil one. Establish your dominion, cast out the enemy from Mary's life. Reveal your Glory, Lord, as Christ conquered the Devil on the cross. In the Holy Name of Jesus, cover Mary with his Precious Blood, deliver Mary, Lord, deliver.'

Then they hummed and their hands started quivering. I felt at peace and thought my troubles were over.

But my troubles were really just beginning.

After the spirit left I went to see Father Vaughan, who was a counsellor. He was a friend of my parents, a liberal Catholic like them, in dismay at some of the teachings of the Church. The first time I saw him he said the spirit was 'auto-suggestion', that my troubled psyche had somehow tricked me into thinking I was possessed by it.

'You don't need prayers of deliverance,' he told me, 'You need counselling.'

I went to see Father Vaughan every week for six months. He wasn't interested in the spirit. He just kept asking me about my feelings. 'You must be angry inside if you thought the spirit wanted you to kill people. What are you angry about?' he asked.

'I don't really know. It doesn't make sense to me.'

'Perhaps it's your mother, or your baby brother that died, or your high school, or the Church?'

While Father Vaughan kept asking me about my feelings and my early life, I kept asking him why he was so sure my problems were psychological and not spiritual. He didn't seem interested in answering my question. We had different reasons for being there: his were for my psychological survival, my reasons were more theological.

I liked Father Vaughan. He was gentle and progressive. In 1976 that meant he had virtually abandoned God for humanism. He didn't really help me understand my experiences, but unknown to him he did a great job at starting the avalanche that dumped God and other spirits from my universe.

Maybe my madness and sanity started in a dimension beyond the reach of the human mind, where millions of billiard balls, or life events, punch and graze each other in indecipherable patterns. Maybe it started without a cause at all, like the big bang, when the universe ballooned out of absolutely nothing. What is it about the art of human meaning-making that compels us to adorn our lives with causes when perhaps there are none? If I compare all my maybes with the events in the lives of others, the picture of why gets even murkier. Many people with comparable traits and levels of trauma to mine never experience madness. On the other hand, isn't there enough awry in any human life to drive us all mad?

2.

THE BLACK BOX

Everyone sees madness through their own lens. Mad people see it through a lens that burns the ground they stand on. Psychiatrists see it through the cool lens of symptoms and pathology. Families see it as disturbing behaviour or the loss of the person they once knew. The public see madness through the rough lens of the vernacular: it is insanity, foolishness, it's wild and uncontrollable.

Madness has been described again and again by people who have never experienced it. Mad people's definition of it has seldom made it into the dictionary or into conversation, media stories, literature or mental health discourse. Our definition of madness can even elude us. We lack a validating language to make meaning from it. Our madness stands outside in the dark, knocking on the door to meaning, struggling to get in. My own stories of my madness struggled to take shape while other people's stories of it took instant inspiration from the dictionary, diagnostic manuals and a wider culture that completely shuns it.

Most of the stories of those who look on, seeing only snatches of madness, portray it as all bad. My story is fuller than the stories of those who looked on. As well as being the most intricate story, it is the only unbroken one, the only story that had a witness present from start to finish and every moment in between. That witness was me.

←——————→

'I want to see you twice a week,' Dr L'Estrange says at the end of the first hour. All winter and spring I see him every Monday and Thursday.

Week after week Dr L'Estrange greets me by gazing at me with his X-ray eyes until I can't bear the silence any more. Sometimes it takes all my energy to suppress the uprising of giggles in my chest and throat. Eventually I blurt out a stream of nervous jabber, sensing I've fallen into a trap, set by his silence, to make me fill the air with the unguarded contents of my unconscious. While he gazes he smokes his pipe and writes his notes in small tidy handwriting. Sometimes he writes copious notes in our big silences. I wonder what he could be writing – that I am repressed, can't free-associate, that my body language is telling him how deviant and perverted I am? Even after I start babbling, Dr L'Estrange hardly speaks. I'm worried he can see into every corner of my mind. Every word I say, every movement I make, the way I sit, where I put my hands, I fear will be used as evidence of my badly diseased mind. He reminds me of a fisherman staring intently into the water waiting to catch the next piece of pathology I float past him.

I make myself sound as normal as possible because I don't want to be judged. I just want to be understood. So I don't tell him the things that are really bugging me like the crush I have on a woman or the fear that I'm not clever enough. So I talk about easier things, like how I don't belong anywhere, how I don't know what to do with my life. I talk about how I hate authority and religion, how I don't believe in God or go to church, how I've refused to go to confession since I was twelve.

I decide Dr L'Estrange is weird and not to be trusted. I want to trust him but I'm sure he follows Freud who had wacky ideas about sex, repression and mothers. I am also spooked – part of me is afraid of Freud and his disciples because they are the secular high priests of the psyche. Other people can only see the surface of you but Freud and his men claim to have special powers to beam into the mind. I think of Dr

ĽEstrange with an uncomfortable mix of mockery and of fear, but also with a yearning to be accepted by him.

Dr ĽEstrange isn't just weird, though. He's even older than my father. Men of fifty are like another species to me. Most of the time we talk past each other.

One winter afternoon after a long silence he asks me, 'Why do you wear unconventional clothes?'

I toss my eyes to the ceiling and swear under my breath. 'Well, why do you wear conventional clothes?' I reply, pointing at his suit and tie.

'We're not here to talk about me, we're here to talk about you and why you're so unconventional. Is it in some way tied up with your rebelliousness?'

'I didn't come here to talk about my clothes.'

'But your clothes can mirror the psyche.'

'Yeah? Well, if my clothes mirrored my psyche then I'd be naked.'

'Mmm. Why do you say that?' he asks, leaning forward as if we are just about to make a breakthrough on my sexual maladjustment.

'Because if I'm stripped of everything on the inside, then I guess to mirror that I'd also be stripped on the outside.'

He leans back and writes several lines of notes.

After a few sessions Dr ĽEstrange tells me I need anti-depressants. 'You're very slowed down and physically depressed,' he says. He doesn't know I am recovering from a night of smoking Buddha sticks laced with horse tranquilliser. The thought of taking anti-depressants terrifies me in a way that recreational drugs never do. What if the anti-depressants damage my brain or change my personality? After days of hesitation I start to take them. All they do is make me feel dopey and constipated so I stop them.

✦————✦

I stop going to see Dr ĽEstrange in the spring and don't turn up to any of my university exams. The next year I go to journalism school, still feeling gloomy. After two months, almost overnight, I don't feel gloomy any more and I decide to leave journalism school. For the rest of the year I feel happy, collecting the unemployment benefit, smoking lots of marijuana and reading anarchist literature with my wild, wacky flatmates. But gradually my inner life splits off from the fun I am having in my outer life. In the privacy of my own thoughts I start to feel troubled again. I decide to go back to university, turn twenty-one and have a wild party. Soon I start to feel empty, like a balloon that has lost all its air and landed all sad and wrinkled in a dark corner.

I make an appointment to see Dr L'Estrange. I haven't seen him for over a year. I'm not even sure I like him but I don't know who else to go to.

'Why do I get like this?' I ask him as I look to the ground.

A short silence while Dr L'Estrange sucks on his pipe. He leans forward frowning, his blue eyes boring into me. 'I think you have a biochemical imbalance in your brain. It's genetic.'

'Does that mean I'm going to be depressed for the rest of my life?'

Another suck on his pipe. 'It depends how your life goes, but you do have a vulnerability, yes.'

I've never heard of a biochemical imbalance before. I thought I got depressed because I am over-sensitive, weak-willed or just totally screwed up. I can change these things. But how can I ever change my biochemistry through my own efforts?

For the first time I feel totally helpless against the depression.

I go home and tell my flatmate Joanne about my biochemical imbalance.

'That must be scary for you,' she says, looking worried.

'Yeah, what can I do? Trying to control my mood is as futile as trying to control the weather.'

I go to my room and lie on my bed. A crack opens beneath me and I topple into nothingness, falling and falling until I crash land in the hospital.

←——→

Someone drives me to the hospital while I curl up in the back seat. A big nurse in a white uniform opens the door and slowly unfolds me. 'Come on, Mary, straighten yourself up.' The nurse takes my arm and walks me into a modern, long, low building called the Canary Ward, near a big medical hospital block. She takes me through the waiting room where sad people sit staring at the walls. 'New admission, Betty,' she calls to the receptionist.

'Oh, not another one, Chantelle,' Betty grumbles and hands her some forms.

''Fraid so.'

Chantelle has big bones and short black hair. She has a strong, wide face and her jaw goes up and down from chewing gum. She reminds me of a discus thrower I know.

Chantelle walks me down a long polished corridor into a pale pink room with a steel bed and a chipped, wooden bedside cabinet. She hands me a white surgical nightie with a back that doesn't do up. Then she picks up her clipboard and asks me some questions, but I have no reason to answer them.

'How about getting into bed?' she asks.

She packs all my possessions into a brown paper bag.

'My things,' I mumble.

'I'm just going to lock them in the property room for safe keeping.'

'But—.'

Chantelle has already left the room.

An hour later Chantelle comes in again. 'Come and meet some of the other patients.'

'I don't want to,' I whisper.

She helps me into a light-blue towelling dressing gown and leads me down the long polished corridor again into the Ladies' Lounge. It's a large room with a green Formica table in the middle, and vinyl-covered steel armchairs of orange, beige and brown, crammed together and backed up against the walls. Sponge rubber spills out from some of them like wounds.

Chantelle drops me into one of the armchairs. The orange swirls in the brown carpet transfix me. They coil into black holes, and half-formed orange letters of the alphabet float like space junk between them. A fluorescent light flickers and buzzes above me. Two women sit talking and smoking on the other side of the room. On her way out Chantelle says, 'Ladies, this is Mary.' They say hi and continue talking.

Their greeting hits me like a large slap. I scream in my head, 'Please don't talk to me!' as I curl away from them. My mind drifts into blackness, then a song I know sung by Art Garfunkel, in a movie about rabbits, plays on the old plastic radio in the corner:

Is it a kind of dream?
Floating out on the tide
Following the river of death downstream...
I drift further into my black box.
Bright eyes, how can you close and fail?
How can the light that burned so brightly,
Suddenly burn so pale?
Bright eyes

My eyes sting because I feel like the rabbit, with the light in its eyes getting duller, drifting down the river into nothing. I curl up in a tight ball, wondering how I can ever get back to my bed.

'Dinner time, ladies,' yells a cheerful nurse.

She stands over me.

'I can't eat.'

She pulls me down the long polished corridor around two corners into the dining room. The other patients are queuing up but the cheerful nurse sits me down and gets me a meal. It's a cold room, like a concrete bunker, with a long stainless-steel bench and hatch. The linoleum floor is swirly greys and whites, like a pot of half-mixed paints. A potato-top fish pie with peas appears in front of me, smelling rotten. The cheerful nurse tells me to eat up but I gag so much I can't get it down.

A male nurse comes around with a tray of orange egg cups. 'Here's your pills.'

'I don't take any.'

'The doctor prescribed them. They'll help you feel better.'

'But—.'

The nurse starts tipping the egg cup. 'Here, put your hand out. That's a girl.'

I stare at the red and white pills in my hand. The nurse puts a glass of water in front of me and waits. His silence is his command. I take the pills.

←———————→

I wake in the middle of the night, filled with foreboding. I jerk with the feeling of electric shocks going through me every time I have a thought. Between jerks I feel smouldering inside my chest.

One of the night nurses comes in and shines a torch in my face. 'Get back to sleep,' she says.

'I'm freaking out,' I say as the torchlight streaks across the wall back into the corridor, followed by the nurse's squeaky footsteps leaving my room.

The next morning Dr L'Estrange calls me into his office. He asks me how did I sleep, have I eaten, do I still feel suicidal, can I reach out to people, do I need a letter from him for the university. I want to tell him about the terrible pain I'm in, about the black box and my devastating discovery that life is a sham. But I don't. I want him to say he understands, that my pain is real, that he will help me fight for the survival of my being. But he doesn't. He just tells me I am very unwell and must stay in my nightie.

After I leave Dr L'Estrange writes his own version of my distress:

Admitted urgently in an acutely depressed state. This had gradually come on since she resumed university at the beginning of the year but rapidly intensified at the weekend when she felt completely cut off from life and people, and had strong impulses to cut herself with a razor blade. She has previously had drug therapy and psychotherapy for depression. She wants to be at university but has failed to sit her exams on two previous occasions. Behind this lies adjustment problems that were present throughout adolescence when she was in constant rebellion. Mary has an inadequate and confused sense of identity. She also has a long-standing picture of being an isolate; tending to live in her own world and always finding it difficult to fit in. In this way she presents a schizoid personality picture.

Diagnosis: psychotic depression.

Dr B. S. L'Estrange

←———————→

It's the middle of the afternoon. I've been in hospital for a day or two and I'm walking in a slow shuffle up and down the corridor with my head flopping forward, like a puppet on loose strings.

Chantelle walks up to me. I know it's her because I recognise her black slip-on shoes and her voice. 'Chin up, Mary. How about coming into the Ladies' Lounge?'

'Um um—.' I can't think of anything to say. I'm stranded inside my own head. It feels as blank as Antarctica.

Chantelle takes me by the arm and leads me to the door of the Ladies' Lounge. All the power in my body is draining out of me. Even doing the slow puppet shuffle and keeping my eyes open is getting too much.

'Here, have a sit down,' she says, 'I'll be back soon.' I stand in the Ladies' Lounge feeling lost and empty, then shuffle back to my room to the safety of my bed.

Later Chantelle comes in, chewing her gum. 'How ya doing?'

'No good.'

'Oh, you wanna mix more with the other patients?'

'It's too hard.'

'Do you often feel cut off from other people?'

'Yeah,' I say slowly. 'I'm like a stone. I'm heavy. I sink. No one can see into me. I can't express myself.'

Chantelle looks away. She's chewing hard and slow. I can feel her eyes and her frown saying, 'You're a strange one.'

She looks back to me. 'Oh you'll feel better soon. Come into the Ladies' Lounge.'

'No thanks.'

'You can't hide away in your bed all day,' she says, striding out of the room.

I bury myself in my bed. If only I could talk to Art Garfunkel about the song. He understood the rabbit. He might understand me.

⟵————⟶

It's morning and I'm still in my nightie, lying on my bed. A stylish middle-aged woman with blonde hair and buck teeth comes to see me.

'Hi, Mary. My name's Pat. I'm the occupational therapist here. We're doing art today. Would you like to join us?'

Before I have time to think of an answer Pat is leading me down the corridor to the OT room. Droopy people like me are sitting in a circle waiting for nothing. She hands out some butcher's paper and a box of cheap crayons. She asks us to draw our feelings.

I draw a picture of me standing alone inside a bubble. It's night-time in the bubble but daytime outside it. I draw myself with no hands or feet or face, and my body is faint except for the black void of my lost self in my chest. A red umbilical cord lies broken at the bottom of the bubble.

In another picture I draw a long tunnel. I've just been whooshed down the tunnel from the everyday world to my private hell. I'm lying at the end of the tunnel with a butcher's meat cleaver embedded in my heart. It has split me in half from top to bottom.

Pat calls us back to the circle and asks us to talk about our drawings. Ruth starts to talk about hers in a quiet voice. 'That's me when my thoughts get all jumbled,' pointing to a big scribble done with a black crayon. Ruth is around my age with brown shoulder-length hair and a frightened face.

'And how do you feel when you're jumbled?' asks Pat.

'Scared.'

'Well done,' says Pat cheerfully. 'Joy, would you like to share your drawing with the group?'

Joy is thin and pale with straight red hair clipped back at the temples. She wears blue plastic glasses and tidy conservative clothes, and clutches a blank sheet of paper. Joy doesn't respond – not even a flicker of a word or a movement. She's a breathing statue.

'Joy?'

No response.

'Let's move on then, shall we? Mary, what about your pictures?'

'Um, um, I'm cut off,' I mumble, looking at the floor.

'What from?'

'The world. Me. Everything.'

'How does that feel?'

'I dunno.'

'I think I might feel sad or scared if I felt that cut off.'

'I don't feel anything.'

'Are you sure?'

I'm saved by the cheerful nurse coming in to announce lunchtime.

←——→

After lunch Chantelle comes up to me while I'm wandering down the corridor. 'Hey Mary, I've taken your stuff down to the ladies' dormitory.'

'Why?'

'We need your room for a new admission.'

'But I can't handle being with—.'

'Look, you've got no choice. You'll get used to it.'

I turn away and start to cry. I don't want Chantelle to see me.

The ladies' dormitory is a long room right up the end of the corridor. There are twelve beds crammed into it. They have lemon or pink candlewick bedspreads on them, with bedside cabinets jammed between them. At the entrance to the dormitory, to the right, there's a room with a desk and a large window in front of it so the nurses can see us in bed at night.

I feel like I'm in a goldfish bowl but I still have my own bed. I burrow under the blankets and stay there for the afternoon.

←——→

In the hospital I start to hear voices that other people don't hear.

It's the middle of my first night in the ladies dormitory and I'm lying awake trembling with the awful knowledge that existence is futile. A booming cacophony of a thousand voices erupts out of the night sky, nailing me to my bed in fright. Then a woman's loud echoing voice comes out of the commotion and sings, 'I'll never go down again.' I cling to her words, wondering where she came from, hoping her song will come true for me.

The next day as I'm walking down the corridor, another voice, all soft and sinister, sneaks up behind me: 'Maaaary.'

I spin around in fright but no one is there.

The sinister voice keeps coming back.

55

'Maaaary,' as I'm getting into bed.

'Maaaary,' as I'm sitting in the Ladies' Lounge.

'Maaaary,' as I'm walking through the town on my first outing after ten days in hospital. I yell at the voice to fuck off. A man screws up his face and goes red, as he passes me. 'Fuck off yourself,' he snarls.

His words stun me like a kick in the head. My brain empties out. I'm unable to move, or to think what to do next. I can't look up. I stand on the street paralysed for some time.

A shop woman comes up to me. She has puffy ankles and navy blue shoes with bows on them. 'Are you all right, dear?'

'Um, um—.'

'Where do you live?'

'Um, um, ah, the Canary Ward.'

'Oh, I see.' Now she understands why I'm so weird. 'Do you have enough money for a taxi?'

I nod. She leads me by the arm to the nearest taxi. She's so gentle, I think, because she's scared she'll break me.

The taxi driver is an old man with a cloth cap. I pay him as he stops outside the main door of the Canary Ward. 'Thanks dear,' he says. 'Now you look after yourself, won't you.'

I walk into the Ladies' Lounge feeling like a frightened cub returning to its cave. Joy is sitting by the door as still as a statue. I go and sit with Ruth who looks nervous and is shaking a lot.

'Hey, what did you think of OT the other day?' she asks.

'I liked the drawing but I don't go for that touchy-feely crap.'

'Neither do I.'

'Have you been in here before?'

'Yeah, a few times. The last time I was really crazy. They gave me huge doses of anti-psychotics but I stayed crazy for months. Why are you here?'

'Because my head's fucked, I suppose,' I say.

We both laugh in a half-power demented way, as though our lives have become such over-the-top tragedies that they now qualify as comic farces.

Over the next week or two Ruth and I become friends. She is gentle and easy to be with. We can be two messed-up people together and know that neither of us minds. Sometimes we just sit in silence together. Sometimes we joke about the staff, or talk about politics or hang out in town together.

←——————→

The days go by and Joy still sits like a statue. I never see her move unless a nurse is leading her somewhere. She never shifts position in her chair or changes the expression on her face.

One morning she is wheeled away in her bed to have shock treatment. An hour later she is wheeled back and sleeps until lunchtime, then a nurse brings her to the Ladies' Lounge where she sits like a stone all afternoon. After lunch on the fourth day Joy jumps out of bed. She's walking and talking. Her eyes are twinkling. She makes herself cups of tea. She plays Scrabble and laughs at jokes. I can't believe the transformation in her.

A few days later Joy is discharged. Ruth leaves soon after. I spend my days lying on my bed, wandering up and down the corridor, sitting in the Ladies' Lounge, going to the dining room and swallowing pills. Eventually I can concentrate enough to watch five minutes of television or read a small article in the newspaper. As the torment and the screaming in my body and soul recedes, I face a new burden. It is boredom – endless crushing boredom.

A few weeks after my admission Dr L'Estrange calls me into his office and asks me how I am. I say I'm really good and I act it too. I don't feel really good but I can't bear being in the hospital any more.

'You can go home today.'

Chantelle gets my stuff from the property cupboard, gives me a prescription and a card with my next appointment with Dr L'Estrange on it. I walk alone down the long polished corridor, past Betty the receptionist, past all the sad people in the waiting room, into the outside world.

I think about all the broken heroes who end up like me, in places like this, seeking their redemption. There is no shortage of myths and legends about people in our kind of predicament – St George and the dragon, forty days in the wilderness, the despair of Job, survival in the trenches. I thought that the psychiatrists and nurses would feel compassion and respect for my desperate struggle; that they would understand I am fighting the collapse of my self and my whole existence. I expected that they would guide me through my despair back into a universe that is rich with meaning. But I'm starting to realise that the staff don't see us reflected in these heroic stories. All they see in me is a sick, deluded, screwed-up twenty-one-year-old who needs their control and containment.

Walking through the car park I know that I am no nearer to recovery than I was before I went in. The only difference now is that I'm on painkillers for the torment. I know that my time in hospitals is not over. I know, with a shiver, that I will be back in a loony bin somewhere, some time soon.

←———→

I've been out of hospital for several weeks. I start to feel a whole lot better and stop taking my pills. Winter sets in. Over the next few weeks the darkness encroaches on my mind, just as it does on the days. I leave my flat and go to live in the sunroom at my brother Sean's flat, where he lives with his girlfriend Tina.

Walking back to Sean's flat from the university, I feel as though I'm trapped in a dreary watercolour. All the colour has drained out of the buildings, trees and sky; everything has an ugly grey wash over it. The trees lean over me, menacing and jeering; the dark sky presses down on me; the low whine of the cars envelops me. When I get home I bury myself in my bed with the curtains drawn so I don't have to look at anything.

It's not long until I'm spiralling into the black box again, where everything is futile except death. My death wish returns stronger than before. It seduces me with the logic that death is my only option. It gives my wrecked life a diabolical purpose.

One cold morning I wake after a broken sleep with more certainty than ever that I have no place in this world that is free of torment. There is only one thing to do. I get dressed and swallow forty anti-depressants. Then I slip out of my flat before Sean and Tina wake.

I slouch my way to the Botanic Gardens to find a hiding place. Up on the side of the hill I find a huge old rhododendron bush with branches that reach down to the ground. I lie under it, curled into a ball, and close my eyes waiting for peace. But after a time I start to jerk and experience the most terrible thirst. Panic rises. I come out from under the bush and stumble down a one-way street towards home. Panic rises again, I'm losing control of my limbs and my mouth is as dry as paper. I go into a dairy. 'Ah, um, raspberry milkshake, please.'

An old man makes me one while I jerk and whimper with panic.

'You all right there, love?' he says handing me the milkshake.

My panic is spiking. I throw some money on the counter and make a jerky exit from the shop. The milkshake wets my mouth but I drink it so quickly that half a block later my mouth feels like paper again. I'm getting confused now and I can't really recall why I'm feeling so spaced out. A few long minutes later I stagger back to my flat. Tina is just closing the door behind her as she leaves for work.

'What's wrong?' she asks.

'I, I, I'm freaking out.' I can't talk properly because I'm jerking too much.

'Sean's gone. I need to get you some help.'

She walks me around the corner to the emergency department, asking me what's happened but I can't talk any more. She helps me up the steps to the reception desk where she explains that she thinks I might have taken something. Then everything goes black as I fall on the floor.

That evening I wake to find myself lying in a strange room, full of machinery with tubes going into me and wires stuck to my chest. Sean is holding my hand. I ask him where I am and he says I'm in hospital. Then I remember.

Dr L'Estrange comes to see me later with a mask on and stands by my bed. 'How are you Mary?'

'Dunno.'

'The doctors who treated you this morning told me you were knocking on death's door.'

'Really?'

'Why did you do it?'

'I don't want to be alive.'

'You need to stay here for a couple of days and then they'll transfer you to the Canary Ward.'

Dr L'Estrange gets ready to leave. 'Stay with it,' he says.

I thank him for coming but I'm not sure if he hears me.

<hr />

Two days later I'm back in the Canary Ward. As I walk in past the sad people in the waiting room then down the long polished corridor I see Joy sitting like a statue again in the Ladies' Lounge. After the admission ritual where I exchange my possessions for a hospital nightie and a light-blue dressing gown, I see Ruth pacing outside my room.

'Hey, Ruth. You're back.'

'Yeah, I crapped out again.'

'Same here.'

'Half the people who were in with us last time are back,' she says. 'Joy's been coming here for fifteen years. I'm really scared I'll still be coming to these places at her age.'

'Yeah, so am I.'

Ruth's eyes fill with tears.

The next day my parents drive two hundred miles to visit me. I see them walking up the corridor towards me. My father's hair is whiter than ever. He's wearing a leather zip-up jacket and beige trousers. My mother's big owly glasses flash in the light, her skirt swishes and she's wearing a patterned satin scarf. They look out of place, like two innocent, happy children who have just discovered the horrors of the underworld.

My parents both hug me and I take them to the visitor's lounge. We talk about my overdose. They tell me I look better than they expected.

'We want you to come home and live with us when you get out of here,' says my mother.

'I don't want to live at home.'

'Look, you've been withdrawn from university, you can't work and you don't have a flat to go to. How will you survive if you stay in

Dunedin?' says my father, knowing I won't have a plausible answer.

'I dunno. Can't I sort my own life out?'

'No, you can't. You tried to kill yourself last week,' exclaims my mother.

My father holds her arm. 'Clare, you need to calm down.'

'You expect me to be calm at a time like this?'

My parents are scared. My mother expresses it for both of them.

We talk some more. I know I don't have any other options. I agree to live with them.

'It won't be forever,' says my father.

'I'm not a kid any more, all right?'

'We just want to see you well and independent again,' says my mother.

Dr L'Estrange calls us into his office. I cringe with embarrassment. My parents are worried raw; my mother gets loud and demanding and my father shelters in rationality and the occasional joke. Dr L'Estrange examines them with his X-ray eyes. They all seem to have forgotten I'm in the room.

As we walk away from Dr L'Estrange's office my mother is angry. 'I don't think that man has done anything to help you and he probably blames me.'

'Calm down, Clare,' says my father putting his arm around her shoulder.

Two months later my parents come to get me from the Canary Ward.

We drive up to Christchurch on a rainy day with all my possessions in two suitcases. I'm already starting to plan my exit from their home as we pass by the fogged-in sea, the wet hills of North Otago and the Canterbury Plains. I've always got on OK with my parents, but at twenty-one it's just not cool to be living with them. I resent becoming their dependent child again. Becoming a psychiatric patient on the cusp of adulthood has thrown me back into what seems like an eternal adolescence, when all I want to be is a grown up.

⟵——————⟶

The Canary Ward was the nicest hospital I ever went to. It was clean and sunny. The bathrooms were private and we didn't have to queue up for drugs. The nurses were never cruel. They never threw people on the floor to inject them. They never locked anyone up. Sometimes they sat with us in the Ladies' Lounge playing cards and laughing with us. One or two of them even asked us how we were feeling.

The next hospital I went to was called Everglade. I hated everything about it.

3.

THE SPINNING KALEIDOSCOPE

I'm in a spinning kaleidoscope.

I cannot sit down, I pace, I run, I feel like a bird getting ready to fly. My whole body zings.

Everything is sacred and sensual. The universe is brimming with beauty and power. I have no fears, no doubts, no tolerance for anything that is less than breathtaking.

Life has an irresistible urgency. I am invincible. I am strong and heroic, rushing into the glorious future with a cascade of ideas that fly for a moment or two then crash.

The kaleidoscope starts spinning faster. My mind loses focus. There are no sequences, no causes or consequences, no depth of being – just a speeding parade of fragmented thoughts, sensations, intentions and movements. The anchors that moor my thoughts to the past and the future have snapped. I'm getting lost in the ever-present.

As the spinning gets faster, the world that other people live in gets unbearably slow. I am too special to belong to this lumbering planet. As my trust in the world recedes and the spinning wobbles my axis to breaking point, my euphoria turns to paranoia.

←———→

I rush around in aimless circles at my parents' house, my mind catapulting to the edge of chaos. I start to throw billiard balls through the air in the back room. I see my father through the glass door on the phone in the kitchen, looking grave.

He comes in and takes the billiard balls from me. 'I've been speaking to the doctor. We think you need to be in hospital. We'll take you in an hour.'

My mother joins us and he goes outside to dig the garden.

'What's he digging the garden for?' I yell.

'Calm down,' says my mother.

'I need to know.'

'He's just planting some vegetables.'

But I know he's not just planting vegetables. He's frantic. Sweat is pouring off his face and he's digging deep. My father is digging my grave.

'I've gotta get out of here.'

'Not long now. Just let Dad finish his digging,' says my mother.

So she's in on it too. I make a run for the door but my mother stands in front of it.

'I've gotta go. Please take me to the hospital. Now.'

She hears my fear and drives me to Everglade Hospital.

As we turn into the main entrance, the mental hospital looks like one of those dark satanic mills William Blake wrote about. It's a grim, grey, three-storey concrete building with a steep roof. It's got a bell tower, tall narrow windows and a huge door at the front. Everglade probably looked grand when it was built but now it looks evil, like a Dracula house.

My mother stops the car. 'God, you're not going in there, are you?' Then I see the sign to the Forget-Me-Not Clinic. It points to the left of the evil building.

The Forget-Me-Not Clinic is a newer wooden two storeyed building; it looks like one of those prefabs that arrive in big bits on the back of a truck. It's plonked in the middle of a grass paddock, just beyond the shadow of the evil building.

'This isn't much better,' says my mother getting my bag out of the car. She looks as though she's going to cry.

It's dark inside. The floor is covered with thin felt carpet patches and it sounds hollow when I step on it. Sad, slugged-out people sit on the chairs and the floor in the corridors. We go around and around. I'm jumping and running, yelling at the patients to get off their arses. My mother gets agitated. 'Where are the nurses?' A patient comes up and directs us to the nursing station. We can see the nurses behind the glass. One or two look busy but the others are lounging in their chairs. They look over to us but it's as if we're not there. My mother gets angry. She raps on the glass. A bored-looking nurse slides the window open.

My mother explains that I'm being admitted. The nurse says, 'Just a minute.' She slides the window closed. We can see her looking at files, joking with the other nurses and making a phone call. Ten minutes later she slides the window open again, 'We've got no documentation.' My mother hands her a letter from Dr L'Estrange to Dr Pilling and she reads it slowly. 'How long has your daughter been in Christchurch?'

'I'm here, you know,' I yell.

'About ten days,' says my mother.

'Yeah, but we need the transfer documents and they haven't arrived.'

My mother is extremely angry now. She says in her most don't-mess-with-me voice, 'My husband has already talked to Dr Pilling. I want to speak to him please.'

My mother waits outside the nurses' station for another forty minutes while I pace around the clinic. Dr Pilling appears with a smile and a handshake. He's about fifty with shoulder-length brown hair and big glasses, wearing a cardigan and suit trousers, sandals and socks.

We sit in his messy office but I can't keep still. 'Don't worry about the transfer documents, we'll sort it out,' he says. While he's reading the letter he asks me about my depressions, my highs, how am I sleeping, am I eating, am I taking my pills and do I feel suicidal.

'Everything's fantastic, the only problem's my father, he's digging my grave.'

He asks my mother about how the family is coping.

'We're very worried and we don't think she's getting enough help.'

Dr Pilling looks at me. 'OK, Mary, I think we need to admit you.'

A nurse takes me to a small, sunless bedroom and gives me a handful of pills. The walls are varnished plywood. There's a bed with a plastic mattress and a cabinet that has a missing castor and a door that won't close. 'We want you to have a very long sleep,' she says. She tells me to put my pyjamas on and takes my clothes away. A few hours later I'm asleep and I don't wake up properly for a week. In between meals, taking pills and visits to the toilet, I'm barely conscious. The darkness presses down on me, my limbs are like lead, my mind sinks like a stricken ship. The world is a receding point of light.

I'm in a pharmacological grave.

←———→

'Medication time,' a nurse's voice sings out.

Since emerging from my long sleep the nurses no longer bring the drugs to me. I have to follow the other patients up to a little cubby-hole. The queue goes all the way around the corner. Two nurses inside the cubby-hole give out pills and syrup. Each person puts out their hands to receive their next dose, puts the pills in their mouth, takes a sip out of a cup then stands aside for the next person in the queue to receive theirs. It's a Holy Communion for lost souls.

One of the nurses gives me a little measuring cup of orange syrup.

'What's this?'

'Chlorpromazine.'

'Can I have a pill?'

'Just drink it.'

The syrup tastes sinister underneath all the saccharin they've put in it.

Next I queue up for dinner in the dining room. A grumpy old woman slaps the food on our plates and I pick up a glass of bright orange cordial and a piece of buttered white bread. I take my meal to an empty table. The mashed potatoes are undercooked and full of hard lumps, the cauliflower is pink and mushy, and the meat sits in a gelatinous sauce flecked with brown. I can't eat it. Most of my diet at Forget-Me-Not consists of buttered white bread and sticky cordial.

←———→

The next morning, still in my hospital nightie and towelling dressing gown, I'm called to the interview room. Dr Pilling and a nurse are sitting in there looking serious. I sit opposite them under a big mirror.

'Mary, can you move over to this chair so people can see you?' Dr Pilling asks.

I am confused.

'You see that mirror there? It's a one-way mirror. There are students and staff in the next room and they can see us but we can't see them.'

'Why don't they just come in here?' I ask.

'Well, there's quite a lot of them and patients can find it intimidating. We're teaching them.'

I give them a droll wave. No one waves back. This must be what it's like to be on TV.

Dr Pilling asks me the questions I have answered so many times before. When did my mood swings start? What happens when I'm depressed? What happens when I'm high? Sleeping? Appetite? Energy levels? Sex? Boyfriends? Religion? School? University? My mother? On and on.

The anti-psychotics have mashed my head, my voice is slurry and my knees jiggle up and down. I feel as though I'm sinking in my own stupor. I ramble through my answers like a revved-up car that's stuck in first and is careening all over the road. I feel like the star in a freak show.

Dr Pilling thanks me and tells me I can leave. I linger in the corridor to get a look at my mystery audience but they stay in their room with the door shut.

←——————※

After breakfast the next morning all the patients meander down to the weekly community meeting in the Great Hall. There's nothing great about it – it's just an oversized room with high windows so the patients can't jump out and the rest of the world doesn't have to look at us. Vinyl-covered chairs line the walls, and a television is fixed on the wall in one corner, high enough so the patients can't interfere with it. We sit or pace, flicking our cigarette ash into giant peach tins. Dr Pilling comes in with some nurses and tells us all to sit. He reads out some notices about groups we can go to, the hospital dance, the restriction on towels because of budget cuts and a reminder to put our plates on the trolley after we've eaten. Several patients have dropped off to sleep. Some of us are still pacing. 'Sit, please,' he says, motioning us towards some chairs. 'Now, do any of the patients here have any issues they'd like to discuss with the staff?'

Silence.

'These meetings are for your benefit. You need to make use of them. Any issues?'

Silence.

'I take it that you're very satisfied with the service at Forget-Me-Not,' Dr Pilling says with a self-assured smirk. 'The meeting's closed.'

Then one of the pacers, an intense, swarthy young man called Jeremy, yells at Dr Pilling, 'Yeah, well, I'm not satisfied. You made me come here. You've filled me with poison and the food is shit. Give me my clothes back, you control freaks, because I'm going home.' Dr Pilling looks full of benevolent concern. He nods at the nurses and four of them drag Jeremy out of the room.

More silence.

Dr Pilling gets up to leave and we follow him out the door.

It's a fine day. We're allowed to walk on the grass and go to the exercise yard. The nurses tell all the people on chlorpromazine to come and get sunhats and sunscreen at the nurse's station. In the queue I start talking to a fat, freckly woman called Glenda who hops from one leg to another. 'Why do people on chlorpromazine need all this sun protection?' I ask.

'Because it makes you fry in the sun.'

I can already feel the sinister orange syrup leaching through my skin and doing its evil alchemy with the sun, while I blister like cheese under a grill.

'Eh, you know the guy Jeremy that yelled at Pill Pusher this morning? He's in seclusion,' Glenda says.

'Just for yelling?'

'Yeah, bloody idiot. Pays to keep your mouth shut around here.'

'Shit, he just wants to go home.'

'Yeah, don't we all.'

A large group of us patients slouch across the grass behind the nurses, towards the exercise yard which is by one of the back wings of the evil building. The yard is enclosed by a high, rusting fence and a gate with a huge padlock on it. As we get nearer I see flaky strips of paint on the bitumen that were once the markings on a netball court. The yard is pitted with potholes as if it has been shot at from the sky. Grassy tufts grow between the cracks. It looks like a no man's land – a space too desolate and dangerous to enter. One of the nurses opens the gate with a key the size of her hand. A line of patients walk into the yard. They wander around it like people too lost to care.

Glenda waddles up to me. 'How's this for a wholesome recreation hour?' She rounds her mouth and puts on a hoity-toity matron's voice: 'In today's programme you will observe a bunch of drugged-out zombies walking around an enclosure with their dicks flopping out of their pyjama pants.'

She points to a young man with tousled hair and red face. A pink roll of flesh is bobbing around at the opening of his pyjama fronts. We both snort with laughter. For a moment I feel alive again.

'Hey, let's sneak off and have a ciggie.'

We sit on the grass behind the recreation hall which is to the right of the enclosure. Glenda asks me. 'What got you into a place like this?'

'I went high.'

'You too. Jeez, my last high was good. Talk about elated. Just danced all the time.'

'Yeah, I do that too. I even danced to the news.'

Glenda laughs. 'Hey, sex is fantastic isn't it? I just about bonked my husband silly.'

'I'd do it with anyone when I'm high.'

Glenda takes a big drag on her cigarette. 'Trouble is, I got the credit card out and just went for it. Bought three brand-new cars, one for me, one for my husband and one for my Mum.'

'I suppose they thanked you by dragging you here?'

'You got it.'

We stub out our cigarettes and walk back to Forget-Me-Not.

'So you've got Pill Pusher for a shrink, eh? Same as me,' says Glenda,

'Yeah. He tries to be all friendly but I don't know how to talk to him. Why should I trust him? He's old. And he locks people up.'

'Just tell him what he wants to hear and you'll be outta here in no time, girl,' smiles Glenda.

←——————→

Since I've come out of my long sleep I've been feeling like a wooden puppet with one blank facial expression and a few stiff movements. I'm an automaton, drained of spontaneity and soul. The drugs have killed my life force. I'm now one of the people sitting around the corridor that I yelled at to get off their arses the day I arrived. I've also got a dry mouth and I'm so constipated I think I'll need a teaspoon to shovel out my shit.

Most of the people at Forget-Me-Not are on high doses of anti-psychotic drugs. They all look wooden like me, but one or two of them have a twitchy face or limb, like androids in the grip of random power surges. Albert's an older patient whose tongue swishes around in his mouth all the time. Glenda says the anti-psychotics did it to him and he can't stop it.

Though the anti-psychotics slug me they make me start to pace and panic. I panic about everything. I panic about nothing. I try to sit but the panic pulls me to my feet and I start pacing again. More panic. More pacing.

'I'm freaking out,' I announce outside the nurses' station, my hands pulling at my hair, my feet stamping on the floor one after the other. Eventually a nurse comes out and gives me extra chlorpromazine.

An hour or two later I bang on the nurses' station window. 'Please help, it's getting worse.'

No reply.

I bang again. A nurse puts his newspaper down and slides open the window. 'What's up with you?'

'I can't stop pacing and I'm panicking all the time.'

He looks at my chart. 'I can't give you any more chlorpromazine yet. Come back in an hour.' He slides the window closed.

'I can't wait that long!' I scream.

He slides the window open. 'I'll get the psychiatrist on duty to come and see you.'

He slides the window closed again.

Half an hour later a woman with a long, serious face and a ponytail takes me into an interview room. 'I'm going to give you an injection for side-effects,' she says.

Half an hour later, I'm feeling high and cruisy.

I pass Glenda in one of the corridors. 'You look better,' she says.

'I reckon you could sell these side-effects drugs down at the pub.'

'People do,' she says. 'I know nurses who steal them from the ward and take a handful of them for a bit of R and R.'

The next time I queue up for medication I'm told I've been promoted to tablets and I've got an extra one. 'That's for the side-effects,' says the nurse.

I take my lithium and the side-effects pills first, then trap the chlorpromazine under my tongue while I take a second gulp of water. A minute later I'm in the ladies' spitting it into the toilet. I go through the same routine four times a day.

Several days later, a nurse comes up to me, playing with her big key. 'Dr Pilling wants to see you.'

Dr Pilling is standing at his desk sorting through a large untidy stack of files. 'How are you today Mary?' he mutters at the files. 'I'm going to discharge you.'

'I want to go home.'

'That's good. Oh, I've found it.' He sits down, opens my file and his face turns serious. 'I think it's timely for me to tell you about the impact your illness is likely to have on you. You have a chronic condition which will recur for the rest of your life.'

'Do I really?'

'The medication can help but you need to reduce stress and lower your horizons. A big career or full-time work probably aren't options, I'm afraid. And you need to think very carefully about having children, in case they inherit your illness.'

I've seen plenty of people in the Canary Ward and Everglade whose lives are like the one Dr Pilling is prescribing for me. They're single, they don't work and they keep going back to hospital. But Dr Pilling is wrong – they do have careers. They are chronic psychiatric patients, schooled in poverty, low status and loneliness, with bloated skills in passive dependence and impotent rebellion. I don't want to be one of them.

'Does anyone recover?' I ask.

'Not usually,' he says. 'I'll see you next week.' He looks up and smiles then starts writing his notes as I close the door behind me.

My mother picks me up to take me home. Her friend Vanessa, who has also been a patient in a mental hospital, comes around for dinner. Vanessa is my mother's age with prematurely grey hair and a commanding verbal flow that spins with humour. We're halfway through the beef casserole when I tell them. 'Dr Pilling said today I've got a chronic illness.'

My mother looks lost for words.

Vanessa says, 'Oh, my psychiatrist used to say that to me too. I remember going to see him, that funny wispy bald head with the part down on top of his ear, trotting along in front of me with his bandy little legs while I followed him to his office. He'd look at me through those filthy specs and he'd tell me I was manic depressive. Never mind the drink. Never thought to ask about the drink, when all I needed to do was dry out. All those years, all those pills, all those visits to that peculiar little man, who really didn't have a clue.'

My mother hoots with delight. 'They are hopeless, aren't they.'

'Of course they are,' laughs Vanessa. She turns to me. 'You'll get better, I know you will.'

Vanessa is the only person I came across in all my years of madness who tells me I'll recover. The trouble is, I don't believe her.

The next time I see Dr Pilling at his outpatient clinic, my parents come with me.

'I'm going back to live in Dunedin next year,' I tell him.

My father says, 'We don't want her to go yet. We don't think she's ready.'

'What will you do in Dunedin, Mary?' asks Dr Pilling.

'Get a flat and find a job. I know heaps of people there.'

'What if you get unwell again?'

'I dunno, there's always the Canary Ward.'

'You don't like living in Christchurch?'

'I don't know anyone here.'

'Mary, you've been very unwell. I agree with your parents. I think you need to stay in Christchurch.'

They all look at me with warning in their eyes, waiting for me to say I won't go.

My anger collapses into humiliation. Tears come to my eyes. I've been ambushed by a gang of middle-aged people who are treating me like a child. Whose side is Dr Pilling on?

Doctor's notes, Everglade Hospital:

Mary seen with parents. Parents are worried about Mary's decision to go back to Dunedin. Discussed this at length and became apparent that Mary really hasn't any plans as to what she will do when she gets there and is really running away from her failure and inability to adjust in Christchurch. She cried bitterly at this point.

Dr P. H. Pilling

←———→

Instead of going to Dunedin, I go hitch-hiking with friends around the North Island for the summer. We head up to a three-day rock festival in the baking brown hills. Thousands of people, squeezed into buses, vans, truck houses and cars, drive up the dusty gravel road to the car park. They gather their packs, their billies and their tents and surge through the gates.

My friend Joanne and I pitch our tent by some other people we know, about five minutes' walk from the main stage. We spend our days getting stoned, giggling, listening to music, looking for water and shade, and buying munchies at the food stalls.

On the last night we take a tab just before the headline act, a band called Split Enz. The crowd is buzzing and suddenly I'm overcome with rapture. The band comes onto the stage at dusk and the hillside erupts with music and lights and cheering.

Move to the frenzy, everybody lose control
Move to the frenzy, it's for the young and the old.'

I dance in ecstasy. The words and the music flow through me. The lights pulse under the darkening sky. The crowd sways in perfect rhythm. I sway with them. The ground disappears and the edges of things dissolve. This is heaven.

Move to the frenzy, where it's all going to end
Move to the frenzy, everybody's round the bend.

A jerking flash of panic.

Another flash of panic, and another, and another, until all I feel is complete terror. 'Get me outta here!' I scream. Joanne and some other friends cajole me to our tent as the terror mounts. It's pure terror with no object or assailant to run from — it's the inescapable terror of being.

'There's no way out.'

'It's OK, Mary. We're taking you to a safe place.'

But the terror devours me and I howl all the way to the tent.

I wake in my clothes. It is daytime and I crawl out of the tent. The others are boiling water in a billy around the fire.

'What happened?'

'Shit, you gave us a fright,' says Joanne, 'When we got you back to the tent you had a fit and conked out. You were frothing at the mouth.'

I join them at the fire and cry. 'You had a bad trip,' Joanne says, and hands me a cup of tea.

←———→

I have an appointment to see Dr Pilling again.

'How was your holiday, Mary?

'Good. Yeah. Not too bad.'

'Where did you go again?'

'Just up north with some friends.'

'And how's your mood?'

'Gloomy.'

'Oh, tell me about that.'

'My life's going nowhere.'

'You said you were going to look for a flat and a job, here in town.'

'Yeah. Haven't got around to it yet.'

Dr Pilling leans forward and asks me questions for another twenty minutes. Then I leave with a prescription for lithium, anti-psychotics and anti-depressants.

Doctor's notes, Everglade Hospital:

Mary is emotionally rather an inhibited and colourless person. I find this young lady very hard going. She gives nothing away. Her mood is very flat. She answers questions monosyllabically. It is almost as if she resents coming to an interview to speak about herself. She appears angry and aloof.

Dr P. H. Pilling

←——→

The next time I see Dr Pilling, my parents come with me. They tell him I'm not getting enough help. He suggests I go to a private day hospital run by nuns. Except the nuns are out the back somewhere doing the accounts or cooking dinner, and most of them have left anyway because they have lost the faith and don't want to be nuns any more. The Gethsemane Day Hospital is staffed by mental health professionals, mainly Protestant ones, whose path to salvation for lost souls like me consists of group therapy, walks in the park, rug-making and Friday afternoon lectures devoted to the new virtues of expressing your inner feelings, blaming your mother and asserting your needs.

It's my first day at Gethsemane. I'm pacing around the nuns' garden when I come across a grotto in the corner. The Virgin Mary stands inside a half-dome of stones, in her usual powder-blue gown with her hands joined in prayer and fake red roses snaking around her ankles. I'm sure she's winking at me, like the Messiah's naughty mum in Monty Python's *Life of Brian*.

A tiny man with a long face and a moustache comes up to me. 'Hi. Mary? I'm going to be your nurse. My name is Rick.'

That means I talk to Rick every day and I go to his group therapy session twice a week.

While I'm at rug-making a few days later, Rick motions me to come over and see him. We sit on a wooden bench around the corner.

'How are you today?'

'Gloomy. I don't have a future. The psychiatrist says I'll never get better, so what's the point in trying?'

'You know, you could take more responsibility for your own life.'

'How? I can't control my moods.'

Rick looks at me with a warning in his eye. 'It's your life. You're the only one that can get yourself out of this rut. No one else can do it for you.'

I sit in silence. It's kind of obvious, but when I became a mental patient all the professionals treated me like I couldn't control my life any more. Until now.

Rick gets up to answer the phone and I go back to my rug, feeling disrupted as though I've just heard someone announce the world is flat after all.

I begin to trust Rick because I can see he trusts me to solve my own problems. I start to feel some hope for my future again.

There are several of us in Rick's therapy group. We always start with a round where we tell each other how we are feeling. David has an amputated arm. During one of our sessions when it's his turn to share, he sits in his chair with his head down, weeping while he cradles his plastic arm. 'I hate my arm. I can't get used to it,' he wails. Saliva falls out of his mouth and his bent torso shudders with grief.

I sit in silence with the rest, feeling both awkward and privileged to be witnessing another person's uncensored despair.

Rick stands up. His face is red. He points his finger at David in fury. 'It's time you came to terms with your amputation. Why can't you do it? You don't want to let go of it, do you? You just want to sit there and suffer. Come on, it's been years since you lost your arm. Move on, move on!'

David sobs even louder, and buries his head in humiliation. I lower my head too, stunned by the cruelty of Rick's outburst. I know Rick is probably trying some fancy trick to shake David out of his despair. But I also know in the depth of my being that what Rick has said is wrong. I can't find the words to raise an objection. No one else does either.

I stop trusting Rick at that moment and for a long time I lose a little bit of trust in myself, because I failed to stick up for David.

←————→

A few months later I leave the Gethsemane Clinic and decide to go back to live in Dunedin. My parents and Dr Pilling think it's a bad idea but I go anyway. Dr Pilling writes a letter about me to my new psychiatrist. It summarises my history and finishes with these two paragraphs:

I think Mary has an atypical bipolar disorder but she also has features of a personality disorder. Her personality adjustment difficulty is very severe and it really goes back to her childhood. I'm not sure whether the family atmosphere can fully explain her degree of personality adjustment or whether in fact her genetic predisposition to manic depression has also had an effect of shaping her personality.

If Mary returns to Christchurch the family have intimated that they would be glad if I continued to manage her. I would be ready to step in if she has any further psychotic breaks and needed the control of this ward.

Dr P. H. Pilling

I don't like Dr Pilling's speculation that I have a personality disorder. Psychotic depression, manic depression and bipolar have been conveyed to me as illnesses; they were not really *from* me, they happen *to* me. But a personality disorder label seems to slander my whole being. There is nothing left of me that isn't sick, twisted or just plain fucked. This means there is nothing left of me that can escape the gaze of psychiatry.

←————→

Everything goes fine in Dunedin. I prefer it there, away from my anxious parents, away from Dr Pilling in the prefab with the hollow floors in the shadow of the evil Dracula building. I even finish a year at university, with only one brief visit to the Canary Ward, and fall for a man called Nick who is pale, with a thick beard and a long brown ponytail. Nick is quirky, he's witty and he tolerates my madness.

There's a new psychiatrist at Student Health called Dr McGeorge and I get an appointment in the post to see him. I walk down there following the same route I took to see Dr L'Estrange, wondering why I've agreed to see another bloody shrink. Dr McGeorge arrives forty-five minutes late and calls my name. I fume as I walk behind him into his office.

'Hello, Mary. My name is Peter. Thanks for coming to see me. I'm so sorry I was late today.' Peter is a youngish man with messy, dark, shoulder-length hair and a beard. He wears a brown leather jacket and sits forward in his seat while he introduces himself. He tells me why he went into psychiatry, that he doesn't believe in just prescribing drugs and he's trained in Gestalt therapy. He has a way of bringing me into his confidence that evaporates my suspicions of his profession and my anger at his lateness. I immediately feel I can trust him.

Peter then asks me about myself, my mood swings, what works for them, what I like and don't like, how my studies are going and what I want to do with my life. 'Have you thought what you would like from me, Mary?'

None of the others have ever asked me this before and I struggle to find an answer. 'Well, I guess I just want to check in with you about my drugs and how I'm doing.'

'How often do you need to check in?'

'Maybe once a month.'

'Sounds sensible to me,' he smiles.

A month later I go to see Peter again. He's forty-five minutes late. Again I walk behind him into his office fuming. Again he apologises and my anger vanishes. It turns out that Peter is always late and we go though the same ritual of apology and forgiveness every time.

One day we go into his office and he sits forward on his chair, ready to bring me into his confidence again.

'Mary, just before we begin, you may find I'm not quite on form today. My father died last week and I'm in a bit of shock about it.'

'Wow, I'm really sorry to hear that. It's OK with me if you're not quite on form.'

I'm bowled over by Peter's honesty, by his willingness to talk to me as an equal human being, by his ability to be vulnerable with me without placing any demands on me. And I wonder why other psychiatrists can't be like him.

———⟶

One night, lying with Nick in bed in the darkness, I tell him there's something I want to talk to him about, something I've never talked to anyone else about, because I feel so bad and stupid about it. I bury my head in his chest and with all the courage I can find, I tell him that sometimes I worry that I'm a lesbian. Nick laughs out loud and tells me how earnest I am. Then he starts teasing me in a fake German accent: 'You have very serious latent psychopathology. You must talk to a psychiatrist about this.'

'No way. Most of them think I'm fucked up enough as it is.'

We both roll about laughing. I feel enormous relief.

Though we live together, Nick wants to keep his distance. He doesn't stick up for me when I need it and he won't introduce me to his family, but I want to marry him. One day I arrive home from a holiday; he is acting strangely but he won't say what is going on.

We get back to our flat, and as I climb the stairs, I see our unmade bed with the two pillows touching each other, both dented in the middle. A terrible truth flashes through my mind and disappears again, until I see him at a party that night with Karen, a friend of ours with crooked teeth. Though Nick and Karen don't talk or look at each other much, I sense there is knowledge between them. Then the terrible truth flashes again but this time it stays with me: it was Karen's head that dented the other pillow.

When Nick comes to bed that night I say to him, 'You've got something to tell me.'

'What do you mean?'

'You know what I mean.'

'No I don't. What are you on about?'

We go back and forth like this for a long time but I refuse to say it for him. Then he tells me and we cry all night. In the morning I go away and never return. Nick goes to stay with Karen and her crooked teeth.

I don't fall in love with any more men after that.

I've got nothing against men. But I have problems with them. I don't enjoy picking up their dirty socks and always being the first to notice the toilet is dirty. I don't like the way they are so inarticulate about their feelings. It troubles me that sex with men is much more of a meeting of bodies than of souls. And it troubles me also that I have been betrayed.

I'm consumed with hurt and rage. My rage continues for months and exhausts me. Slowly I start to slide into the black box again.

4.

A WOUND UNDER SIEGE

I'm back in the Canary Ward. My flatmates found me mute in bed one morning. I could hear them calling my name but they were so far away and I didn't have any words to answer them with. It was as though burglars had broken into my mind, stripped it of everything, and pulled all the blinds down on their way out.

I lie in my hospital bed between starchy white sheets for days. Most of the time I am a vast nothingness; all I am aware of is the shape and weight of my body, my rapid shallow breathing and the black space inside my head. I have no thoughts, I have no intentions, I have no name. Words and images are the blocks I make meaning out of. They are my world. Without them I am lost in space.

But there are also times when word and images attack me like missiles that come from nowhere and explode in the core of my being.

Nick is arched over me, stripped back to the muscle without hair or skin or fat. I am terrified; he is far too naked for me. He tries to kiss me but his lips are raw and bleeding. I squirm and turn my head away. Then he ejaculates blood all over me.

Insects have laid eggs in my brain. They are hatching and the larvae are eating through my brain. Their pale wet bodies are about to burrow out through my ears.

My beautiful baby niece Siobhan is lying in the sun. Hard hands pick her up and stretch her out on a table. Then an axe chops off her head and it rolls onto my lap.

These detonators keep playing and replaying in my head while a monotone chant of despair rises and booms in the ruins – I must die. I must die. I must die.

Then the explosions and booms fall away and I'm back in the vast nothingness again.

I drift until I hit the turbulent terror of my nihilistic existence. I know I have to find words in order to find my world again, so I try to make thoughts and hold onto them, but they splinter and get sucked up into the blackness.

A young nurse crouches by my bed. 'Mary, I've come to take you for a walk,' she says in a soft voice. She slowly peels the pink candlewick bedspread off my head and cups her hand on my shoulder. 'Let me help you up,' she whispers, slipping her other hand under my back. I sit in a slouch as she removes the bedspread. Then she helps me off of bed and holds me by my arm. I take slow little steps and can't bring myself to look above the ground. We shuffle down the long polished corridor, past the waiting room, through the car park and onto the lawn.

The nurse doesn't say 'chin up' or 'hurry up'. She doesn't say a thing. She's just there being kind, gently holding my arm and guiding me forward. She's the best nurse I've ever known.

←———→

I drift for days in the vast nothingness. Sometimes I think I'm lying alone on a raft in the middle of a huge empty sea. Sometimes I'm on a spaceship whirling into a remote lifeless galaxy. Sometimes I'm just in my hospital bed as the apocalypse erupts in my head.

Then one afternoon the world I share with others starts coming into view. It's as though my face has been buried in the ground and the hand that held it there has let go. Gradually the ground beneath me comes into focus. As I rise above it I see more and more of the ground until

I get a bird's-eye view of the whole landscape. I start off seeing little chinks of light and by the end of the day it is trickling into me. I even get up for half an hour and sit in the Ladies' Lounge.

The next morning, Chantelle the discus-thrower lookalike comes up to me. 'Hey, Mary, Dr Lackland wants to see you.'

'Who's he?'

'He's your new doctor.'

Chantelle steers me down the long polished corridor, past the waiting room into another corridor where the doctors' rooms are. Dr Lackland is about forty with ash-coloured hair, watery blue eyes and a red nose. He wears a bright smile and a herringbone suit jacket.

'What happened to Dr McGeorge?' I ask.

'Oh, he can't be your doctor any more because you've come into hospital.'

Dr Lackland looks through his notes then looks up. 'You've been very unwell but it's good to see you looking so much better.'

'Yeah.'

'Can you describe what's been going on?'

I tell him in a monotone about the vast nothingness, the terror, the repulsive images and the words that get jammed in my head. Then I ask him if he knows what it all means.

'What you've just described is a distortion of reality. It's happened because your brain chemistry is out of balance. What I need to do now is review your medication to make sure you're on the right ones to correct your imbalance, like insulin does with diabetes.'

Dr Lackland gives me a reassuring smile.

I feel uneasy but I don't know why.

←——————→

In the Canary Ward there's a nurse called Felicity who has a serious intelligent face and doesn't huddle with the other nurses. One day Felicity comes to sit beside me on a wounded chair in the Ladies' Lounge. She puts her knees together and straightens her gold-rimmed glasses. Her dark greying hair is cut like a pudding bowl. 'How are you getting on?' she asks in a well-modulated voice.

'I'm a lot better but I still I feel like a stone.' By now I've learnt not to say too much because the nurses look at me like I'm weird.

Felicity looks into the distance, her forefinger crosses her closed lips while she thinks. 'Mmm, that's interesting, where do you think that feeling comes from?'

'I dunno. My brain's fucked, I suppose.'

'I guess a stone feels cold and heavy and lifeless,' she says

'Yeah, I guess so.'

'Did you ever feel like that when you were little?'

I can see where she's heading – straight for my mother.

'No, not really.'

Most days Felicity comes to sit beside me. 'Have you ever thought about doing psychotherapy?' she asks one day.

I tell her it didn't do me any good. 'I'm not sure if I believe in all that stuff. Freud's wacky and he's too negative about people. I prefer Jung – he's more of a mystic.'

'Your unconscious has an enormous influence on you. Psychotherapy can help you understand it better. I've been doing therapy for years,' she says.

'Yeah, I found a book called *The Discovery of the Unconscious* in the library,' I tell her. 'But the unconscious isn't a discovery – it's an invention. You know, like God's an invention.'

Felicity says she believes people come to the Canary Ward because of unconscious conflicts and psychological dysfunction. She says if people did more therapy they might not need to take the pills.

I like Felicity, but it's scary and confusing talking to her. All the other psychiatrists and nurses say I've got a biological imbalance that I need to correct with pills. Felicity is saying I've got deep personality problems and I need to undress my head in front of some wacko psychotherapist for years if I am ever to recover. What a choice.

———

Things start feeling bad again. One day I'm sitting on a bench in the hospital garden when I come to the realisation that I have murdered someone. It was so brutal I have suppressed any memory of it until now.

Fragments start coming back to me, thrusting the knife into her soft flesh again and again, her blood spilling everywhere, her eyes frozen open with terror, then burying her body under a house and hiding the evidence. It's a waking nightmare.

I groan with horror and remorse covering my face with my hands. A nurse comes over to see what's going on.

'I've done something terrible. I've gotta go to the police station to make a confession.'

'How about having a lie down?'

'I'm a murderer.'

'You're a sick girl.'

'Please take me to the police station.'

'Take it easy. I'll be back.'

He walks away while I fret over my recovered memories. A few minutes later he returns with a shiny white pill for me to take.

The white pills turn the twisted torrents of my thoughts into a paste that takes an age to squeeze through the trenches in my brain. It's not so much that I stop believing I'm a murderer, it's more that my thoughts don't connect enough for me to sustain a complicated story any more.

←——————*

The next time I see Dr Lackland he tells me I have a new diagnosis. 'Your EEG results are consistent with temporal lobe epilepsy.'

'What's that?'

'It's a non-convulsive epilepsy. You don't lose consciousness or have fits but you may have strange sensory experiences, like hallucinations. Some people get a feeling of déjà vu, or they might feel intense fear or joy. These results probably explain some of the sensory or cognitive distortions you've been experiencing.'

'Does that mean I don't have manic depression?'

'Well, it certainly means there's something else going on, though it may not be the full explanation. But the good news is there's a drug that treats both temporal lobe epilepsy and swings in mood – it's called carbamazepine. I think you'll do much better on it than lithium.'

Dr Lackland looks excited, like he's just hit the bull's-eye.

'You mean I've been on the wrong drug all the time?'

'Yes, but I believe we have the right one for you now,' he says, smiling with conviction.

I start the carbamazepine straight away. Several days later Dr Lackland discharges me from hospital, telling me my moods are unlikely to trouble me any longer.

It doesn't take long for me to realise the carbamazepine is no more effective than lithium.

←——————→

It's two months since Dr Lackland discharged me and put me on carbamazepine. One evening I visit my close friend Louise. She has her own battle with despair but she doesn't go mad. She can always get up in the morning and go out looking like an ordinary person even when she feels barren inside. Louise understands my enormous struggle because she struggles herself. She understands it with empathy and immense respect.

As I walk in her front door she's playing Verdi's *Requiem* on her stereo. Louise hugs me then stands back with her hands on my shoulders. 'You look awful.'

'It's bad.'

'Sit down and I'll get us a cup of tea.'

Alone in the lounge I sit on an old green sofa and put my head in my hands. Verdi's *Requiem* comes back into focus. Its dark power floods me with anguish. Suddenly I can't stand the intensity of it any more. I stand up just as Louise is coming in with the tea.

'I've gotta go.'

'Hey, what's the matter?'

'The music.'

I'm already out the door sprinting through the streets, somehow believing the music will shake out of me and die on the footpath behind me. But it doesn't. Louise catches up with me and hugs me. 'I'm sorry. I didn't realise.'

'It's so bad.'

'I've turned it off. Come back to the house.'

Louise hands me my lukewarm tea. 'Mary, stay the night with me. I'm worried about you being alone.'

Louise gets into her side of the double bed and I burrow into the other side. She holds me close and strokes my hair while I whimper into the pillow.

The trouble is few people understand. I can't find anyone in my lucky family who has suffered like me, except perhaps my grandfather in the trenches. My grandfather never talked about his suffering but after he dropped dead at the Returned Servicemen's Association, I read the World War One poets, novels, histories, my grandfather's postcards home, and his intelligence reports. Though I've never been inside a trench, I've come to see my madness as trench warfare of the mind. The networks of trenches, knee-high with mud and barbed wire are like the nerve pathways in my mind as they clog up in the tangle of my despair. The men in the trenches and I are both trapped in the shelter of our dugouts: me retching at my own decaying spirit, they at their comrades' decaying bodies. We know our respective wars might kill us; they certainly will not be quick or easily won. But we are often past caring.

I leave Louise's flat the next afternoon to go to my drama class in the university. It's my turn to recite a poem. I've chosen a grim World War One poem that mirrors how I'm feeling. As I walk to stand in front of the class I feel raw, as though someone has peeled my skin off me.

I say the poem in a tight monotone, staring at a picture hook on the far wall, hoping that no one will notice that I feel like the soldiers running from the shells and the gas:

But someone still was yelling out and stumbling
And floundering like a man in fire or lime. . .
Dim, through the misty panes and thick green light

As under a green sea, I saw him drowning.
In all my dreams, before my helpless sight,
He plunges at me, guttering, choking, drowning.

As I'm saying it my terror mounts, at the poem and at how much I identify with it, and at the faces in front of me, some cringing, others uncomprehending.

I sit down feeling like a wound under siege, then go home and wrap myself in the cool bandages of my bedding.

⟵——⟶

The next morning my flatmate sees my desperation and takes me to the Canary Ward. A nurse says, 'Wait in the visitor's lounge, please. Dr Lackland is fully booked today but I'll tell him you're here.' I wait in the visitor's lounge all day huddled on the floor behind a chair, as my distress engulfs me. I feel like a long piercing scream, all screaming on the inside of me and out of the pores of my skin. My screaming and my self are one. This is pure pain.

At five o'clock Dr Lackland comes along and snaps at me to get up. I drag my way behind him and he tells a nurse to put me to bed. I have never, ever been in so much shame.

Guilt swoops down on me and pecks me to bits as I lie snared between my sheets like a whimpering animal. I am full of red-hot blame at myself for everything. I can't bear being so thoroughly bad. I am carrying hell around inside me.

Dr Lackland is in his office writing his notes:

On arriving on the ward, spent the entire day curled up on the waiting room floor behind a chair. Could not talk. Impression of over-dramatisation but with underlying gross psychological turmoil. For admission.

Dr M.T. Lackland

The next day Dr Lackland tells me I've been histrionic.

With one word he inflames my biggest fear – that my mood swings are my fault. With one word he gives external legitimacy to my private terror that I have used my mood swings to manipulate my relationships and escape my responsibilities. More often the shrinks have called me delusional, psychotic or depressed. These labels console me that my problems are not my fault. Mostly, mental health professionals reinforce my belief that I can't control my problems, but occasionally they decide I'm putting it on. I never understand how they decide whether I'm putting it on or not. Do they think I'm putting it on when I'm more florid than usual in my expressions of distress or when my behaviour doesn't fit my diagnosis? Do they start to blame me when they're tired and grumpy? Do they lash out in frustration when they see me returning again and again with the same problems?

←——————→

'I want to die.'

I'm sitting in the Ladies' Lounge with Maria with my head in my hands. Guilt continues to swoop down on me. 'It's all my fault. I need to die.'

Maria strokes my back. She's in her late thirties – dark and elegant with the fear of the hunted in her eyes. She doesn't argue with me.

It isn't that I want to die, I just can't stand the pain of being alive.

'I've tried so many times I've lost count,' says Maria. 'I hate myself so much, it feels like I'm clawing myself from the inside out. I just want to end the torture sometimes.' Maria is warm and lively and always ready to help out but I know she suffers more than just about anyone. She can't remember when she last felt comfortable with her own existence. Sometimes I get glimpses of Maria's rage at herself when, through the crack of her door, I see her slamming her head into the wall or biting her arm until it bleeds.

We patients talk about suicide the way inmates in prison talk about crime. Maria has the most expertise. She has a broad understanding of all the different methods, their shortcomings and their advantages, and the tricks you can play to ensure success. I'm just an apprentice who soaks up Maria's knowledge.

'Slashing your wrists is too slow,' says Maria. Jill tells us that anti-depressants are good but you have to take a lot of them. I tell them forty anti-depressants weren't enough to kill me and I've moved on to thinking I'll go alone to the mountains to die of hypothermia. 'Oh no,' mocks Jill,

'I'm going for comfort and style. I'll do it in my own bed, thanks, with my hair done and my lipstick on, not in a stinking bush shirt under a dripping rock on a mountain pass.' We all howl with laughter, until a nurse pokes her head in and tells us to tone down.

We need the option of suicide because it is the only power we have left when the pain gets too much. Suicide isn't just giving up, it's also the ultimate way of giving the finger to the demon inside you. Most of us don't kill ourselves. Instead we use drink, drugs, sex, cutting, cigarette burning or any other mind-altering activities. Sometimes we use them to kill the pain. At other times we use them to feel something – even if it's more pain.

<hr />

Things are tough for most of the patients. Jill is bringing up two children on her own and has been abused in every way possible. Her parents got drunk all the time, her uncle raped her, her father beat her, the school expelled her and she became a prostitute. Then she met a good man and tried to live like Mr and Mrs Normal. But the man turned out to be violent and she was left with the children. Jill is eaten up with anxiety and depression. She's scrawny with peroxided hair and heavy make-up. Her eyelids droop and her voice is slurred by psychiatric drugs.

But Jill has spirit, she is brave and treats us all like her comrades. Maria and I are sitting with her in the Ladies' Lounge again. Jill lights a cigarette, sucks hard on it and blows a stream of smoke out of her nostrils. 'You know, some of the staff here are crazier than the patients.'

Maria and I laugh in agreement.

'We're the sane ones,' she announces drawing hard on her cigarette.

Maria and I cheer.

'You two are fabulous.'

I sleep beside Jill in the ladies' dormitory. That night I hear her sobbing in the dark. The night nurses are too busy knitting in the Ladies' Lounge to notice her. I wake Maria and we go and sit with her.

'You're strong, you'll get through it. Don't let those bastards get to you,' we say.

Her sobbing dies down. 'Thanks, girls,' she says. We give her a hug and get back into bed.

←———→

'Visitor for Mary,' calls a nurse. I walk down to the visitor's lounge.

It's Brett, a Christian cartoonist who is trying to save me from my troubles in a gentle and unobtrusive way. We talk a lot about religion and madness. I tell him I'm not a believer. He doesn't seem to mind.

'Do you want to come with me to see a Christian healer?' he asks. It's the anthropologist in me that agrees to go, rather than a person in search of healing. The next week he comes to get me. The church is packed with people singing the roof off and flinging their arms in the air. The healer gets up and rants about Aids. Then he thunders on about all STDs: 'No, they are not sexually transmitted diseases. They are sexually transmitted demons that prey upon people who have turned their back on the Lord and indulged in sins of the flesh.'

This is hugely entertaining for me but I do my best not to show it.

Later the healer calls on people to come up to be healed. I go up to the front with Brett, feeling the awkward irony of a heathen pretending to be a believer. We explain what the problem is. The healer says he has healed many people like me. He puts his hands on my shoulders, closes his eyes, lifts his face to the heavens and yells, 'Lord Jesus, banish the spirits of manic depression and inadequacy from this young woman.' I wondered where he got 'inadequacy' from – I had not listed it as one of my problems. Then the healer throws me back into some people's open arms and I somehow end up on the floor. 'Go, you are healed,' he bellows. I feel no different.

←———→

I've been out of hospital a few weeks and I'm sitting in Dr Lackland's office telling him that nothing helps me.

'Would you like to try group therapy?' he asks. 'It won't cure your illness but it may help you deal with it. You know, come to terms with it.'

I reluctantly agree and he refers me. The group meet once a week down at the university. Around six of us sit in a circle with two middle-aged female psychiatrists. The other people in the group suffer from things like shyness, anxiety and low self-esteem. They all have jobs and money and houses. None of them have had years bouncing in and out of the mental health system. I wonder what I'm doing there.

David, a balding intellectual man in a tweed jacket, starts ruminating. 'I can't stop thinking about her, but I can't bring myself to talk to her. I hate myself for not having the guts to go up to her.' His face is getting red and creased.

'How long have you had feelings for her?' I ask.

'Five years, three months and thirteen days.' David's face gets redder and even more creased and he crushes his hands together into a ball. 'I'm so angry with her. Sometimes I think she's just a whore who's playing me along.'

'That's so sexist,' yells Jo, a young radical feminist with flaming cheeks and bright blue eyes. 'It's men like you that have totally screwed me up with your fucking madonna-whore thing, putting her on a pedestal in one breath and in the gutter the next.'

'Oh, I didn't mean to offend.' David stares at the ground.

The psychiatrists are silent.

A woman called Cheryl in stockings and a flowery print dress starts crying.

'Would you like to share your feelings with the group, Cheryl?' asks one of the psychiatrists.

'I'm scared. Angry people make me scared.'

Jo glares at her. The psychiatrist asks Cheryl to address the person who scares her directly.

Cheryl keeps crying. Jo keeps glaring. David is still staring at the floor.

And so it goes on while the therapists sit there calmly orchestrating the eruptions of raw torment without any show of compassion or affirmation. I wonder what the group members feel they have in common with each other and why they want to flagellate themselves in front of a couple of shrinks? This is not the way I want to resolve my problems. I want the opportunity to organise my life and take myself into the future, not to sit and talk to troubled strangers and smug 'experts' about how awful things are.

After a few sessions I decide to leave the group. I tell them why. Of course, the psychiatrists disagree with me. 'You've got problems, like all the other people here. We think you could benefit from this group.'

'Goodbye and enjoy your discussions,' I say.

Life's bad, really bad, and no pill or person or deity can make it better.

I should be at my lectures but I'm sitting in my flat feeling empty and hopeless. Maybe looking at television will make me feel a little bit better. I turn it on to watch a documentary about dolphins. The presenter walks into a dolphin marina in Florida. It's hot and cloudless and the water sparkles. A sick dolphin drifts on its own around the bottom of a big pool. Some men in white shirts and ties wearing sunglasses are examining it from poolside and sprinkling some powder into the water. They keep peering at the dolphin and step back every time the dolphin surfaces and the water threatens to wet their feet. The presenter says the dolphin died a few days later.

I turn off the television, feeling more disillusioned and desperate than ever.

The next day I have an appointment with Dr Lackland. He asks me why I didn't like group therapy. I tell him they were the worried well and I don't have the same kind of problems as them. He gazes at me and chews the end of his Biro while he waits for me to talk.

'I first saw a psychiatrist seven years ago and none of the pills really work.'

'You could be in a worse state without them.'

'What's worse than never being able to hold down a job or your studies and spending half your life in hospital?'

'We want to help. You're depressed about your life. We can help you come to terms with it.'

'Yeah, but talking never helps either. I've told the same story to over twenty psychiatrists. None of them have ever given me any new insights or useful guidance.'

'We need to clarify how realistic your expectations are. I'd like you to commit to talking with me once a week for the next six weeks.'

'OK,' I say.

I go away wondering if it is my fault the psychiatrists don't help me. Part of me wants to spill all my pain at their feet. Another part of me watches from the wall and savours the irony of two people talking past each other. The psychiatrists, because they know they are right; me, because I know we are both equally fallible. I want to trust psychiatrists but I can't because they claim such a monopoly on insight and knowledge.

←———→

My moods are swinging all over the place. None of the pills work but Dr Lackland keeps prescribing them anyway. I frequently stop taking them. Sometimes I stop them because I feel good again. Sometimes it's because they make me feel like wood. But at other times my motivation runs deeper than these rational assessments. That's when not taking the pills is the only act of will I have left open to me. I can't will myself to be stable and I can't will the pills to work but I can throw them in the rubbish bin and head down to the pub. I often end up in hospital a few days later and Dr Lackland complains to me about my non-compliance.

←———→

I'm sitting in my room staring into the garden. It's raining and misty, the grass has grown higher than my window sill and the clothes on the line are drooping so much they're brushing the grass. I should be studying but I feel like lying on the floor and howling.

Louise comes to see me. Her short hair is dripping and her warm kind eyes settle on me curled up in my chair. 'How are you today?' she asks.

'Not good.'

She takes her coat off and shakes her hair. Then she gives me a long tender hug and sits down.

'This crap has been going on for seven years and it's not going away. I went through my diaries for the last twelve months – most days I can't function. I can't live like this.'

'Has your death wish returned?'

'It's there all the time. I don't see what I've got to live for. More of this crap. That's what the shrinks tell me. Then my bloody parents tell me just to get on with life and not worry about my future. It makes me get in such a rage with myself. I just want to put me outside myself and beat me up. Because I can't just get on with life like they can.'

'They haven't been through what you have.'

'I think I'm jealous of them because life's never totally decked them. Me, I'm like a boxer in a ring who gets knocked out, staggers up and then gets decked again and again.'

'I've seen you struggle for a few years now. You've fought hard. I think you've got battle fatigue.'

'Yeah, you're right.'

'Maybe you need to stop fighting and just go easy.'

After Louise leaves I lie on my bed and relax. All the fighting drains out of me. Yeah, I'm a survivor, but I'm a deeply tired one. Fatigue floods every corner of my being. And I sob for hours at how impossible my life has become. I have a university record that's long and distinguished by the number of courses I have withdrawn from for medical reasons. I get the sack from jobs for not turning up, reading the rosters incorrectly or not smiling at the customers. I leave other jobs because I'm too depressed to do them. I can't find a partner I want to stay with or who wants to stay with me. Everything is slipping away from me and I'm saturated with a sense of loss. It's not so much my past or present I grieve for but my future.

5.

THE ZOOMING TURBOJET

It's a new year and I've just found a flat with Dave, Liz and others, high up in the bush behind the big swimming pool. I've been on holiday in the North Island and I've joined Dave and Liz for the long drive to Dunedin in time for enrolment day at university.

The world is starting to look so radiant and beautiful again I can't bear to look at it. The colours are too rich, the trees too sacred, everything too infused with godliness. Looking at the world is like looking straight into the eye of the sun.

We're driving through the countryside. I'm quietly spinning. The ends of my nerves start rising out of my skin. As we drive across the smooth arcs of the hills, down into the curves of the valleys, and over the bleached hilltops, everything is so sensuous I start to ache with desire for the contours of the human body.

'Those hills are so erotic it hurts,' I tell Dave.

He smiles and scans the hills, looking confused.

The next day we catch the ferry to Picton. As we drive through the bursting yellow hills of Marlborough, I listen to Mozart's Flute and Harp Concerto on a Walkman. The music is too heavenly to contain within my being. It makes me dizzy with delight; it surges into the core of me and bounces off the hills into the bright blue sky. It's so unbearably beautiful I'm floating on the satin sound of the flute.

I remove my head phones. 'This music is amazing, it's blowing me away.'

'Yeah, not bad, eh,' says Dave.

'*Not bad*. Fuck, is that all you can say. You don't know how to listen.'

'Yeah, we can't help it if we're normal.'

Everyone in the car cracks up laughing.

I enrol at university again. All I want to do is have fun. I go to parties and dance until after the music stops. I go to the pub and leap from one table-top to another until the bouncer throws me out. At five a.m. I put the stereo on full blast until my flatmates rush in to turn it off, frowning and holding their ears. Passing an antique store I see a blue-and-red soldier's uniform in the window. It has two rows of brass buttons going down the front and red stripes down the sides of the trousers. I want the uniform so much I spend half of my first-term student allowance on it. The uniform is so much fun to wear. People give me funny looks and I return the favour with an exuberant wave and a loud hello.

I'm ecstatic most of the time, but I'm alone. Other people are too slow and serious for me – I'm like Charlie Chaplin quick-stepping it in a movie where everything else is drifting at quarter-speed. I'm so ecstatic, spinning so fast, the core of my being disappears.

Catching my thoughts is like trying to catch fish with my hands in a raging current. Everything is a blur. I can't read or work or sit and watch TV. I can't reflect on the past or see how the present conspires to create the future. I'm living in an ever-present that blinkers out the past and the future and leaves me with such narrow vision all I can see is a streak of speeding thoughts. Sometimes my thoughts speed so fast I can't understand them.

I'm like a turbojet zooming through the desert, sides shaking, seams bursting, on the verge of rupturing as it nears the sound barrier.

←——→

I'm pacing back and forth between the living room and the front door of my flat. Thoughts are ricocheting around my head like randomly lit fireworks. Dave and Liz look concerned and suggest I take some chlorpromazine.

Fuck them – they want me to take chlorpromazine – I love them all – my body is bursting for sex – I feel wonderful – shallow and bright like tinsel – I won't take the chlorpromazine.

Dave passes me in the hallway.

They're trying to destroy me – they wouldn't kill me – yes they would – feel so fucking wonderful – lost myself – gotta get out of here.

Dave puts some music on.

The music's coming from the mouths of the gods – why the fuck don't they turn it up – gotta get some sex – no depth to this feeling – flatmates plotting something – I know it – gotta get out of here – they love me – I love them – gotta get out of here.

It's 'Planet Clare' by the B-52's.

I'm an alien from another planet – these bloody humanoids so slow and dull – gotta get off this planet – a spaceship is gonna pick me up – I'm special – I'm spinning I'm spinning – it's fucking wonderful.

Dave walks back into the kitchen and I follow him.

It's fucking scary – they want to get rid of me – the music is sacred – it's too quiet – an insult to the gods – must turn it up or bad things will happen – gotta get out of here – find the spaceship.

My flatmates are gathering in the kitchen, communicating in secret codes, nodding, raising their eyebrows at each other. I see the kitchen knives sharpened and winking on the wall magnet above the bench.

Dave takes down one of the knives. Now I understand what's going on: they are planning to kill me. I run away in terror through the cold dark streets. Dave catches up with me, puffing, pleading with me to stop. He sticks his arms into the air and tells me to feel him for knives. I can't find any. He calms me down and walks me to the emergency department.

The emergency nurse puts me into a room and shuts the door. I spin around. Everything is infused with holiness. Even the chrome and the white Formica glow from within. I am getting lighter and I feel my feet starting to leave the floor. I am the Virgin Mary ascending into heaven. At that moment a psychiatrist comes in. I bolt from the room and run through the corridors until a security guard catches me. The psychiatrist sends me to the Orchard Hill mental hospital in an ambulance that winds through the dark country roads like a shining beacon, while I prepare for my ascension through the metal roof, up into the endless night sky.

A male nurse takes me from the ambulance into a modern one-storey building with high windows and a locked entrance. He shows me my room, and tells me to get undressed. He gives me an injection. It's supposed to be chlorpromazine but it feels like he using all his strength to force marzipan into my bum. The injection hurts like hell. 'Now go to bed and stay there, please.'

But I can't stop pacing around and around the corridors.

'Get back into your room,' the nurse says.

I keep pacing.

'If you don't go to your room now, I'll drag you there and lock you in.'

'Don't lock me in. Please don't.' I'm getting scared.

I run back to my room and pace around inside it terrified that the nurse will come with the big key to lock me in. Then I start to fall into an anti-psychotic torpor and sleep.

The next morning I wake with the sunlight splintering through the windows, evil as a nuke. There are patches of white light on the floor. I jump over them fearing that if I step onto any of them I'll be blown to bits. As I weave through the safety of the shadows in my stained light-blue dressing gown, I grab a young nurse by the arm. 'Help. The sun's trying to kill me. This madness is destroying my life.'

'Not to worry, you'll get well again soon.'

A few days later the ambulance winds me back through the country roads to the Canary Ward in the city.

←———→

Chantelle, the discus-thrower lookalike, takes me to the ladies' dormitory. The drugs are slowing me down and I feel like wood again, but my mind's still speeding and jumbled. I'm still avoiding the sun and I'm too scared to see my flatmates in case they knife me.

It's evening and I'm getting ready for bed. The long polished corridor turns into a glowing ramp and the ladies' dormitory at the end of it becomes my private spaceship bound for Mars. I sit on my bed listening to the low whine of the engines, feeling the solar winds lash at the outside of the spaceship, waiting for the big bump of the landing. But I fall into a drugged sleep before I reach my destination.

←——————→

It's my birthday. My voice is slurring and there's no spring left in my walk. I don't think my flatmates want to kill me any more. Dave, Liz and my other flatmates bring me a square birthday cake with dark grey icing all over it.

'That looks like a chunk of roadside.'

'Yeah,' says Dave, 'it's a memento of all the roadside you've trodden in the last few weeks.'

'We thought it best not to bring a knife with us, so you'll have to provide one,' says Liz, smirking.

I laugh, overcome with gratitude.

We go outside and cut and eat the cake on a verge of grass by the car park. It doesn't taste like roadside at all. The cake is moist and delicious. Even the icing tastes good.

←——————→

They've let me out of hospital so I can go to my flat and get some of my things. I'm waiting at the bus stop beside the big swimming pool to go back up to the Canary Ward. The bus is straining to get up the hill. I put my hand out and it screeches into the bus stop. 'The hospital please,' I tell the bus driver. I take a seat. Across the aisle I see someone familiar. It doesn't take me long to realise it's Jack Nicholson. He's wearing a lumberjack shirt and moleskin trousers and his thinning brown hair is slicked back with Brylcreem. He's unshaven and he's got the same sinister glint in his eye that he had in *The Shining*.

What if he's planning to kill me? I feel uneasy, so I move quickly down the aisle to another seat. He follows me and sits across from me. I'm starting to feel scared. I look at him out of the corner of my eye. Jack stares straight ahead, fixing his gaze in the distance while he fiddles with the zip on his carry-bag. He's planning his attack. He's reaching for the gun in his bag. I panic, ring the bell and leave my seat to stand up the front. I get off at the next stop. Jack stays on the bus.

Alone on the footpath I try to calm myself. 'He doesn't even know me. Why would he want to kill me? What's a film star doing on a bus in Dunedin?' Perhaps it isn't Jack Nicholson at all. I'm confused and spooked as I climb the hill to the Canary Ward.

I walk past the waiting room, down the corridor into the Ladies' Lounge. A woman who has just been admitted to hospital looks exactly like my mother. She doesn't recognise me. Maybe she isn't my mother. Maybe she is my mother and she's pretending she doesn't know me.

The next day I sit in the Ladies' Lounge still trying to figure out if the new woman is my mother. A nurse comes in and asks some people to play cards.

Three women seat themselves at the table. As the nurse starts to shuffle the cards I see her hands turning into feet. I whimper like a dog and run from the room, away from the private freak show of my mind.

←——————→

I discover that there are words used by mental health professionals that carry enormous authority. One word they have appropriated is 'insight'.

I sit with Dr Lackland in his office, staring at the flax bush outside his window while he looks through my notes. 'Mmm, you seem to have a lot of insight for someone with your diagnosis,' he says. 'It's quite atypical.'

'What do you mean?'

'Most manic people don't think they're manic, they just think they're feeling incredibly good. But you seem to recognise the need for help.'

I say nothing.

I leave Dr Lackland feeling uncomfortable. He's anointed me with insight, like a priest who anoints one of his parishioners as a devout believer. Mad people with insight are considered less mad than the others, just as devout parishioners are considered less sinful than the lazier ones. There's a big difference, though. Sinning is a matter of choice, but insight isn't. People are seen to have the capacity to assess whether they have sinned or not and can defend themselves against such an accusation. But mad people who are seen as lacking insight cannot defend themselves against their accusers. Any denial that they lack insight is normally used as evidence in favour of it. Unlike sinners, people labelled with lack of insight lose their right to negotiate reality.

←——————•

I find it easy to talk to the cleaners about my distress because they're so ordinary with it. Every morning they came in with their dry mops to restore the polished lino. Sometimes Iris, a plain, short, middle-aged woman, comes up to me and asks me how I'm doing. 'You'll get through it, love. My husband did,' she says. 'It's hard for you lot in here. You're pretty brave, you know.'

Why couldn't the professionals say things like this, I wonder.

'You know, the doctors never talk to us cleaners,' she says, 'but I reckon we could tell them a thing or two. "Get off your bloody perches and come down to our level." That's what I'd say to them. You and me, we're at the bottom of the heap here.'

Of course, I agree with her.

←——————•

'Mary, you're being inappropriate,' warns Chantelle a couple of days later as I pace around the Ladies' Lounge.

'Whaddya mean?' I ask.

'You know what I mean.'

But I don't know what she means. Maybe she means I shouldn't yell at the announcer on radio about what a bigot he is. Or she may mean the soldier's uniform I've just put on. Is it because I'm smoking a pipe? Maybe she thinks it's because I'm pacing the room.

I learn that the term 'inappropriate' is a nursing tool to control behaviour on the ward. In all the times I hear the staff call myself or others inappropriate, they never once describe the behaviour they're criticising or tell us what appropriate behaviour would look like. It's a vague, global put-down that gives us little opportunity to disagree or to behave differently.

The standard used for appropriateness by the staff is the sane people's standard. But how can mad people conform to this standard? There's not even one standard of appropriateness for sane people. Appropriateness is largely governed by context. Sane people kneel in church, they yell obscenities at football matches, they shriek like wounded baboons when they make love, and shoot each other in wars. Yet in most contexts these behaviours would be considered inappropriate.

It's in the context of my depression that I stay in bed and don't look people in the eye. It's in the context of my highs that I dress flamboyantly and rush around. It's in the context of my paranoia that I take evasive action against those who threaten me. The nurses consider all this behaviour inappropriate, but it's perfectly appropriate behaviour for people when they're mad.

———————

I first notice Brooke sitting in the Ladies' Lounge joking with the nurses. She laughs with her whole face, like a clown. Her brown curls bounce and her clear blue eyes meet mine as I walk in. 'How long have you been here?' she asks.

'Two weeks.'

'I just arrived yesterday. I'm gonna flunk university again if I stay here too long.'

'I've hardly been this year.'

'This'll be the third time I've flunked.'

'Same here.'

Brooke and I become good friends. She's zany, messed up and irresistibly likeable. Brooke takes me away from my earnest ruminations. I help to bring Brooke back from her torments about her family and the sexual abuse she suffered at the hands of her father.

Brooke is curled up in the corner of the Ladies' Lounge.

'Is the abuse stuff getting to you again?'

'I can't talk about it,' she says.

'You don't have to.'

'I'm disappearing.'

'You're here, and I'm here too.'

Brooke sobs into my shoulder and I stroke her back. Slowly, she starts to feel she's taking up space again.

←———→

Felicity the nurse walks up to me. 'Mary, we've decided you could benefit from going to Mr Wilson's new Social Skills group after lunch. Would you be interested?'

I'm bored so I agree to go.

Five of us sit in a circle in a small room – me, Brooke, Anne and two others. Anne is a middle-aged woman with dark greying hair and lagoon-blue eyes who's full of obscure wisdom.

Mr Wilson, the psychologist, comes in wearing corduroys and horn-rimmed glasses that were probably fashionable in 1950. Without introducing himself he says, 'Today we're going to video you in pairs introducing yourselves to each other, then we're going to play it back and give each other feedback.'

'Whoop-de-doo,' says Brooke. All the other patients snigger except Anne.

Mr Wilson looks uncomfortable.

'I can't allow myself to be videoed. It's too dangerous,' says Anne. 'You'll have to excuse me.' As she rises from her chair Mr Wilson says he will come and see her later. Anne casts him a dark look and leaves the room.

We do the introductions exercise with Mr Wilson operating the video. I feel stupid and self-conscious in front of the camera. Brooke uses it as an opportunity to do her haughty headmistress routine. After we play the introductions back Mr Wilson gives his feedback.

'Mary, I think you could project yourself more. Any other suggestions for Mary?' No one says anything.

'Brooke, it helps in social situations to show more warmth and to get onto the same level as the other person. Do you understand what I mean?'

'Yes, Mr Wilson,' she says stifling a giggle.

'Yeah, Brooke, I notice you're a bit up yourself on the ward,' I tell her. By now we're both working overtime to stop giggling.

'Mmm, that's interesting,' says Mr Wilson, looking at Brooke's feet, 'You might want to reflect on that, Brooke.'

There's a short silence, then Mr Wilson says he'll see us next week.

As soon as we've closed the door behind us, Brooke and I erupt into squeals of laughter. 'You bitch,' Brooke giggles as she shakes me by the shoulders.

←——————×

'How was Social Skills?' asks Anne.

'Hilarious.'

'You need to watch Wilson.'

'He could do with watching himself – in a video, I mean.'

Sitting together in a corner in the visitor's lounge Anne tells me her husband walked out on her, leaving her to bring up several children. She soon cracked up, though Anne doesn't quite see it that way. 'The KGB started spying on me because I've got some information they need.'

'What kind of information?' I ask in all my naivety.

Anne looks straight at me to alert me of the gravity of the situation. 'Oh, I can't tell you that. You'd get caught up in this terrible thing.'

'I see.'

'They contacted me after my husband left. I've been avoiding them ever since. The only reason I come in here is to hide from them. But I've found out there are a couple of staff members who have connections with the Soviet Union so it's not as safe as I thought it was.'

I figure not to ask her who the staff members are.

'So you can see why I wouldn't be videoed. My cover could be blown.'

'How do you cope when you're not in here?

'I've got other hiding places. I keep away from my children. It's to protect the younger ones but I know the oldest one is involved. He's a good boy but they've corrupted him.'

'Has he told you he's involved?'

'No, nothing like that. You just know these things.'

'Yeah.'

'If all else fails I've got a stash of pills hidden behind a brick at home.'

'Well, we've all got that option.'

'No, I'm not suicidal. But if the only way to keep the information from the KGB is to die, then I'd do it.'

As I listen to her complex and intriguing story I see how much Anne has had to carry on her own – her children, her poverty and the knowledge that the KGB are after her. She carries all of it with the dignity and the seriousness such burdens place on good people. Everything she says makes sense to me, though we're living in different movies. She's the wronged hero in an obscure psychological thriller and I'm the fucked-up daughter in a Sunday-night drama.

Later Chantelle comes into the kitchen while I'm making a cocoa. 'So Anne had a long chat to you today?'

'Yeah, she did.'

'What's with you? Are you just really patient or do you believe all that stuff?'

'I dunno,' I reply.

Chantelle walks out before I have time to say anything else. Stirring my cocoa long after I need to, I wish I'd said to Chantelle that Anne is brave, and wise in her own way. She has twice the imagination and intellect of most of the staff, who believe the KGB are safely tucked away in the Soviet Union. Her only failure is that her reality is hers alone, without any of the privileges that come from consensual reality, like the reassurance of social acceptance, the belonging that comes from common knowledge, and the sharing of the burden of responsibility.

＜————✳

One night Brooke and I leave the ward to go out for beef stroganoff and a bottle of wine. We're having so much fun we decide to pick up some beer and go back to her flat. It's a dilapidated bungalow behind the university. None of her flatmates are home.

'Oh, she's so gorgeous, I've got a massive crush on her.' Brooke's talking about a young trainee psychiatrist at the Canary Ward called Dr Virtue.

'Brooke, she's straight.'

'No, she isn't.'

'But she's got a male partner.'

'Doesn't mean a thing. I can spot 'em a mile off.'

'How?'

'I've got an inbuilt gaydar.'

We both double up with laughter.

'I reckon you could be a friend of Dorothy too,' she says, pointing at me.

'I don't know anyone called Dorothy.'

Brooke lies back on the floor and laughs with her whole body. '"Friend of Dorothy" means gay, you drongo.'

'You think I'm gay?'

'Well, are you?'

'I don't know.'

Suddenly I'm overcome with a tender yearning for her. She sits up and we look into each other's eyes – Brooke's eyes shine with mischief while mine flood with longing. As she runs her fingertips over the back of my hand I shiver with desire.

The spell breaks when Brooke does a loud burp; she starts to look pale and uncomfortable. 'I think I'm going to be sick,' she says.

'I don't feel too good myself.'

We stagger into the bathroom and vomit together into the bath. Mushrooms float like withered little umbrellas in two tracks of lumpy sludge that join near the plughole. Later, in celebration of the bond we forged that night, we call ourselves the spewing sisters. But we never look into each other's eyes again.

✦————✦

Brooke and I both leave hospital a few days after we vomited in the bath.

A week later I go to my next appointment with Dr Lackland to talk about my problems but I don't know if I should trust him because I know so little about where he is coming from. I ask, 'What do you think is a well-functioning human being?'

'Why do you ask that question? I think you're worried I'll judge you.'

'Yeah, I am worried about that. I want to know if your ideas on

107

human beings are compatible enough with mine for us to be able to talk about me. I mean, how do you ensure your values won't impose on mine?'

'Let me assure you, it's not my job to judge you,' says Dr Lackland. 'I'm here to help you know yourself better.'

'But what if you judged me without knowing it?'

'That was below the belt,' he laughs, as though he has suddenly realised I'm a precocious brat. 'You do need a high degree of control in your relationships, don't you. We need to explore this further. Maybe you want to know my views on human beings so you can disagree with me.'

I go home angry that Dr Lackland didn't answer my question about human beings. I know this behaviour well; whenever I ask a psychiatrist a searching question they either respond by asking another question or use my question as evidence of my pathology.

That day Dr Lackland writes in my notes:

Requesting my views on life, sex, religion etc. Why she needs to know my views? Feeling of powerlessness that she knows little about me and my beliefs. Theme of control in relationships and how vulnerable she feels when she cannot label people. For further discussion – importance of her control issues. Blood levels satisfactory.

Dr M.T. Lackland

←——→

I want to get help for my moodswings because they make me suffer and interfere with my life. I want them to go away. Failing that, I want the strength and wisdom to deal with them in the best way possible. I want to transform my weakness into a strength. But mental health professionals appear to see only my weakness. I can recall only two or three out of maybe a hundred professionals who have acknowledged my strengths. Even these people do not say the things I most need to hear: that I'm doing well in tumultuous circumstances, that these circumstances are enabling me to develop my strengths, that my strengths will help me to create a better future for myself. Some of my friends and family say these things to me but why couldn't the professionals? I know there is something wrong with a service system that requires only my incompetence to be part of it.

At first I think mental health professionals have the answers for me. I think they must be knowledgeable, wise and strong. I believe they can help me with their pills or with their guidance. But all they do is provide a pillow when I'm in a crisis. As time goes on I know they are running out of ammunition in the battle to stabilise my moods. I am becoming one of their chronic patients.

←———⁎

The next week I go to see Dr Lackland again terrified about my future. 'What's going to become of me?' I ask.

'Why is that worrying you today?'

'It worries me all the time.'

'We're here to help, you know.'

'The word for me is "chronic", isn't it?'

'Oh, I don't use that kind of language with my patients.'

After I leave Dr Lackland writes in his notes:

Mary has finally accepted, emotionally, not just intellectually, the long-term nature of her illness and disability.

It's a breakthrough, according to Dr Lackland. I no longer resist the hard truth; I'm learning to accept it. In his notes Dr Lackland anoints me with a new-found insight because I now know what he has known all along.

But neither of us knows that my last orbit through madness and my final admission to hospital are only three months away.

6.

MAKING FRIENDS WITH MADNESS

I'm back in the Canary Ward. Brooke, Anne, Richard and I are sitting in a huddle in the Ladies' Lounge. 'We're all in here because we're too sensitive,' Brooke says. 'We're the normal ones. It's the people who put us here that should have their heads read.'

Anne looks at Brooke as if she's just announced a new discovery that grass is green. 'God, how long did it take to work that one out? I know why I'm here. Just ask the KGB.'

'Yeah,' I say, 'they've put a few people away.'

Richard is in hospital because he tried to get his wife and children out of bed at 3am to drive them to the North Island to protect them from nuclear threat. He paces around the ward cracking jokes in a powder-blue dressing gown. He throws his hands in the air. 'I'm here because I'm mad,' he yells, and leads us laughing out onto the balcony. We line up at the rail facing the road, which is about ten metres away. A woman and a little boy are walking past. 'Listen to this,' he whispers as he cups his hands around his mouth, 'It's great to be mad, you should try it sometime,' he bellows. The woman picks up the boy and runs. We laugh so hard we can't stand up. Richard keeps slapping us on the back telling us how fantastic we all are.

←———→

The only people who really understood were other mad people. People like Richard, Anne and Brooke knew – more than anyone. Over the years I met many good people who were mad like me. Their madness had taken them to a foreign land where only mad people could go to. Some of them stayed in this mad land for a long time while others got out and kept returning to it. Mental health professionals stood at the border trying to pull people out of the mad land, even the ones who wanted to stay. They knew the mad land as a bad place where people get lost, sometimes forever. But most of them had never been there. My peers showed me that the mad land, for all its perils, had some of the most enchanting scenery in the world. Like a land that has mountains and ravines, rivers and caves, blinding sun and swirling storms, the mad land could be a place of beauty as well as danger. My peers helped me to understand that I was not alone in the mad land, that there was a whole tribe of us who had been there and seen many of the same things. Things that other people did not easily understand. Things they feared and denigrated.

By now I was starting to think hard about madness and to unpack its social construction. Most people's responses to madness and mad people are based on a bedrock of belief that usually lies under the surface of everyday consciousness; the belief that madness is wrong, meaningless and has no value. From it comes a tangled array of responses like fear, pity, discrimination, exclusion and the coercion of mad people. Joe Public may be full of crass language, like 'psycho', 'barking' and 'axe murderer' but the traditional mental health system could be just as invalidating once you dig beneath the smooth surface of diagnoses, therapeutic language and institutional rituals.

I was still a privileged citizen after I went to see Dr L'Estrange for the first time. Taking anti-depressants didn't put my social status into a nose-dive either. But that all changed the afternoon I was first admitted to the Canary Ward. Hobbling through the doors past the sad hollow people in the waiting room, past the fed-up receptionist, down the long polished corridor into my little room, I entered a system that stripped me on both sides of my skin. First came the induction ritual where I was stripped of my clothing and possessions. This was just a taste of things to come. Over the following weeks and years a deeper stripping took place as I lost possession of my credibility and dreams.

Fortunately, I'd never taken too much notice of authority figures and I often disagreed with professionals' versions of my past or with their assessments of me on any given day. But as the years went by and I lost hope, the professionals and I started to agree about my future – as a chronic psychiatric patient.

It would be wrong to attribute all the stripping of mad people's credibility and dreams to mental health professionals. Discrimination in all its other guises, and madness itself, can be just as corrosive. Nothing was more profound for me than the stripping I experienced in the black box. Sometimes our families, friends and others strip us of our status. Worst of all, we can make our own contribution by believing other people are right about us, or by still believing what we thought about mad people before we became mad ourselves.

Becoming 'one of them' was instructive. Faced with my sudden drop in status, I had three choices. I could decide there had been a terrible mistake and that I wasn't really 'one of them'. Or I could come to the cruel realisation that I *was* 'one of them'; they were bad so I must be too. Or I could accept becoming 'one of them', deciding that they were OK after all and I was too.

Some people never get beyond the first or second explanation. I was lucky enough to latch onto the third explanation almost straight away. It was easy for me because I possessed middle-class confidence coupled with a desire to be different. These attributes gave me permission to explore the idea that madness might have value and meaning.

But none of the professionals I talked to believed there was anything good about madness. Mood swings were bad and had to be got rid of. It didn't matter to them that some of the most intense and powerful experiences of my life happened while I was mad. Some of those experiences were enlightening while others threw me into terror, confusion and despair. But I came to see that even the bad experiences had value – just as grief does, dying in pain for a just cause, or the precarious path towards spiritual enlightenment. The difference between these states and madness is that society legitimises them and allows for the possibility of growth or recovery.

I learnt over the years to make some meaning from the enigma of my own madness through words and metaphors. With enormous effort I wrote my journal in tiny handwriting, crouched in the ladies' toilet in the hospital. I learnt to make meaning, not in spite of my madness but because of it. It was not the kind of meaning that answers ambitious intellectual questions such as 'Why?'. Like haunting music or poetry, the meaning I found was saturated with soul. It was an intuitive expression of being without the labour of logic.

My madness took me places I had never been. It showed me the universe without its clothes. It stripped my mind of all its chattels. It rubbed my nose in the divine. It turned the lights off all over the undulating continent of my brain. Many people pass through this territory at some time in their lives. Most manage to skirt their way around the edge of it and look on with dread at a distance. But those who are forced right into its belly come out with richer pictures of a being that has been lost and found again.

The tragedy is that not many people understand these pictures. Like the paintings of some abstract artists, ordinary people look at the subjective pictures of madness and think they could have been done by a child of three. But I wanted to understand the gift of being in a world that is too beautiful to look at, to discover the lessons inside the black box, to re-enter the glory of rising into heaven and to find a map to navigate my spaceship to Mars. I was a lost explorer in the extreme zones of existence, wandering around the uncharted edges of human experience with no one to guide me.

So I sought guidance in conversations with friends and in books. I read the ideas of Thomas Szasz, Michel Foucault and RD Laing. I read the autobiographies of mad people. And I soon discovered that the existence and nature of mental illness is highly contestable.

I read that madness is not a biological illness but a socially constructed idea that has been used for centuries to banish a group of people who don't conform – by killing them, burning them at the stake, locking them up or forcibly treating them. I also read that some cultures valued madness by making spiritual leaders out of people who experience voices and visions.

I read that mental illness was invented by psychiatry a couple of hundred years ago. They took some inspiration from the Greeks who thought madness originated in the humours of the body. To this they applied the scientific tools honed in the Enlightenment. Believing they could uncover The Truth through experiments and rational inquiry, they established themselves as the experts in reasoning about madness.

Two hundred years later, biological psychiatry has the technology to peer deep into the brain. One person wrote they have discovered the brain has more neurotransmitter networks than all the roads and tracks in the world put together. Scientists have signposted all the major junctions and analysed the traffic that passes through them. They can see a billion traffic lights blinking in different junctions of the brain every time someone thinks or moves. And they can spot some of the traffic lights that signal madness. But are they really uncovering The Truth?

I read somewhere else that trying to understand madness through biological psychiatry is like trying to understand the Mona Lisa's smile by analysing the chemicals in the paint. Madness is an enigma that defies every clever theory and all the advances in technology.

Some of the people I read claimed that madness is not an illness because you can't see it through a microscope, the way you can with cancer or heart disease. But I figured that even if you could see madness through a microscope, you couldn't tell whether the cause of what you are witnessing was biological or not. Madness could be like crying with sadness or blushing with embarrassment – it is a psychological process that has some biological effects. But biological effects do not necessarily have biological causes.

Most of the people who wrote about the myth of mental illness didn't question the concept of physical illness. But I was intrigued that some writers thought that physical illness is as socially constructed as mental illness. They claimed that physical as well as mental illnesses are judgments, not facts. It's a fact that fast-dividing cells invade other body tissues in cancer but cancer is called an illness not because of what you see in the microscope, but because the fast-dividing cells threaten something that matters very much to us – our health and our longevity.

In a similar way, it's a fact that hearing voices that others don't hear or believing things others don't believe are events that do happen to some individuals. This is easy to verify. You just have to observe those individuals or ask them. But attaching the label of mental illness to these facts is purely a judgment about them. I discovered that mental illness has no real meaning outside the context of our social relationships and how we understand some of the things that matter to us, like productivity, communication, independence and status.

Many of the people I read debated the question, 'Does mental illness exist?' But they didn't always distinguish between its existence as a fact and its existence as a judgment. It was easy for me to see that mental illness is not a fact, but that didn't mean it could not be a good and helpful judgment. So the more interesting question for me was, 'Is mental illness a good judgment?' There are a thousand answers to this question. My own answer was that labelling my madness to be mental illness did not help my recovery. And here is why.

Once I was labelled with 'mental illness' I was seen as a helpless bundle of needs without competence and rationality. I was handed over to experts who colonised my story of suffering and condemned me to a predetermined pathway of recurring or deteriorating illness. They had exclusive rights to administer powerful treatments and to remove my freedom if they perceived me as a danger to myself or others. All they required of me was my passivity and compliance. I knew this regime was the logical consequence of the mental illness label and the belief system that underpinned it. And I knew it was wrong. It may not have always looked wrong on the outside but this regime was just as oppressive as locking mad people in attics, once you got beneath its cloak of benevolence.

For a time the idea of a biological illness was of some help to me. Biology absolved me from responsibility because I didn't see my biology as my self, but as the container my self sat in. But when professionals suggested my problems were psychological, they didn't relieve me of responsibility because I saw my psychology as mingled with my self, inside the container. The biological view made me a victim of my pathology, whereas the psychological view made me a more or less unwitting perpetrator in my own demise. Thinking about my madness in this dualistic way, I preferred to be its victim, rather than its perpetrator.

But I soon discovered that it didn't matter whether biology or psychology won the battle for possession of my troubled mind. They were two sides of the same coin. Professionals who used either frame of reference were equally preoccupied with pathologising my madness and with their futile attempts to get rid of it.

Knowing that mental illness was not a fact, and seeing it instead as a questionable judgment, allowed me to totally rethink madness. It led me to ask, is madness such a bad thing? Why shouldn't psychiatry and society allow people to be mad if they're happy that way and not harming others? Isn't it more damaging to crush our madness with toxic, invasive treatments than to live with it and understand what it is trying to tell us? How different would our experience of madness be if it was valued and given status?

After a lot of reading and thinking I wrote in my journal:

I have been told again and again that I have a serious problem that needs to be eliminated with expert help. But now I'm starting to think that my mood swings are not an illness, but a strange and inexplicable minority experience that has been captured, impounded and colonised by the psychocratic regulation of reality. Like colonised indigenous people, I have been denied what is truly mine. The psychocrats with their monopoly on knowledge and their power have alienated me from my mood experience.

How different my mood swings would have been if 99% of the population had extreme mood swings instead of the 1% that do now. Society would be organised around this vast 'normal' labile majority. Perhaps people would even be socialised into experiencing and channelling their mood swings in acceptable ways as other universal attributes like sexuality are. And for the small stable minority maybe there would be a diagnostic category called Mood Inlability Disorder (MID) – 'Patient is incapable of experiencing the full range of normal adult moods'.

So, after several years of trying to push my madness out of my life I had to find a place for it. Living against my madness and fighting it with pills was not working. My madness was like a boarder coming to live in my house who turned out to be a foreigner from an enemy country. The knowledge that I might not be able to evict him meant I had to make peace with him and learn to understand his language. Once I got to know the boarder he was no longer the stereotypical enemy but a complex character who deserved some respect. Even if I could not stop my madness I could change the way I viewed it and live *with* it instead of *against* it. I could even change the experience of being mad, or I could lessen the threat that madness made to my inner life. I needed to find a place for my madness instead of allowing psychiatrists to make their futile attempts to get rid of it.

I could see the terrible suffering that madness brings. But was it the madness itself, or the oppression, stigma and lost opportunities that robbed people of a good life? Was there a more constructive way of looking at madness than the 'illness' view perpetrated by psychiatrists? How could I live a good life and still have periods of madness? Could I change the experience of my madness so that it was not so disabling or distressing? No one I talked to had any answers to these questions. Some did not even understand the questions. So I struggled with them on my own.

I'm out of hospital again. Richard and Brooke have also left but Anne is still in there. My flat mate Dave and I are slouching around the house on a wet Sunday afternoon. 'There's a docudrama called *The Wheelchair Republic* on TV,' says Dave.

We switch the TV on and sit in our bean bags drinking tea. The Walking People's empire has just been taken over by the Wheelies who brandish guns and megaphones from their wheelchairs while they herd the Walkies into restricted zones.

In another scene a Walkie is going into the Wheelies' headquarters to ask for special dispensation to work in paid employment. He has to crawl around the building because the ceilings are too low for him to stand. He keeps knocking his head and an inconsiderate Wheelie rides over his hands. By the time he gets to the employment office he's angry and in a lot of pain. He finds some other Walkies crouching in the office; they are wearing crash helmets and protective clothing.

'Go, Wheelies,' yells David.

'Imagine if they made one about the lunatics taking over the asylum,' I say.

'We'd announce that the loonies'll make all the decisions from now on and non-compliance from professionals will be punished with heavy doses of drug therapy.'

'Or, you could do McCarthy-style interrogations on psychiatrists who express any disbelief in their patients' realities: "Dr X, you were overheard saying you do not believe Patient Y when he tells you he's an insect. Shame on you. You're employment contract is terminated."'

'Yeah, and we'd send him off with a diagnosis of "Professional Thought Disorder" so he'd never get another job. Oh, and we'd make him take the bus home while we drive around in his flash car.'

We laugh so hard our bean bags disappear from under us.

———————

A few weeks later Brooke rings me to say Maria is dead. She went into her back garden, poured petrol over herself and lit it. I cry for an hour after I put down the phone. But I also know that not all suicides are equal; for some it becomes a reasonable wish. After years of trying and of treatment, nothing else could relieve Maria's unrelenting torment.

Soon after Maria dies, a friend of Dave's dies in a mountaineering accident. Dave is also a mountaineer when he's not studying. He's a serious man who's prone to dark moods that bow his wiry young body. One night sitting by the fire, he counts how many friends he has lost to the mountains and I count how many I've lost to suicide. It's about the same number.

'Why do mountaineers do it?' I ask him. 'I think you're all courting death.'

'The risk is definitely part of the appeal.'

'Attempting suicide is probably as life-threatening as going on a risky mountaineering expedition, but no one tries to stop you, do they.

Because mountaineering is heroic. They tried to stop Maria killing herself by forcing her into hospital under the Mental Health Act. She hated it.'

'Yeah, but when we go on an expedition we take precautions. Suicidal people go all out to kill themselves.'

'But you're only talking about a difference in intention, when the outcome could still be death in both cases.'

I stare at the flames searching for something more to say and after a couple of minutes I find it. 'I think the reason we don't stop mountaineers is that we assume they have free will. Mad people, we assume, don't have it, which provides the justification for forced intervention.'

'That's interesting,' says Dave. 'At high altitude you can get serious hypoxia which stuffs your cognitive functioning and makes you hallucinate. A mountaineer can't have much free will in circumstances like that.'

I keep staring into the fire. A helicopter, carrying a psychiatrist and nurse, appears in my mind. It's hovering near the top of Everest to rescue some severely hypoxic climbers from their madness. They take the climbers kicking and screaming back to the psychiatric hut at base camp where they lock them up until they're fully re-oxygenated. The psychiatrist is worried one of the patients will try to climb to the summit again once he's released, so he puts the patient on an Altitude Restriction Order to ensure he fully complies with his oxygen requirements and doesn't go above 7000 metres.

I share my imaginings with Dave and we snigger at how ridiculous it is.

But the joke doesn't settle the matter for me. I bend towards the flames again in concentration and finally ask: 'What's the difference between a psychotically hypoxic climber at 8000 metres and a psychotically suicidal person at sea level? Why do we make a necessity out of forced intervention in one case but find the idea so ridiculous in the other?'

←———————→

By now I'd started to make some sense of madness and to understand what was wrong with the mental health system. I knew there had to be a better way of responding to madness but I couldn't find it. So I kept searching library shelves for the answer, not quite knowing what I was looking for. Then one day, a few months before my last admission, I noticed a book called *On Our Own: patient-controlled alternatives to the mental health system* by an American called Judi Chamberlin. I opened the book and scanned the introduction:

For too long mental patients have been faceless, voiceless people. We have been thought of, at worst, as subhuman monsters, or, at best, as pathetic cripples... It is only with the emergence and growth of the mental patients' liberation movement that we ex-patients have begun to shake off this distorted image and to see ourselves for what we are – a diverse group of people, with strengths and weaknesses, abilities and needs, and ideas of our own... Our ideas about psychiatry, about the nature of mental illness, and about new and better ways to deal with people undergoing emotional distress, differ drastically from those of mental health professionals.

With these words, I knew I'd struck gold. I'd already read several autobiographies of mad people who wrote vivid descriptions of their madness and how they were treated. But this was the first time I'd read anything by a mad person that challenged the ideological foundations of psychiatry through an analysis based on her own experience. It was my introduction to the mad movement.

Chamberlin started by writing about her own experiences in the mental health system. It resonated with my own: her initial hope that professionals would help her; her growing awareness that they were controllers rather than healers; the crumbling of her personhood as the hospitals took away her possessions, her liberty, her self-belief and the hope that she would ever recover.

Chamberlin's experience was worse than mine: she was held down and forcibly treated, locked in rooms and told she would never leave the hospital. She recovered some years after her hospital admissions in an alternative setting run by ex-patients where she was respected, listened to, free to come and go and able to express her feelings. In the book she described alternatives run by ex-patients in the USA and Canada where participation was entirely voluntary, everyone could both give and receive help, and there were no hierarchies. Suddenly, after years of wondering if there was a better way, I had found it.

This book validated the experience of madness more than anything else I'd ever read. It slammed the medical model and argued passionately against the power of the mental health system to force treatment on people and control their lives. That system needed to be replaced by responses that respected the experience of madness and let people choose what worked for them.

I never took Chamberlin's book back to the library. It still sits on my bookshelf, browned at the edges, one of those rare books that showed me a new world rather than a familiar world revisited. Between the lines it showed me I could do something good with my madness, that there was a place in the world for mad people to critique the mental health system, to organise, and to come up with better responses to madness than hospitals, drugs and coercion.

I didn't know it at the time, but *On Our Own* became the launch pad for my life's work.

←——————→

One day I watched Dave weed and dig the vegetable garden. It had been lying fallow for a year. He came up to me and said, 'The soil's good, it's had a break.' Then I realised my madness was like the soil lying fallow. Sometimes it stripped me bare but it was also the beginning of renewal: every time I emerged from it I felt fresh and ready to start again.

My madness did not just take away, it gave to me as well.

It was like a prolonged and brutal rite of initiation that came close to destroying me, before I discovered what it gave me. Though on the surface madness took away some of my competence, like thinking straight or talking, it gave me a route to a deeper competence, like a richer understanding of life and the ability to face existential terror. It also give me strength – the strength to withstand the terrible grief I felt, to keep looking for answers, to put my life back together, to know that if I could survive years of madness I could survive almost anything.

Professionals told me that my madness had slowed the job of growing up but I knew that in some respects my madness accelerated my maturity. It quickly taught me the grown-up virtues of resilience, acceptance and self-reliance while many of my friends were still living in youthful innocence. But it also delayed my passage to the adult roles I wanted, such as the skilled professional, the fulfilled lover and the caring parent. Added to this, I came out of my madness with a huge deficit of good experiences which I knew I had to plug with hope, fulfilment and success.

Madness also gave me compassion where once I may have felt a range of pettier responses like fear, pity, impatience or indifference. Through the struggle to find dignity in my own suffering I learnt to encounter others who suffered as inhabitants in my world rather than as aliens in someone else's. Compassion drove me further than an equal regard for individuals who suffered: it added clean energy to my sense of social justice. Madness gave me the experience of being 'othered'. It removed me from a life soaked in privilege and allowed me to see that privilege from the outside-in for the first time. It gave me a position on the poorly mapped margins of society where mad people were starting to peg out their new subdivision of shared experience, knowledge and power.

Madness also gave me an understanding of how limited human beings really are. We often congratulate ourselves because we can think and make informed decisions. The black box, although it terrified me at the start, is still there behind everything I know or think I know. The black box is my metaphor for many of the things we cannot congratulate ourselves for – what we don't know, what we cannot know, and the stories we make up to fill the void.

Madness gave me insight into the illusion of control – how most of us walk around every day thinking we are in control of our existence. It is not until something threatens our existence that we truly understand we are at the mercy of countless forces that could turn on us at any time, like gravity, oxygen, life experience, spirits or our genes. Madness taught me that there are many things I cannot control and that good health, wellbeing and life itself are not part of a predictable design but accidents waiting to be nurtured.

Another lesson madness gave me was to understand that stability and well-being are a luxury to be thankful for. It was a luxury to wake up in the morning and know that I could get through the day and do all the things I set out to do. It was a luxury to feel at peace for a sustained length of time.

But my madness only gave me these things after a long struggle. At first, it completely bowled me over. And I let it because I did not know my own power. To escape the turmoil I got drunk. Drinking thawed the frozen wasteland my madness had turned me into. I felt warm and hopeful again. I could laugh, find meaning and feel affection for people. But after hours of it I slipped into a haze of confusion and grief. The next day I would go back to the pub and do the same thing, and the day after that. Drinking was like scratching a sore – it gave temporary relief but it lifted the scab and made the sore weep.

It took me several years to stop drinking during my madness. I quickly understood that drinking made my madness worse but it took a lot more than understanding for me to stop it. It took a belief in my own power and the hope that my life could someday be worth living. Without these beliefs my drinking continued because there was no point in stopping it. Once I saw the point in stopping drinking I had no difficulty in enduring my madness without it. From that time on I drank only to enhance pleasure, never to kill pain.

Gradually I learnt to prepare for the storms before they gathered full force. I came to know that they would pass. I took shelter from stressful events. I made myself comfortable as I could be. I learnt to breathe slowly and deeply when my terror at the futility of everything rose up in me. I got better at knowing the right time to go back into the open when the storms subsided.

I also learned how to slow the whirring when the lights got too bright and the world whizzed and sparkled. I turned the music off and went to quiet places. I refused drink and drugs and didn't go to parties. I tried meditation. I learnt the dosage of drugs that enabled me to slow down without the intrusion of too many side effects.

Between episodes I became tidy and well organised to compensate for the chaos of my madness. More important, getting up at the same time every day, making my bed, tidying my room, making lists and planning my day was a way of telling myself that I wasn't mad on that day. It showed me that I could go through all the ordinary routines that mark sane people's days.

After eight years, I felt as though I had been in a boxing ring with a prize fighter who knocked me to the ground time and again. But I kept getting up and slugging it out, trying different tactics, trying to duck the punches, trying to believe I would win. I don't know if I did really win; it was more like the prize fighter lost interest and walked out of the ring. My madness did not go overnight but it gradually subsided over two or three years like a ball that bounces less each time it hits the ground.

←——————*

I'm back in the Canary Ward, back in the black box, curled up in my bed with my eyes shut. I'm trying to catch my thoughts but they keep sliding off into nonsense so I try to make some sense of things by taking bits out of nonsense and putting them into a story:

An old woman and her granddaughter lived by a great ocean. Every day the old woman went fishing. She yelled in awe to the ocean, 'Let me take the life out of you with my net.' She always returned with fish and cooked them for herself and her granddaughter. One day she gave some of the fish to her granddaughter and said, 'Cook these for yourself.'

The girl wailed, 'I can't.'

The old woman replied, 'You must find your own power.'

But the girl didn't understand and went to bed hungry.

That night the girl woke from her dreams to a booming voice from the sky: 'You have the power of the old woman and the great ocean flowing into the core of you. Now, take meaning from the rawness of life and cook it for yourself without fear.'

At first I just repeat the words over and over to myself to ward off the chaos. Later I realise the words have arranged themselves into a coherent story that's telling me that life dishes up all kinds of raw experiences, but the quality of them is in the cooking. I have the power to transform my madness into fine cuisine. Maybe I even have the power not to go mad any more.

Ten days later I leave hospital for the last time.

7.

RISING FROM THE ASHES

Recovery is not just a phase that follows when madness has subsided. The seeds of madness and recovery can be sown in the same soil of inheritance and experience. And recovery starts to take root as soon as madness flares. Madness rages through the internal landscape like a bush fire. But well before the last plume of smoke has risen, new growth is getting ready to rise from the ashes.

Recovery does not necessarily mean the end of madness. It's true that recovery is a return, but not always from madness itself. Recovery is a return to a good life. Some people reconstruct a good life for themselves by making space for both madness and sanity. Other people reconstruct a good life by leaving their madness behind.

Nor is recovery simply the triumph of strength over weakness or good over bad. For there is an element of strength and goodness in madness. The problem with madness is that it maroons us in a place where there is room for only one. Recovery repairs the bridge to belonging.

←———→

I soon noticed that mental health professionals and the people who wrote books about madness were preoccupied with the origins of madness, but no one showed much interest in the origins of recovery. Psychiatric pessimism threw its dark cloak of denial over my recovery when I was told I had a chronic condition that would dog me for the rest of my life. Professionals had a language for psychopathology that filled volumes but they had virtually no language for recovery.

But understanding the origins of my recovery was just as important to me as understanding the origins of my madness.

When my mother left me feeling abandoned at kindergarten and the tonsils hospital, she returned and my security was restored. When I smashed my face into the merry-go-round, my parents were there with their arms out to comfort me. When I saw Mount Taranaki rise out of the sea after living in a foreign land, I felt the joy of coming home to a place where I belonged. When I pulled my pants down in the creek for some boys in exchange for the eel and worried that I had committed a mortal sin, my mother relieved my burden by making light of it. When Father Dempsey told me my mother was cracked for not believing in the Resurrection, she stood up for herself and defended me. When I encountered tragedies including the death of my baby brother, I saw that people survive them. When I absorbed stories about heroes who faced adversity, they almost always overcame it. When I was unable or unwilling to follow the paths that others had made for me, I learnt to create my own truth.

But my capacity for recovery did not just precede my madness, it lay within it. My recovery began to show itself where my madness began to show itself – in the black box. At first the black box terrified me with its profound nothingness. But I learnt to find peace in it. Over the years I learnt to stop curling myself up into a terrified ball and started to let myself just float in the blackness. The black box slowly changed from a dungeon of existential terror to a metaphor for the mystery of life and the uncertainty of knowledge. Black became my colour of spiritual peace.

So, the internal template for my recovery was laid down before my madness showed itself and continued to work its transformative magic even in my darkest moments. But recovery needs more than the self and its templates from the past to take root; it needs to happen in a world that gives hope, connection, opportunities and resources to people, just as soil does to plants.

Most of all I needed to be in a world where people believed in me. One person who never wavered in his belief in me was my brother Sean.

Sean was quiet and slow to judge people. He was accepting to the point of naivety and blind to people's baser motives. To others he was an unusual, enigmatic young man who hardly spoke. To me he was my oldest friend, a soul mate, the person who accepted me no matter what kind of state I was in. And acceptance was what I craved for most. He sat with me in silence and held my hand while I was in distress. He smiled at me and called me zany when I was restless and elated. And he kept me in his sight without interfering when I was spinning out of control.

As children we played in the sandpit and built grass huts together. As teenagers we got drunk and stoned together. We discussed the Vietnam war, drugs, long hair, world poverty and the environment. Then he left home to study and dropped out to shovel coal. After several years of soul-searching he decided he wanted to be a social anthropologist – not an elite highbrow anthropologist but an egalitarian one who could communicate his big ideas down at the pub or in women's magazines. He thrived on his studies, married a young Samoan student called Asi and had a beautiful baby called Siobhan. He wrote a book. Then he got the job of his dreams doing social science research for a natural history television programme. Sean was more than a friend – he gave me unconditional support during my years of madness. He also became a role model – the kind of person I could be if only my life would come right. I looked on his life with admiration and some envy.

In the last year of my madness I decided I wanted to write a self-help book for people with mood swings. It grew out of my realisation that the mental health system did not have many answers for me and from my dawning belief that we mad people had to find the answers for ourselves. Drawing on all the reading and thinking I'd done, I wanted the book to promote alternative ways of viewing mood swings and to include the combined wisdom of people who had experienced mood swings on how to manage them. I went to Sean for advice and support. When I doubted my ability, he told me I could do it. He sat with me and we discussed how to find people to interview, how to interview them, where I might find funding, how to get free publicity, and how to write a synopsis and find a publisher. I didn't ever write the book but the planning of it, with Sean's support, gave me some hope and steered me in the direction of my future work.

While I was working on my book I struggled with dread and despair. I felt as though there was a glass wall between me and the rest of the world; it looked like a distant planet at the end of a telescope that flickered in and out of focus. The isolation was too painful for words. One morning I woke in a total blur. I went to see Dr Lackland and said, 'The only drug you have given me that works is anti-depressants. You keep saying I shouldn't have them. But why should I be depressed if I don't have to be?' He prescribed me a cautious dose and warned me about going high. I still felt a veil of dread enclose me every morning so I put the dose up.

In a few days the veil of dread dissipated. Everything looked crisp and new. It was like coming out of a dungeon into a wide, open, sunny space. All the pain that had sat inside me like an old lump had disappeared. I felt happy and hopeful. I realised that it had been many months since it had felt OK to be alive.

The anti-depressants worked like magic. My madness was the rabbit in the top hat that disappeared. Occasionally the magician slipped and my madness came back but with an extra wave of his wand, or an extra pill, he made it disappear again. I couldn't believe that after all these years I could get up every morning and expect to get through the day without any difficulty. I couldn't believe that the simple act of taking some pills every night could change my whole experience of life. It just didn't make sense. I had spent the previous year or two trying to make friends with my madness, striving to find a positive place for it in my life, questioning psychiatric orthodoxy. The pills were magic all right, but on one level this was deeply disturbing. No one knew how the magician did his tricks, or why they worked on some people and not others. All I knew was that they were not *my* tricks, that two small pills had more power than I ever did to put my madness to rest.

The power of the pills gave credence to the view that my madness was a physical aberration. I didn't have a problem with this view because it did not necessarily invalidate my experience. Olympic athletes and geniuses also have physical aberrations associated with their rare talents. It was naming the presumed physical aberration associated with my madness as an illness that I had a problem with. But my tolerance for ambiguity enabled me to continue taking the pills every night believing they would deliver me a better tomorrow than my madness ever did.

But I worried a lot about the pills. How could I know they weren't doing silent and deadly damage to my brain cells? What if they totally disabled my brain's already limited ability to regulate my mood? What if I became psychologically dependent on them? What if they worked just because I believed in them? None of these questions stopped me from taking them, because the pills were like a life raft that enabled me to return from the wreck my life had become. Perhaps I would have eventually found my way back without the pills. Perhaps my madness was due to subside anyway. I didn't know for sure. All I knew was that shortly after starting the pills my life became manageable again.

———✕———

I had been taking the anti-depressants for about three months when Sean went missing. We were all on holiday together and he went tramping for a couple of days with our younger brother Liam. It was an ordinary day in early January. The heavy rains had stopped and a big cloud curved across the sky like a smudgy fish skeleton. My sister Lucy pulled me from a late-afternoon sleep to play with a frisbee on the lawn. Asi was putting some washing on the line and Siobhan was playing at her feet. Our ordinary day ended when we saw a cloud of dust coming up the gravel road. A white car with blue stripes and a red siren turned into our driveway.

I ran inside, too terrified to hear the news that visiting policemen are famous for, and sat suspended in the still gloom with my hands over my ears in a desperate bargain with fate. There was a long ominous silence broken by the faint wailing of a child. Asi came inside. I jumped up like a petrified animal who has nowhere to hide. 'Sean's been washed down a river and they can't find him,' she said.

The police took us to the local garage to collect Liam. He said the river was raging, Sean had a heavy pack on, he went down like a stone, came up once and never came up again.

After a day or two of searching the local policeman came round and said Sean's body was probably out at sea. He explained that the river would have stripped him of everything, first his life, then his clothes and pack, even his wedding ring. A farmer did find his pack nine months later, several kilometres downstream. In it there were some clothes, his sleeping bag, some rocks and his pipe, all in one piece.

Some friends came around and reassured us that drowning is a nice way to die. The procession of his life would have rolled in front of him like a movie, from his birth all the way to the river, they told us. He would have just faded away.

An old Irish priest came round and gave a more mystical account of Sean's death. 'I once talked to a man who nearly drowned in a lake,' he told us. 'When he decided he was done for, he looked down and saw himself submerged in the water. He said that the valley and the mountains were glowing with an unearthly light. And he knew this was his homecoming, so he started to enter the unearthly light, while his cocoon, stripped of its soul, lay dying in the water. When they rescued him, the man felt sad that they pulled him from that heavenly place. And do you know what? He never feared death again. You can be sure now your Sean has gone to a better place to be with his Maker.'

Other people's romantic notions of the drowning experience didn't convince me. Some years later I looked up some medical texts and people's near-drowning experiences to try to understand what had really happened. Sean was up to his chest in water when the river bed disappeared under his feet. I could see him tossing in a vortex of speed, twirled with darkness and diffused light. Maybe he hit the bottom and scudded down the river at the speed of a man falling off a cliff. I could sense his last thought – his pack was dragging him down and he had to get it off, but his arms couldn't move through the wall of water. I could see him, with the stabbing pain in his ears and eyes, gulping in his last fatal breath of water as he flailed towards the light and broke the surface, rasping as his throat refused to open to the air. The whirling water pulled him down again. Through his wild thrashing, a pain blasted like a thousand sirens in his chest. Then the blackness of unconsciousness would have encroached, first around the edges, then towards the centre until the last speck of light vanished.

My friends and the priest were wrong about drowning; there is no nice way to die, because all our reflexes are designed to stop us consenting to it, just as gravity is designed to stop us floating away.

All I knew was that a young man lay at the bottom of the ocean being taken apart piece by piece. He would never see Siobhan grow up, would never finish his studies or grow old. His young life had been snuffed out in the time it takes to boil a kettle. I didn't think he was in a better place and it dawned on me that I was now the one to be envied. My life was still full of possibilities. For the first time I saw the absurdity of the self-pity that had limped behind me through my years of madness like a mangy dog.

And I remembered the song from the rabbit movie I'd heard on the radio in the Ladies' Lounge, the afternoon I was first admitted to hospital.

Is it a kind of dream
Floating out on the tide
Following the river of death downstream. . .
Bright eyes, how can you close and fail?
How can the light that burned so brightly,
Suddenly burn so pale?
Bright eyes.

I had always thought the song was about me, but it was really about Sean.

The day after Sean went missing, we drove to the river. Liam led us down the bank to the place where they began their fateful crossing. I saw a small smooth stone where my brother had made his last footsteps. I picked it up and fitted it into my hand. It felt as though Sean had handed it to me and said, 'Go and do the things I never will.' My own problems receded while I embarked on my mission to keep his spirit alive in everything I did.

Sean had a clever and creative mind. He loved ideas. He loved to bend and stretch them. He loved to make new ones. He was never satisfied with orthodoxies and always wanted to see beyond them. We talked ideas from a young age, breathed in the same influences, knew the same people. We understood each other and where our ideas came from. Sean was tolerant and tender-hearted. He was always kind and slow to anger. I wanted his ideas and values to live on in my own life. Sean did as much to enable my recovery dead as he did when he was alive.

Though my grief was enormous it never collapsed into madness. My days of tears and overwhelming sadness did not lead me into the black box. Grief did not besiege me with existential terror, endless despair or profound isolation. My grief was a daylight experience: the rest of my world stayed visible and solid while I was going through it.

When people die they leave a space for others to inherit. I grew into some of the space that Sean left, though I have never quite known what to name it. All I know is that it was a more liberating space than the one I had been confined to during my years of madness.

←————→

Soon after Sean died my friend Louise came around one night and said, 'I've heard about a job you might be interested in.' I was not a good catch for an employer. I was twenty-seven with no qualifications, no skilled work experience, serious mental health problems and a long history of dropping out. Despite this I was employed for six months to write a self-help manual for unemployed people funded by the government. It was the first job I had enjoyed and succeeded at.

Through the contacts I made researching my self-help book I became a committee member of the local mental health association, a non-government education and advocacy group made up mainly of professionals and family members.

The Orchard Hill Hospital, where the ambulance had taken me the night I was ascending into heaven invited the committee to visit. We drove out there on a crisp winter's day – over the hill, past the bays and into the green hinterland. It was built in the 1960s with low-lying villas sprawled around in large paddocks. We filed into the administration block and waited for the head nurse, Brian, a colourful, energetic man with a reputation for manic sprees.

We trailed after Brian through many of the villas. Occasionally I came across patients I knew. One of them was Richard. 'Hey, good to see you,' I called out to him. I slipped away from the cluster of talking heads and went over to him.

Richard was pacing around the villa in a mania that had gone sluggish from the drugs. 'Hey, nutcase, are you a spy now?' he asked.

'No, of course not.'

'We were told to behave because some important guests were coming through, and who should turn up but a fellow nutcase,' he laughed.

'It feels really weird. I dunno where to put myself.'

Brian called me over to say they were moving onto the next villa and I said goodbye to Richard.

Brian and the other committee members walked into each villa and said bright hellos to the patients. Then they huddled in corners to have conversations with the staff so that the patients couldn't hear. I stood awkwardly on the edge of these conversations, like an imposter knowing I did not belong there, sensing that my presence there was a betrayal to all my fellow mad people.

I left the hospital feeling phoney and unsure of myself and it took me some time to figure out why. I knew I could never belong with the professionals. They would never let me belong but more important, I didn't want to. To belong I would have to sweep away all traces of my madness and adopt a new knowledge that put madness at a distance, that saw it as a tragedy which afflicted others, that regarded it as an intellectually vexing problem which only science or professional reasoning could solve. But I also knew I didn't want to continue being a patient either, because that was a role that saddled me with passive incompetence and a dismal future. It was not shame that repelled me from the patient role, but the knowledge that it would take me nowhere.

My work in the mad movement would create a new role for me

but I didn't know it then. All I knew was that the roles of patients and professionals were separated not just by their different functions of helper and recipient, but also by entrenched inequality. Moving from one role in the direction of the other one, as I did that day at the hospital, was untenable. I had to find a new role where I could be both a mad person *and* a valued competent person. At that time such a role could not exist inside the knowledge and power structures of the mental health system. The mad movement had shown me that this could only happen outside the system.

←——→

Before I finished the handbook for unemployed people I went to a Mental Health Foundation conference in Wellington to represent the local mental health association and to find people and information that could assist with my self-help book. I imagined rows of smug, haughty professionals looking at me as I walked in thinking, 'What's she doing here?' I nearly didn't go. But my father, who was a health professional with an interest in patients' rights, persuaded me. I arrived at the conference feeling like a beggar gate-crashing a ball.

To my relief, all the professionals I met there seemed pleased that someone who received services was at the conference. Peter McGeorge, the psychiatrist at Student Health who had always treated me like an equal, came over and welcomed me. I started to relax. Then I went to the talks and heard some things that made me feel alienated. I heard that psychiatric patients are too docile to complain. I heard the system turns away from people with severe mental illness because they were not as interesting to treat. I heard that compulsory admission can be a useful therapeutic tool. I heard some good things too, about the need for patients' rights and the plans to close down the old hospitals. But mainly, for the next three days, professionals talked about people like me as if none of us were in the room, as if we weren't able to speak for ourselves, as if we couldn't even hear. I felt totally invisible.

During the conference I met only two other mad people. One was a plainly dressed, middle-aged woman who campaigned against psychiatric drugs and handed out screeds of badly photocopied papers.

The other was an articulate and energetic woman who had set up a support group for people with agoraphobia. I told her how invisible I felt. She knew exactly what I meant. 'They're so paternalistic, especially the medical model people,' she said. 'More of us need to speak out.' So I went for it. At the final plenary I got up and talked:

A few years ago I went to a public meeting where a psychiatrist talked about community care. At the end of his talk the psychiatrist asked for a breakdown of who was at the meeting. He wanted to know how many GPs, psychiatrists, nurses and social workers were there. He asked if any family members were there. He even asked if any clergy or trade unionists were there. But I remained silent and unrecognised because he didn't think to ask if there were any patients there.

A few years later I am at this conference, still silent and still unrecognised. But this time I feel I must speak.

What you professionals plan and implement affects me greatly and the thousands of other psychiatric patients in this country. But where are these people? Why aren't there more of us at this conference? How can you provide an adequate service to people like me if we don't get our heads together at conferences like this?

Why does the psychiatric system, in the eyes of many of its consumers, fail to serve them as well as it could? I suggest there are two important reasons for this failure. First, we patients have not organised ourselves as a force to be consulted with. Second, you professionals and planners have not really thought to consult us.

When I go home I'm going to start a consumer group. And when you go back to work I hope you remember to involve us in your planning and at your meetings and conferences.

My request to you is this: take us seriously, encourage us to talk, and above all listen – listen to what we have to say.

I got a long clap. The woman from the agoraphobic support group stood up and cheered. Several professionals came up to tell me they agreed with everything I said. That day I decided to put my self-help book on hold. At the conference I discovered the door to a new world that had been closed off to mad people by centuries of discrimination. It was an empty world with very few travellers in it – a world where we

135

mad people could organise and stand up for ourselves, where we met as equals with professionals and other sane people. And I was determined to help open its borders.

A couple of months later I visited the Mental Health Foundation in Auckland and asked them if they would provide office space for me to research the experience of mad people and start up a group of patients and ex-patients. They agreed. A month later I moved to Auckland. Dunedin had become my city of ghosts. In my new home city there was no past to haunt me, no street corners where my brother once stood, no roads leading to the Canary Ward, no neighbourhoods saturated with bad memories. I had arrived, not just to a new city, but to a new life beyond trauma and loss, to begin my work in the mad movement.

8.

PSYCHIATRIC SURVIVORS

I arrived in Auckland late in 1985 with my backpack, my weekly benefit cheque and a draft proposal for funding to research the experience of mad people as an information base for our advocacy. I hadn't been admitted to hospital for nearly a year and felt ready to make my contribution to society. I'd always liked a cause – world hunger was my first at the age of eleven. At thirteen I moved on to the Vietnam war, then onto saving a lake from being flooded for a greedy aluminium smelter. At university it was nasty nukes, racist Afrikaners and sexist men. But the injustices in the mental health system and discrimination against mad people didn't even make it onto the outer edges of the social justice radar screen. I had found a gap that needed to be filled.

The Mental Health Foundation gave me office space – but they gave me much more than that. Through my association with them I gained a ready-made credibility in a world where mad people had very little of it. The Foundation also gave me contact with people I might have never met otherwise – not just influential people, but other survivors who like me were looking for a better world.

I began by reading research on psychiatric patients. It turned out that our experiences were as underrated in mental health research as they were in mental health services. All the research was done by well-meaning professionals and academics who saw us as vulnerable people who could not determine our own best interests; mad people did not have needs like everyone else but 'felt' needs, implying that professionals were the final arbiters on what our 'actual' needs were. Of course, none of the researchers whose work I read ever identified as mad people. None of the papers mentioned consulting mad people about what should be researched and how it should be done. Mad people's experiences were often totally silenced in the research, smothered by the assumptions and analysis of the researchers. Or it was distorted because the questions asked were not necessarily ones that were important to mad people, and the interpretation of their responses was monopolised by professional researchers who arrogantly believed their reality was closer to the truth than the lived realities of the people they were researching.

One report I read was about people I had been in hospital with in Dunedin in 1983. I don't recall being interviewed for it. It was done by social workers who designed the research, selected the patients, interviewed them, interpreted their comments, made the recommendations and wrote up the results. The people I had sat with in hospital seemed to die on the page. People like Richard pacing in his dressing gown, Jill sobbing in the dark, Maria who bit herself until she bled, Brooke who helped me laugh at my despair. The report's portrayal of them reminded me of dead butterflies behind glass arranged in tidy rows with their wings pinned down. I couldn't find them bleeding or sobbing or laughing anywhere among the tables, percentages or wooden prose.

But that was one of the better reports I read. Though it reduced mad people to specimens it did so gently, without annihilating our human status. I read another report about a service for people who had left hospital. It read like an invitation to a subtle form of genocide. Not the type of genocide that kills the bodies of a whole class of people, but the type that kills their reputations and the value others see in their lives. It described a typical client group entering the group homes with a long list of deficit-ridden insults. The typical patient was described as 'single (if married has not been able to sustain a relationship), long in contact with the psychiatric services, of limited intellect, possessing strange behaviour, paranoia, schizophrenia, nowhere to go or nobody to be with.'

There was no way I could do my research in the way that professionals did theirs. But how *was* I going to do it?

As I was finishing my proposal someone suggested I get advice from a researcher at the university who had just completed a sociological study of a psychiatric hospital. After losing myself in a chaotic network of dark narrow corridors I knocked nervously on the researcher's door. A serious, middle-aged woman with thick, unfashionable glasses let me in, her mousy hair pulled back in a severe ponytail. She sat behind her desk in a light green suit with her framed degrees behind her, looking pale and self-assured. 'You've got to be credible,' she said, 'Even more so than others, given that you're an ex-patient without research experience.'

I nodded, unable to think of a quick response.

'You've got to be able to defend your methodology. If you want mental health professionals and academics to take you seriously you must ensure bias doesn't sneak into your research. You don't want them to dismiss you as a disgruntled ex-patient with an axe to grind.'

She then explained to me how I could minimise bias and said goodbye. I left her feeling even more nervous, and struggling to articulate why I felt slightly patronised and dissatisfied.

I followed her advice. Not because I wanted to. Not even because I had to. I followed it because I knew of no other way. My research proposal was to interview a representative mix of fifty mad people, found through the 'snowball' method where the people I interviewed recommended others to interview. The interviews were structured into question areas decided on before the interview phase started. I was then to collate and analyse the answers, make generalisations from them, fill it out with quotes and stories and put it all into a report.

My proposal was funded by a philanthropic organisation and a short time later I started. The first person I interviewed was Gerald, an imposing man from the waist up with impaired legs and a stumbling walk. Gerald had done some work speaking to community groups about patients' rights. His own story was a good illustration of why they are needed. His deep voice filled the room as he gave an eloquent account of his experiences:

'Oh sure, I've been beaten up by staff. At the secure hospital there was a rule you had to strip naked in the corridor, leave your clothes out, go into your room totally naked, and get your pyjamas on and go to bed. I found that really hard to do because of my physical disability so I took my clothes off in my room. I had three buttons undone on my shirt and they literally ripped my clothes right off me, pants and all, testicles squashed. It was standard practice.'

Gerald had spent many years in and out of hospitals, often as an involuntary patient: he had never had legal representation or seen a judge about it. He hated the coercion and neglect he had experienced: 'In seclusion I belted my head on the concrete floor and did myself a bit of damage. Nobody came in, nobody could even hear. I'm totally against seclusion – it aggravates a person's illness. A nurse should be assigned to someone to be in constant contact with them.'

But it was not just the blatant abuse and neglect that Gerald hated – it was also his loss of credibility: 'The doctor would say to me, "You're looking well today." I'd say, "I feel terrible." He'd say, "No you don't."'

Gerald told me his mental illness had had a worse effect on his life than his physical disability. Here was an energetic, intelligent man of nearly forty, living alone, unemployed and on a benefit, who had given up hope of getting a job, who longed to have a partner and children. It shouldn't have had to be this way.

Gerald was nearly in tears. I sat quietly with him. 'What bastards,' I said. 'Gerald, you and I are going to make sure this kind of thing never happens again.' Gerald nodded but I could see he was a defeated man.

←——————*

As I began my interviews I met another mad person called Hank, who was setting up a group called the Mental Health Activists with the manager of a non-government community mental health service. I thought about grafting my efforts onto this group but it didn't take me long to see it would never work. The manager dominated the group, despite her good intentions about empowering the survivors. She said she was only there to support us but her behaviour said something different. She facilitated a planning meeting for the Mental Health Activists. Several mad people came to it at my invitation. The manager often disagreed with us and didn't write some of our ideas on the board. Some of the people I'd invited started getting angry with her but she couldn't understand why.

The final straw came when Hank and I decided to write a letter to the local newspaper about the lack of housing for survivors. We discussed it with the manager. 'You people can't write a letter – you don't have sufficient experience and the letter would be bad PR for this service,' she said. Her words landed on me like a heavy blanket; once again a mental health professional was telling us we were incompetent. But something in me had been stirred by my reading about the mad movement and I sensed she was wrong about us. Later I told her the group I planned to set up needed to be completely independent of mental health professionals, and I would no longer take part in the Mental Health Activists. At the time I wrote:

I've decided to leave the 'shelter' of the Mental Health Activists, and set up a group independently. I wasn't looking forward to telling the manager this because she is defensive and has her heart set on a patients' group that is associated with her service. Then something clicked. I realised my apprehension about telling her showed more clearly than anything that I, and the others, have perceived her to be the group's operator. Although it is called a patients' group, implicitly – and sometimes not so implicitly – the manager has taken the reins. How did this happen? Both the manager and the survivors – including myself a bit – believe in some dark corner of our minds that survivors don't know what is best for them or how to go about getting it. That is why the Mental Health Activists could never succeed.

I had learnt my first big lesson. Mental health professionals had no place in a psychiatric survivor organisation. The structural inequality in their relationship with mad people destroyed their ability to share power. It also destroyed the ability of mad people to expect this of them.

The second person I interviewed for my research was Veronica, a witty, eccentric woman in her late forties. Veronica dressed like a scarecrow in colourful, dishevelled clothing. She chain-smoked, inhaling with every breath, her cigarette squeezed between her fingers while it bobbed rhythmically in and out of her mouth. We sat for an afternoon in her living room as she talked about her life, swerving from one compelling story to another – funny stories, sad ones, angry ones, stories full of wit and novel insights.

Veronica first became suicidal at nineteen after breaking up with a boyfriend but her problems escalated when she married an alcoholic. She then lost custody of her son who was now at a boarding school. Stress tipped her into her mood swings: 'I'm a shy, unconfident person, and I have little power as a woman in my situation. All these things make me vulnerable.'

I asked her if she agreed she had a mental illness. 'Yes I do,' she said, 'but it depends on whether you want to get involved in other states of mind or not. Half the population is taking LSD to get into the same state I'm trying to get out of!'

Veronica talked about her experiences in the mental health system. She was still fuming over her most recent admission to hospital:

'Two policemen came and picked me up because I wouldn't let anyone into the house. I think I was quite within my rights not to have anyone in the house. I was forced to go with them and the actual examination of me was a complete and utter farce. I was put in the prison cells for one night. I'm not complaining about the fact I wasn't well but the method – I had no advocacy, I was entirely defenceless. Two young doctors came and wrote busily about me in my cell. They said hardly a thing to me. They didn't ask me any questions. They hardly said a thing to the judge and on those grounds I was committed. I got stroppy and asked a nurse – she told me I was committed because I dressed strangely and abused my neighbours.'

Veronica talked about being in seclusion without toilet facilities and peeing on the floor because the staff didn't check her regularly enough to let her out in time. She talked about drugs and how in many cases they violated people's bodily rights. And she talked about the nurses who sat smoking in the office reading about the cardboard characters they had created in the patients' files, while the real live people milled around waiting for the nurses to come and talk to them. I agreed with Veronica that the files are not really about us. She said hers might as well be thrown in the rubbish bin – they knew so little about her because they never really tried to find out.

'I no longer trust doctors. If you come up with a difficult question they either ignore you or mow straight over you. I no longer find them honest. I no longer find them informed. I find they know a lot about drugs and nothing else. There should be a multi-faceted approach in psychiatry. People are too ready to supply drugs as the answer to patients problems. Drug therapy is a lazy way of dealing with people's emotions. Staff are ill-equipped to deal with people's emotions. It horrifies me. I'm lucky – I've had psychotherapy. It was very positive, supportive and encouraging. Someone could see my point of view for a change.'

Veronica talked more about her life and how it had been devastated, not just by her mood swings but by the way other people had treated her:

'I was a teacher until ten years ago but I don't know if I could get a job again after being a committed patient. I'd probably have to lie about myself. I'd like more status in the community. The drugs and stresses in our lives tend to make psych patients unassertive. To be in a job where I had to be assertive would be very hard – I don't think I could do it.

'I feel close to tears when I think of the effect my manic depression has had on my life and my child's. I've lost self-esteem, confidence – yes, tremendous loss of hope, loss of power and loss of respect from everybody. I lost all my friends and never regained their trust and respect. I've written my family off. I haven't received any real lasting help from anywhere.'

←——→

As I was starting on the interviews I received an invitation to speak to the staff at a community mental health service about my work. A nurse ushered me into the front room of an old brick building. Serious-looking, casually dressed people sat in chairs in a circle drinking coffee. The psychiatrist in charge welcomed me and the others murmured in appreciation. I talked to them about my research and the organisation I planned to set up. I could see they were interested but I struggled to communicate with them from the perilously narrow shelf of territory I stood on where I could show myself as both an ex-patient and a competent person at the same time, without denying either. It was uneasy work. The staff said things like you're so brave, good for you, and haven't you done well. I felt like a child being praised by over-caring parents. The staff were more enlightened than many professionals but I could tell they weren't used to dealing with people like me in a competent role, just as I wasn't used to talking to people like them behind 'Staff Only' doors.

Something I said got them talking about the problems they had getting some of their patients to accept their illness. I felt discomfited and lost for words. The ex-patient part of me felt like an unwilling eavesdropper on a conversation that belittled my peers and could have been about me. The competent advocate part of me searched for an authentic critique of their conversation, fearful that my silence signalled my agreement. Somehow I found a question that integrated my ex-patient identity and my competent advocate role: 'Have you ever thought that *not* accepting their illness may be a help to them?' No, they hadn't thought of that. 'What an interesting thought,' one of them said. Another one said that acceptance was vital for complying with treatment and getting better.

With that question and their responses, the territory I stood on became a little wider.

←——→

Next I interviewed Hinewai, a thin, haunted Maori woman in her late thirties who lived in a boarding house and blamed herself for bringing shame on her family.

'I was in the female secure unit,' she told me. 'The closed wing had seven cells with nothing but a plastic mattress and, if you were lucky, a blanket and a pillow. Girls were locked in those cells for thirteen and a half hours out of every twenty-four. There were no toilets in the cells so we had to ask the staff to let us out. Sometimes the staff were too busy playing cards or having a smoke. On at least four occasions I was forced to go on the floor like an animal. It was the ultimate in degradation.'

Hinewai wiped her eyes and rolled a cigarette. 'We spent the rest of the time in a small dayroom. There was a small courtyard to walk around if the weather was fine, but we could spend weeks in that wing without getting any fresh air.'

'What was the open side of the ward like?' I asked.

'It wasn't much better. It was still locked but you could wear clothes. There was nothing to do on the open side except watch television and smoke. If you were good you might get up to two hours ground parole in the afternoon. Most of the nurses never had time to speak to the patients. You're basically there to look after yourself. Most of the girls were drugged up to four times a day. One of my friends was on thirty-one pills a day.'

'Did you ever complain?'

'There was a lot of physical abuse from the staff. You couldn't have any emotions in this ward. Crying got one woman put in an arm lock and thrown into seclusion. Twice I was stripped naked by male nurses and dragged down the corridor by my ankles. When I got the police to investigate they said they wouldn't lay charges because I was a committed patient. So the physical abuse just continued.'

Hearing Hinewai and the others talk, I wondered why the whole community wasn't outraged by the way people have been treated in the mental health system. Maybe they never got exposure to these stories. Maybe they thought it was OK because mad people weren't full members of the human race.

←——————×

People started to invite me to meetings and to sit on committees to represent the views of people on the receiving end of services. After one meeting at the local psychiatric hospital I noticed a sign by the side of the hospital driveway. It was big and black with silver letters that reflected in the dark: 'Caution Patients'.

A few weeks later a journalist interviewed me for a feature on advocacy in the local paper. 'We need a photograph,' she said.

'I've got just the backdrop for you.'

The journalist, the photographer and I met at the 'Caution Patients' sign. 'What got you into this work?' asked the photographer.

'Being in places like this where nothing is expected of you but to stay sick, and wanting to prove them wrong, I guess, and to stop them from treating people so badly.'

'My aunt died in here. She never got out. How come you got out?'

'I don't really know, ' I said, 'but I thought, bugger it, I don't want to go on and on being the recipient of a system that requires only my disability to be part of it. People like me have got something to give to places like these, not that we're grateful or anything.'

The next day the photo appeared in the paper – me standing with my arms folded looking staunch beside the 'Caution Patients' sign. 'Watch out – we're going to change things,' the caption read. 'Mary's time in psychiatric hospitals taught her about powerlessness and she is now determined to change the balance.'

←——————→

I interviewed many others. They all had similar stories to tell. Many had never talked about their experience in one sitting before, to someone who took them at their word. Some cried as they talked about all the pain they had endured. So much of it was not due to the experience of madness itself but about their experiences in hospital, their lost opportunities, about once promising young lives that had fallen into unemployment, poverty and loneliness. They talked again and again of hospital staff who took their dignity away or never talked to them, the overuse of drugs, of seclusion, the trauma of compulsory treatment, the lack of psychotherapy and support, and the lack of information about drugs and side-effects. So much of their suffering could have been avoided if the mental health system and the rest of society had genuinely responded to them.

Although many felt a deep vein of disappointment and at times outrage about the way they had been treated, most of them came from ordinary, conservative backgrounds and were not politicised by anti-establishment views. They did not have a framework for thinking about what was wrong with the present set-up or how the world could become a better place for them. Instead, some excused mental health services or blamed themselves for the way their lives had gone.

I interviewed Jack in his smoky council flat as he sat breathlessly on his sofa, an oxygen tank gleaming like a bomb in the corner. He told me, 'People have breakdowns because there is a weakness in the personality and habits of the person. Patients have to be controlled more as children rather than reasoning adults.'

I asked him how the staff should treat patients. 'The staff appear to be offhand, almost heartless,' he said. 'But there must have been a reason they are like that – it must be for the patients' benefit.' Later I wished I had asked him if he felt as responsible for his emphysema as he did for his madness, though I suspected he didn't. Or if he thought the respiratory medicine staff went out of their way to be heartless for his benefit. Again I suspected he would have said no.

Then there was Dermot, a gentle and guilt-ridden ex-priest, who talked about his experience of seclusion. 'I was stripped naked and there was a mattress on the floor, a blanket and a potty. On one occasion they put me there for a month. I accepted it. I didn't hammer on the door. I just felt, I'm in here for a reason, I must have put myself in here.'

And there was Shirley, a timid over-medicated woman who had been in the mental health system for years. 'I don't really know anything about my condition. I peeked at my file once and it said "schizophrenia". I don't think it was the proper thing for me to do,' she said.

'Are you satisfied with the information you get on your condition?' I asked.

'Yes, I'm pretty satisfied.'

Most of the people I interviewed were older than me – people in middle age who had more life to look back on than I did. Though my own madness seemed to have subsided at the age of twenty-seven, I worried that my life could still unfold like theirs, that I would grow old with thwarted potential, raging with regrets about a life not fully lived. I could see that people like Gerald and Veronica raged with regrets, at least from time to time. I could see that others like Hinewai felt a quieter grief. But some said they were satisfied with their lives, lives that no one else could have envied. They were the people like John, Dermot and Shirley who felt they didn't deserve anything better.

I knew it was time for mad people to show mental health professionals and the world that we had something to give; we could organise, challenge them and engage in debate as their equals. But most of the people I interviewed did not feel ready for this. Though they felt harmed by the mental health system, most had not analysed the ideologies and practices that had created this harm, or thought about the changes that were needed. Instead, some blamed themselves for the way their lives had gone.

Through the research, I wanted to satisfy my youthful craving for new knowledge and a new vision for a better world. I wanted to make a powerful statement for change. But after several interviews I began to wonder if the research was going to deliver what I was so impatient for. Many of the people I had interviewed did not share my passion for change. And I continued to doubt the research advice I was given; it was becoming more important for me to tell our truth in our own way to mental health professionals than to dilute it to suit their biases or expectations. For a couple of months I felt as though I was stumbling around in a great fog with no answers.

Some of the resolution to this confusion came from feminist literature on research, which critiqued the conventional kind of research I was doing and explored alternatives to it. Feminist researchers claimed that research on women was typically done by men who either distorted or omitted their experiences. Men in their research on women often had complete control over the topic they were investigating, the questions they asked and the analysis of the responses. I could see with a new clarity that mad people, just like women, were powerless in the research process.

In the research I was doing I too had control over the topic, the questions I asked and the analysis of people's replies. Initially I thought my status as a mad person would save me from distorting or omitting their experience, and to a large degree it did. But I was not always so sure. For instance, one man I interviewed said he always locked the doors when he was inside the house in case the Security Intelligence Service came to take him away. The research method I was using gave me the power to dismiss his experience as paranoia, in order to fit it in with my own world view. I did not want to have that power over my peers; it replicated the power mental health professionals had over me.

I was not even comfortable assuming the role of researcher when I was among my peers. Their opinion of me was far more important to me than the opinion of professionals. The last thing I wanted to do was give them reason to think I had climbed the social ladder and was no longer one of them, as I wrote at the time:

At first I assumed that other survivors would treat me as one of them – a comrade. But after my initial contact with them in the role of researcher, I am not so sure. For instance, today I went to meet a group of survivors about the research. Why did I leave my black briefcase at home? Why was I reluctant to bring my diary out and hand around my clean typed research information sheet? Because these things are symbols of professionalism.

The final resolution came one morning as I woke in the dark to see a small strip of light appear on the eastern horizon. Another way of doing the research shone in my head as if someone had planted it there overnight. Like a precious seed I nurtured it into an alternative research proposal – a variation on participatory action research. The research would be controlled by a group of survivors who would have the final say over the design, the topics to be discussed and editorial power over the reports. I would be the overall coordinator and compiler of the information, but this could be shared with the other survivors.

Participants would be encouraged to write a journal on an agreed topic, to be shared with other participants. The group would meet among themselves to share their views, starting with reflection on their experiences, moving on to their positions on issues, then on to possible action to bring about change in the mental health system. Examples of issues that could be taken up were compulsory treatment, legal advocacy, housing shortages or shock treatment. The survivors group was going to be the kernel of a survivor-run advocacy organisation.

This methodology addressed all the misgivings I had about the conventional research I was doing. It allowed a creative process to take place rather than one that was pegged down with conventions about bias, objectivity and truth. I would no longer be presiding over other people's experiences but joining with them in a search for meaning and solutions. People would not be selected semi-randomly, but for their commitment and ability to take part. All the participants would be on an equal footing as both researcher and researched. They would all have continuing involvement in the research and contact with each other, giving them more opportunities to enhance their understanding. I wrote a critique of conventional research and a proposal for the alternative research and called it 'From Taking Snapshots to Making Movies'.

It was an ambitious proposal that needed extraordinary commitment from thoughtful and reflective people to ever have a chance of working. And it never happened. It stayed on the page like a lesser version of Leonardo da Vinci's helicopter; ahead of its time perhaps but difficult to get off the ground. At the same time, other events and issues started to take up my time and the establishment of the survivor advocacy and support group happened without it.

←——————→

We had our first meeting in February 1987. Several of us sat around in a tiny sitting room and talked about our experiences with the mental health system. We talked about things that should never ever have happened – the insensitive remarks, being held down and injected, solitary confinement, over-drugging, being written off as human beings. We talked about what a strong collective force we could be. We yahooed about the patients taking over the asylum. We erupted with the heady excitement of people who had just found freedom.

Debbie was a big woman in cheap, colourful, market clothes, about my age with red hair and warm shining eyes. She came from a high-achieving middle class family; now she was on a benefit and lived by herself in the council flat where we met. She made everyone welcome. As people downed their instant coffee and sucked on their cigarettes Debbie held the floor with her breathtaking stories. She named our group 'Psychiatric Survivors'. Week after week we met in Debbie's flat as we supported each other and plotted to change the world.

One of the early regulars was Kahu, a strong, young Maori woman who had come, full of youthful hope, to the big city to get a job. But the job never happened and she was taken away to the mental hospital. She now lived in a run-down inner-city boarding house. She hated it there. 'If we had a choice about where to live the boarding houses would be empty,' she said. Kahu was a rouser – full of humour and a positive anger. 'We can do it,' she kept telling us, 'this is fantastic.' We all agreed.

Glenn was another early member. He was a tall, dark, young man who had been kicked out of medical school. His psychiatrist told him he had schizophrenia because his family was dysfunctional. He had taken Glenn off all his drugs and was doing some re-parenting on him. The psychiatrist told Glenn not to visit his parents; they lived down the road but he hadn't seen them for over a year. We could all tell that Glenn was having a hard time. He had a wild, bewildered look in his eyes, like a man being chased by his own demons. Glenn would slip in and out of our conversation but we carried him with us with the gentleness and respect of people who knew, without affirming or denying his reality. When he lay on the footpath outside, staring at the stars, we understood and waited by him until he got up. When he went into hospital we walked beside him as he shuffled around in a state of siege – the demon of his madness now crushed by the demon of anti-psychotic drugs.

My work in the mad movement started alongside another group of people seeking partnership and self-determination – the indigenous Maori. In many ways their cause paralleled our own, both in its timing and in the similarities of our grievances. Madness had been colonised by psychiatry and indigenous cultures had been colonised by western expansionists. But there was an interesting and uneasy twist to this parallel; from the point of view of the indigenous movement I was one of the colonisers, but in the mad movement I was one of the aggrieved.

I grew up in the South Island where very few Maori lived. At school I was taught that New Zealand had the best race relations in the world. Though the British settlers and the Maori had fought each other in the nineteenth century, I absorbed the mythology that Maori were now a happy lot – just like white people, a bit poorer perhaps, but how they could sing, play rugby and do the haka. All the children in my class were white, until one year a young Maori girl named Aroha was put in the same class as me. I was immediately drawn to her. She was gentle and friendly, easy to talk to. I was drawn to her difference – her smooth, glossy, brown skin, her wide smiling face, her thick blue-black hair and her bottomless brown eyes. And I loved the stories she told me about her people who fought against the British, her grandmother back home with the tattoo on her chin, and her sister who sang beautiful Maori songs on stage.

At eleven I was innocent about the divisions created by ethnicity and class. I also knew little of Aroha's world. But Aroha knew my world. She knew I lived in a flash two-storey house with leafy trees and a high hedge. She knew I had white professional parents. She knew she didn't belong there. I wondered why she didn't want to visit, why she always wanted me round at her house in a treeless street full of peeling bungalows. I felt welcome and comfortable in her home but she did not feel the same in mine. Knowing Aroha taught me the disturbing lesson that I had some privilege, but more than that, it taught me that others who lacked this privilege were not comfortable with it.

As a teenager I went to meetings in cold community halls to oppose the All Blacks playing rugby with South Africa in the era of apartheid. At one of these meetings a lone Maori woman at the back stood up full of bitter passion and said: 'You fellas are worried about what's going on over there in South Africa. Yeah, we all know it's bad over there but why don't you look at your own back yard? We signed a treaty with you lot. And what did you do? You stole our land, you forbade us to speak our language, you stood by while we lost our culture and our pride. How can you sit there and go on about whites in South Africa when you've got a lot of cleaning up to do right here in Aotearoa?'

Rows of troubled pale faces took their gaze off the woman and turned towards the front as she stood shaking with anger. It was the first time I had heard such anger coming from a Maori person and I struggled to understand why she felt so strongly aggrieved in a country with the best race relations in the world.

This was the beginning of the Maori revival and most of the white people in the cold hall didn't understand. Some tried to comfort the woman. Some told her how much worse it was in South Africa. Others said the point was that Maori had always been able to play for the All Blacks – no black people had ever been allowed to play for South Africa. Another said it was time for her to move on from the past. Of course these were not the things the woman wanted to hear; she wanted people to hear the truth in what she had to say. She left the meeting and never came back.

Years later I thought of the Maori woman at that meeting as I struggled to get my truth heard at meetings of mental health professionals. And I thought of Aroha who felt an alien in my house, just as I felt an alien in rooms of mental health professionals who were oblivious to their own power and privilege.

By the time I started my work in the mad movement the Maori revival had gathered force. Maori protests were common. They were setting up their own schools and health services. Many were learning their language and returning to their tribal heritage. The government had set up a tribunal to investigate breaches of the Treaty of Waitangi, signed in 1840 between the Maori chiefs and the British Crown. The Treaty was beginning to be a cornerstone of government legislation and policy, a belated attempt to honour its undertaking to Maori that the Crown would act in partnership with them, protect their culture and property, and ensure them the same rights as other citizens. Gradually, I began to understand Maori grievances. A key to this was the acknowledgment of the immense power white culture and its institutions had in New Zealand – a power so immense that it covered every inch of our white imaginations and cultural landscape. I had not even imagined that a conquered culture lay beneath this landscape until the Maori revival began to break its surface.

Another key to my understanding was the realisation that Maori culture was fundamentally different from my own individualistic, progress-oriented, materialistic culture. Maori had a collective culture where the individual who stood alone was nothing. It was a culture with a deep attachment to the past and to the spirituality of the land. It was also a deeply injured culture determined to revitalise itself.

My experience of madness and my work in the mad movement

helped me to understand Maori grievance perhaps more than anything else did. Being a white person on the receiving end of Maori grievance enabled me to understand some of the defensiveness, bewilderment and vulnerability mental health professionals might feel when they were challenged by mad people. How professionals, like white people, generally think they are doing good. How it takes time to break the habits and attitudes of generations. How unhelpful it is for people to be told they are doing it all wrong without offering some clues on how they could fix this. How fate rather than virtue determines whether we are born or sorted onto the side of the oppressed or the oppressor.

←———×

After Psychiatric Survivors was formed, we joined a new advocacy coalition named the Auckland Mental Health Interest Group. The people in the coalition were mainly mental health service providers who were frustrated with the poor state of mental health services in Auckland. But we soon became just as frustrated with the Auckland Mental Health Interest Group as we were with services. It lacked a strategy and coordination, and made virtually no progress on any issues all year, despite all the meetings. In fact, the Interest Group behaved very much like the services it was trying to improve. We sat at meetings with them where everything was discussed – money, politics, facilities, plans – everything but the pain of the people we were all supposed to be there for. Our major frustration, though, was the way our voice was marginalised by the Interest Group. They set the agendas, chaired the meetings and dominated the discussions. We were a small minority, a new stakeholder that would not have been represented on such a group even two years beforehand. As the others talked, we survivors felt as though we were almost drowning in their entrenched conservatism and patronising attitudes. When we did get the opportunity to express our views, we soon felt submerged again by the powerful voice of the status quo. The professionals at these meetings pronounced their views from a high sturdy platform built by historical privilege, education, money and authority. We survivors were just starting to find ground to stand on.

After some months we decided to withdraw from the Interest Group.

I explained that we were doing it because the group was making no progress and our involvement was tokenistic. I said that though we were leaving we did not want to lose contact with them, we just wanted the contact to be on our terms. I was not prepared for the vitriolic response I got. An angry bewildered-looking woman with wild hair pointed her finger at me: 'How can you expect us to keep going without consumer representation? That's the reason we're here – to help consumers!' She didn't seem to recall that she had been 'helping' consumers all her professional life without our representation. Or to question the group's tokenism if she thought consumer representation was so vital.

Then a wholesome woman from a church-based service said with a reddening face, 'I'm angry with you. What you are doing is deeply selfish. We all have to make sacrifices to do what is good, sometimes at great personal cost!' I was stung into silence by her remark, desperately trying to understand why she thought I was deeply selfish. Later I realised she said it because she hadn't understood a word of what I said. A heated discussion swirled around me. Several more people criticised me for our decision.

Later, after discussions with others in Psychiatric Survivors, I wrote a proposal setting out the terms on which Psychiatric Survivors would rejoin the Interest Group: a paid survivor to coordinate survivor involvement in the group, at least fifty per cent of the members to be survivors, fifty per cent of meetings to be hosted and chaired by survivors, and regular educational seminars run by survivors for other group members. We knew the proposal was futile and we never sent it. For its day, the proposal was pushy and radical – most of the Interest Group members would have flipped if they had been presented with it. Though they understood that mad people need to have a say, they had a long, long way to go to understand what true partnership really meant.

←———→

Housing for mad people in Auckland was a growing issue. We at Psychiatric Survivors decided to tackle it. I went to some boarding houses and listened to the stories of the people who lived in them. One of them was Steve, who had spent most of his twenties in the mental hospital. Steve was a talented pianist whose only contact with his family was through a post office box. He wrote to them to ask them to come and see him but he never got a reply.

Steve greeted me and we sat on the veranda while he rolled a cigarette. 'I'm in a room with five beds,' he told me. 'One man goes to bed at six o'clock in the evening. We can't turn the radio or lights on in case there's a fight.' He took a deep draw on his cigarette and looked into the distance. 'You know, doing nothing is hard – it gets boring here. All the people I know are on the injection. I can't play the piano after midday because the TV is turned on but I don't want to sit around watching TV all day. I don't go out much because I can't afford to. Sometimes I take pills from the chemist just to stop the boredom.

'This is the best boarding house I've been in. The manager at one of them sexually harassed me. He used to call out to me at night to come to his room. It was really bad. I was quite sick at the time and didn't know what I was doing.'

I asked Steve what kind of housing situation he would like. 'I'd like to get a group of us together to rent a house with back-up from the mental health service.'

'What's stopping you?' I asked.

'The medication makes me complacent and lethargic. I feel as though this is my lot in life and I might as well accept it.'

I heard similar stories from other people living in boarding houses – of being forced to work for no money, of chronic boredom, lack of privacy, stolen possessions, sexual abuse, foul food and flea-infested rooms. Most of them agreed that boarding houses were even worse than being in hospital.

Later I visited Leota, the manager at Steve's boarding house. He was a handsome, curly-haired, Pacific Island man who took me to his gloomy office in a large basement stacked with second-hand furniture. An untidy desk shone in one corner under a naked light bulb. Leota sat behind it. I could see he was a good man but he looked depressed and powerless. 'This place is understaffed,' he said. 'The people here need help on a one-to-one basis but I'm one person with eighteen residents.'

'Do they ever complain?' I asked.

'No, their self-esteem is too low. These people have no jobs and no interests. They have low motivation because of the drugs and their low self-esteem. They have no choices. They are the forgotten people. Quite often I feel the people here would be better off dead, there is so much unhappiness and emptiness in their lives.'

I left Leota and the boarding house people with a great weight on my mind. But I also had a renewed sense of mission. After months of sitting in my office and being with survivors like me, who were putting our lives back together, I was reminded of why I was doing my work – to create a world where life for the 'forgotten people' would be worth living. Leota's comments also made me confront my own past in my journal later that day:

The manager's comments about the ex-patients being better off dead took me back to the years when my mood swings were at their worst. What if they had remained that bad for the rest of my life? Would I have been better off dead? Yes, I think so; the pain would have been too much for me to bear.

Though I could feel Leota's despair and relate it to my own life, I felt unease at his attitude towards the people in the boarding house. I didn't doubt his compassion for them but I wondered how much hope he could pass onto people whom he thought would be better off dead. I wondered how the men would have felt if they knew what Leota thought. I remembered how the hope of others was sometimes enough to keep me alive when I had lost all hope myself, and I wondered how much inadvertent harm the good Leota might be doing.

Two weeks after I visited the boarding house I woke to the radio news. Through my half-sleep I heard that two men in Steve's boarding house had been stabbed to death with a carving knife by another resident. By mid-morning Opposition politicians were calling for an inquiry into why 'dangerous' psychiatric patients were allowed to wander free in the streets. 'Shouldn't they be locked up?' they asked.

'No,' I replied on the television news that night, 'Psychiatric patients are no more violent than anyone else.'

In the media over the next few days, and in my journal, I asked the questions that didn't seem to occur to ranting politicians or the public who voted for them. Would the murderer have gone crazy with the carving knife if he lived in a community that wanted him? If he had some money in his pocket? If he had really mattered to another person? If he had had something worthwhile to do with his days? If help was there when he needed it? It was impossible to know for sure but the murders might not have happened if the man had been a valued member of his community. In all my time in psychiatric hospitals I had not seen one act of violence by a mad person. What I saw much more of was the antithesis of violence – extreme passivity, a deadly stillness and silence created by madness, drugs and loss of hope.

The murders at the boarding house catapulted me into the media. I spoke to newspapers, magazines, radio and television, and the more I did it the more exposed I felt. It wasn't coming out as a mad person that got me. It was when I stumbled with my words, when I felt I didn't know enough to comment, when I said something that later made me cringe, when I was misrepresented by journalists – these were the times when I felt exposed. I was more concerned about exposing my incompetence than I was my madness. Media exposure also changed other people's view of me. I sensed they saw me as invulnerable, an expert, sure of every word I uttered and as totally thick-skinned. But I wasn't.

Though I made progress with my work in the first few years I continued to experience the aftershocks of my madness. My mood swings were not severe enough to put me into hospital but they sometimes disrupted my work, my concentration, motivation and confidence. I struggled on in the early years, going to work when I could at my office in the Mental Health Foundation. The staff there were tolerant and respectful. They didn't pressure me to turn up or put me down for my aberrant behaviour when I was manic.

In the midst of all the trauma and upheaval, I berated myself for the slow progress I was making in my work but I also knew that I had set myself demanding and difficult tasks. I was constantly searching for new ways of understanding the world. I was not content to do things the way other people did. People said I was hard on myself but it wasn't so much myself I was hard on. I was hard on the known world, bored by and disappointed with it. The mental health system, conventional research and the models of advocacy I saw around me did not have the answers for me. But finding my own answers was hard brain-breaking work. I felt that in rejecting conventional truths I had marooned myself on an empty beach where I was free to create, but the price I paid was isolation, pain and losing my way.

I also continued to feel overwhelming grief at the loss of Sean. Usually, I could hold it together but occasionally a memory, a comment or a song flooded me with immense sadness. At first I struggled to absorb the totality of his absence. Sometimes I caught myself planning to tell him something when I realised he was not there. I raged at the spaces he no longer filled, leaning against his living room wall, beside his partner, bending over to his daughter, sitting opposite me at the table. Gradually, the shock of his absence gave way to quieter grief as I grew more accustomed to life without him.

←———→

My mother Clare and I were drinking a gin and tonic around my parents' dining table in Christchurch. 'I can't believe he's been dead for two years,' she said. 'If it weren't for the photos I'd start to forget what he looked like.'

'Yeah,' I said. 'At first I could remember the little details, like the hairs on the back of his hands and the way he sniffed. I could imagine him walking right up to me. But I can't reconstruct him so easily any more. Some of the bits are missing.'

'Oh yes, I hate the way he's just fading. I want to keep holding him fresh in my mind.'

'As time goes on, do you think the fading memories become part of the grief?'

Clare took a sip and frowned. 'Yes, because they give you the sense the person is slipping even further away. But I think the fading memories are also part of the healing.'

159

I looked at the photograph of him above the mantelpiece. My eyes prickled and the picture clouded over. Clare took my hand. 'You're a tender one. He was too. A couple of old souls looking for a home in the world.'

＿＿＿＿＿

Woven through all my years of madness, occasionally on the surface, often hidden even from me, was my uncertainty about my sexual orientation. Resolving it was part of my recovery. When I first started going mad I didn't know any 'out' lesbians. From a distance lesbians looked grim and butch to me. My friends joked about them. I didn't want to be a lesbian because of the stigma. I had never heard or seen anything that was positive about lesbians – no lesbian love stories or songs, no appealing lesbian role models. Being a lesbian also meant I wouldn't be able to have children. So I had boyfriends instead.

Most of the time I did a reasonable job at convincing myself I was a heterosexual. But sometimes my fear of wanting women broke through my heterosexual veneer. I didn't discuss it with anyone. I especially didn't discuss it with mental health professionals.

As the years went by I got to know some lesbians. They weren't all grim and butch. Some of them were beautiful. Some were fun. Some were strong and assured. Most of them were feminists. Slowly I realised that lesbians could be good and happy people too. Then, soon after I moved to Auckland, it happened. I fell into the arms of a woman. I never had sex with men again.

Being a lesbian in the lonely sprawl of my new city gave me a community. It was a closed community, staunch and edgy like a large gang, but based on feminist ideals rather than criminal intentions. The price of belonging was the denouncement of men, butch clothing and short haircuts. The benefit of belonging was a ready-made community founded on principle rather than just preference. Feminist principles gave me another framework for thinking about madness. I could see clear parallels between the subjugation of women and the oppression of mad people.

Around this time I was interviewed for *Broadsheet*, a feminist magazine, and discussed the relationship between feminism and our movement:

I see the psychiatric patients' movement arising from the same well of discontent as feminism. I became interested in feminism as much through my experience as a psychiatric patient as through my experience as a woman – though as a patient my powerlessness was more pronounced. Feminism has a tremendous amount to offer in the creation of a psychiatric patients' movement.

I'm concerned with far more than patients' rights in the narrow sense, I am interested in patients taking power back – and knowledge. The prevailing belief that there is one external truth independent of human perception places knowledge on a hierarchy. Sane men in suits have 'right' knowledge. They are elevated in the hierarchy. But women and psychiatric survivors are lowered in it. Those at the top are given wide-ranging powers to regulate reality. Man has dominion over woman. Mental health professionals have dominion over survivors. There isn't even a word for patients that doesn't put us in a relationship to the system that dominates us.

By the end of 1987 many more people had become involved in Psychiatric Survivors. Debbie's living room was too small so the weekly support groups continued in the basement of a boarding house run by the Baptist Church. A smaller group of us focused on advocacy. I was still the only waged person involved in Psychiatric Survivors, paid through grants and a government work scheme, and still working from the Mental Health Foundation. Although we had become an incorporated society we were not much more than a loose collection of like-minded people.

Mental health issues had been getting a lot of media exposure since the murder in the boarding house. A television documentary team talked to Debbie and me about what it was like to be a psychiatric patient and why we weren't getting a fair go. But Debbie didn't appear when the documentary went to air. I phoned her the next day and I could tell she was down and disappointed that she had missed out on appearing. A few days later she walked to a bridge that crossed a motorway and jumped off it to her death. I got the phone call at work the next morning. Debbie, so full of stories and laughter, intelligence and generosity was dead at the age of thirty. She left behind a poem about herself, written in the past tense:

I postured
I performed
I manipulated
I had to
I role-played
I demanded
I made excuses
All because. . .
But I loved
I tried
I wanted
I was human.

Debbie was buried in her home town by her large family, but Psychiatric Survivors remembered her at a special meeting down the road from where she jumped. We were all shocked and sad, some of us reliving the horror of our own perilous dances with death, all of us more determined than ever to create a world where people like Debbie didn't have to die.

Over the next few years, as Psychiatric Survivors sometimes lost its way in the distractions of power struggles, personality differences and mental health politics, I remembered Debbie. I remembered her because by some twist of fate I had survived my suicidal urges and she hadn't. I remembered her because I still had the power to intervene in the world and she didn't. I remembered her because she was the compass that pointed to the real reason I was doing my work – to make the world a gentler, more just and nurturing place for mad people, so that we didn't have to suffer so much or die before our time.

9.

THE SOWETO OF THE INSANE

Two people, Rod and Corinne, helped me to take Psychiatric Survivors from a weekly support group to an advocacy and support service employing four people in just a few months.

Rod was in his early forties. I first met him at the Mental Health Foundation office in the middle of the winter. He wore shorts and sandals, and was alert to the point of agitation, with hard-bitten fingernails. 'I want to do some advocacy work and see if there's an opportunity to do it in Psychiatric Survivors,' he said.

'That's great.'

'Yeah, well, I've experienced depression most of my life. I developed a drug habit when I was a teenager and to cut a long story short I ended up spending six years in prison for drug offences. Since then I've had several admissions to Carrington Hospital.'

'Was prison much worse than being in hospital?'

'Hell no. Prison was better. I was able to study in prison and improve myself. I was beaten up by the Police on the way to the hospital and we sat around all day in there drugged and doing nothing.'

'Really? What have you been up to since you got out?'

'I've been a union delegate and got involved in tenants' rights. It's given me a clear political analysis. You need an understanding of how the system works and who has the power. It's taught me how to fight and be persistent. I really want to use my skills in the mental health system.'

Here was a gentle compassionate man who hated social injustice and possessed an analysis that so many ex-patients lacked. 'I'm really keen,' I told him.

Within a week I met Corinne at a meeting about women in mental health services. Wearing a check woollen shirt and boots, she looked as though she had just come out of the bush, but she had a sophisticated mind and could see right through the world according to psychiatry. After the meeting I introduced myself and we talked alone.

'I was diagnosed with schizophrenia and I spent most of my twenties in and out of Carrington,' she said. 'It all started as a teenager when I was admitted to a psychiatric ward. The psychiatrist was so nice when Mum was in the room but when she left he turned into a cursing foul-mouthed monster. Maybe he'd just read a book on how to provoke passive depressive clients into talking or maybe he was just a sadistic prick. Whatever, I just shrivelled up inside myself and created a wall of silence to protect myself.'

Worse was to come. Corinne was locked in seclusion, given shock treatment without her consent and was doped up for years on drugs that crumbled her teeth and numbed her spirit. Corinne opened her bag and pulled out a notebook with a poem she'd written in it about those years.

I lost myself
I was 'reshaped' to fit a different mould
I was devalued
I was given up on
I was left on the rubbish heap to rot
I forgot how to trust myself.

'I like it, I've felt the same way,' I told her, handing back the notebook.

'You know, I've got no thanks to give to the mental health system and I really want to help change it,' she said.

'Do you want to join Psychiatric Survivors?' I asked.

'Sure,' she said.

Rod and Corinne burned with the energy and enthusiasm that comes from finding a purpose after years of believing there was no hope. They wanted to change the mental health system without putting any brakes on. They hatched a plan for Psychiatric Survivors to set up an advocacy and support service at Carrington, where they had both been patients.

'I don't think we've got a hope in hell of getting into Carrington,' I told them. 'The superintendent is an incompetent paranoid old bugger who thinks patients' rights is a communist plot. He'll barely let me into the building.'

A few weeks later the superintendent of Carrington was sacked after one scandal too many. Peter McGeorge, the psychiatrist I'd been to at Student Health in Dunedin was appointed to clean the place up. Now was our chance.

We walked up the wide asylum stairs to Peter's large office. As he emerged from behind his wide heavy door in his leather jacket, he greeted us with a smile that cut its way through his tidy facial hair. 'Great to see you all. It's been a while, Mary. Have a seat,' he said.

Rod explained what we wanted to do.

Peter took us into his confidence. 'What you're suggesting is just what this place needs. I'm still coming to terms with what a sick institution this is. You wouldn't believe some of the things that go on here.'

'Oh, yes we would,' said Rod

Peter agreed immediately to Psychiatric Survivors basing itself at the hospital to provide support and advocacy to the patients. He said the hospital would provide office space and clerical support. Rod and I had found independent funding for our wages and Corinne's were to be paid through the hospital's social work department. We moved into the hospital at the beginning of 1988.

Carrington was a large nineteenth-century yellow-brick building – a grand architectural masterpiece on the outside and a sad testament to the apartheid of mad people on the inside. Its proud exterior concealed a century of paternalism, neglect and abuse – the dungeon with the manacles bolted to the wall, the bare solitary confinement rooms built like bunkers, the desolate dormitories, the lost souls who wandered without purpose, the custodians who were beyond caring.

We felt like an activist group operating out of the Soweto of the insane. Once we lived in places like these; now we came to the hospital every day to challenge the powers of the custodians there. We were paid to do it and we were free to leave every night. The irony of it filled us with subversive delight and a renewed determination to liberate the asylum.

But the irony did not delight many of the staff. Most of them could barely put up with people from Psychiatric Survivors coming to hospital planning meetings, having an office inside the hospital and visiting patients on the ward. So our presence in the staff cafeteria was a bridge too far for some of them. After we arrived some staff members made a complaint to Peter McGeorge about the risk our presence in the cafeteria posed to patient confidentiality. Translated into honest English this meant they could no longer moan about the patients or poke fun at them. Peter ignored their complaint and we kept going to the staff cafeteria, sometimes bringing one or two of the patients with us.

The patients in the hospital welcomed us. They couldn't believe that we had once been patients like them and that we now had jobs to advance their interests as they saw them. A revolution was beginning.

✦————✦

Other people joined Rod, Corrine and me at Psychiatric Survivors, running support groups, helping with the advocacy, doing the administration. Some were paid, others were volunteers.

Annie and Janie were middle-aged identical twins. They both had jobs and owned houses until they went mad within a few months of each other. Now they were unemployed and living in a boarding house together. I first met them when they came to my flat wanting to get involved in Psychiatric Survivors. They both had light brown hair, freckles and small alert blue eyes. They were dressed in cheap trackpants with cigarette packets bulging out of their pockets. Though they looked the same they had different personalities. Annie was energetic and funny; she talked for both of them.

Counting on her fingers she said, 'We lost our jobs, our houses, our money, our families and our friends. What else is there to lose?'

'Shit, not much,' I said.

'Oh I forgot, I've got two pairs of second-hand trackpants, a jersey, a jacket. Hey, I've even got three pairs of knickers from the Salvation Army. Cigarettes, toothbrush, four books, a pair of pyjamas, my birth certificate and three dollars in the bank. Of course I haven't lost everything. What an ungrateful tart I am.'

Janie and I laughed.

'Oh, I forgot to mention my sheets and towel.'

Janie said, 'They're not yours. They belong to the boarding house.'

'Not once I leave that dump for the last time. They'll be going with me!'

Life started looking up for Annie and Janie. They got involved with Psychiatric Survivors and Rod helped them find a flat owned by a local church group with the rent subsidised by the government. People in the church visited and made friends with them. They worked every day at Psychiatric Survivors as volunteers, running support groups, representing survivors on committees and helping with the administration.

<hr />

Every Wednesday morning all the paid workers and volunteers, including any interested members came to the coordinating-group meeting at our Carrington office where the decisions about Psychiatric Survivors were made by consensus. We were ideological pioneers, exploring new frontiers where there are no hierarchies and no oppression. We rejected the arrogance, paternalism and domination of the psychiatric system and other social institutions. None of us wanted to be the boss or tell others what to do.

We started coordinating-group meetings with a round to say how we were. Tom, one of our new advocates, started. He was a conservatively dressed chain-smoker with bulging green eyes and a voice that had been poshed by childhood elocution lessons.

'The tardive dyskinesia is really bad. I can't even write out the advocacy forms, my hands are shaking so much. Oh yeah, I've put my name down for a subsidised house. The garage gets a bit cold in the winter. It'll be great to have a house with rooms and a carpet and a heater. Wow.'

Rod said he was still reducing his anti-depressants but he felt anxious a lot of the time and despaired at how powerless the patients in the hospital were.

'Things aren't too bad here,' said Tom. 'I don't get too deeply involved with the patients' personal problems. We've gotta get rapport with the doctors and not come over as anti-authority. They mean the best you know.'

Rod was active in left-wing politics before he cracked up, but the hospital was a large part of Tom's life. He spent years as a patient there and was fond of it. Yet the hospital had profoundly damaged him; they filled him with drugs that damaged his brain, they left him on the street with nowhere to live, they told him he would always be too sick to do paid work and condemned this intelligent man to years of industrial therapy, putting pegs into packets for a dollar a day.

As Tom talked I wondered why he defended the hospital so much. Maybe he had authoritarian parents and transferred his loyalty to the mental health system when he first encountered it as a teenager. Perhaps it was because the staff at the hospital had given him the message that they were indispensable to his survival. Maybe they'd been just good enough to Tom for him to feel grateful for their small kindnesses. Perhaps he grew attached to the staff because they were among the few role models in his life he could look up to.

It was Annie's turn to speak next. She rubbed her hands with glee. 'I've had a ripper of a week. Janie and I moved into our new house on Friday. I can't believe our luck. We've been trying to get a flat in the private sector for years but I'd go to the land agent and as soon as they found out I lived in the bloody boarding house they said they couldn't help us. Bastards.'

We all cheered for Annie and Janie.

'We got into the house and there was all this furniture and plates and sheets there. The church gave it to us. We were so stoked.'

'So you own two pairs of sheets now,' I yelled across the room. 'That's getting close to middle-class, isn't it?'

Annie pointed a triumphant finger at me. 'Wrong. Middle-class people have to pay for their sheets. I'm special – I get mine for free.'

Tom did a wolf whistle, Corinne said, 'Nice one, Annie,' and the rest of us roared with laughter.

Tui, a new volunteer, spoke next. She was a young Maori woman with large frizzy hair.

'I feel a bit stink,' she said, staring at her lap. 'I keep wanting to burn myself with my butts. It gets real bad when I'm alone at night.'

'Why don't you come and stay with us for a few nights?' said Annie. 'We can make up a bed on the sofa. I've even got a spare pair of sheets,'

Tui smiled and looked up. 'Would that be OK?'

'Yeah,' said Annie, winking at her. 'Just don't burn the house down when you're playing with those butts, all right?'

'No way,' smiled Tui, her eyes meeting Annie's for the first time.

←———→

Most of the wards at Carrington were shaped like a big T, with a long corridor running down towards the dormitory. First there was the nurses' station, then came the little kitchen which was locked most of the time so the patients couldn't make a mess or burn themselves. The drug room was opposite. Then came the dining room which always smelt of overcooked cauliflower. Next up the corridor was the patients' living room which usually had a ripped pool table in the middle and people sitting on chairs, chain smoking and looking blankly at the wall. Next were the bathrooms with no shower curtains or door locks. They faced the laundry, the property rooms and the seclusion rooms. At the end of the corridor came the institutional sleeping arrangement for boarding-school children, the homeless and the mad – the dormitory.

But by the time Psychiatric Survivors arrived there was a new ward at Carrington – run by Maori for Maori. Although it was imprisoned in the same architecture, the Maori ward was radically different and we liked the sound of it.

The ward was run by an activist called Titewhai Harawira. She had rare presence. When she stood to speak, tall and dignified in her long garments, her black hair flowing, her green eyes flashing, her mouth lined up for combat, the room hushed and waited. Her speeches were radical and uncompromising and extraordinarily powerful. White people needed to move over and give Maori the resources they had stolen from them. Maori must create their own world. 'Keep away from us,' she warned the hospital authorities. 'You have no business interfering with our service.'

Rua, a member of Psychiatric Survivors who later became our Maori networker, arranged for us to pay the Maori ward a visit. We were given a big welcome by the elder, the staff and the patients, followed by a cup of tea and a table loaded with food. Then we all sat around on cushions with the staff and patients and sang to guitars. The walls were covered with traditional Maori art and bright contemporary posters. This wasn't like a ward at all, it was more like a big family where people spoke in Maori if they wanted and did things the Maori way. People talked about the patients coming alive again, like Sleeping Beauty, after their medication was reduced, and some of them came off it altogether. A lot of the patients who had been in the hospital for years were starting to recover. We could see the staff at the service were excited about it. We came away thinking this was the kind of service we would like to use.

After the visit Rua told me about her life. Her father had died in prison when she was seven, leaving her mother with several children. She lived in foster homes and was first hospitalised at fourteen with both mental health and drug problems. In her late twenties she went to university to do Maori studies. It changed her life. For the first time she took some pride in who she was. Rua was tall and well-built, an open, good-natured person with a large stockpile of jokes. But she had also seen the hard end of life and knew how serious the situation of many Maori survivors was.

Rua taught me many things. She taught me the Maori language though I was not one of her most gifted students. She taught me about the world of Maori survivors, how they were victims of a breakdown in their culture that started with colonisation and worsened when Maori migrated to the cities after World War Two and lost their extended family support. She talked about the collective grief and anger felt by Maori at the loss of their sacred land, their language and other treasures.

I told her about my Irish ancestors who suffered in a similar way, and wasn't it ironic that when they arrived in New Zealand on their sailing ships, they did the same things to Maori as the English had done to them.

'Many of us grew up deprived and abused and alienated from our culture,' Rua said. 'So what happened? We turned to fantasy, drugs and alcohol and we poured into the mental health system. Trouble is, the mental health system has never helped Maori. It's treated us as physical beings in isolation from our culture and beliefs and the spirits.'

'A lot of white survivors object to the narrow focus of psychiatry as well,' I said.

'Yeah, that's true, but I reckon the system is even more damaging for Maori. First thing is, we go crazy more than white people because of colonisation. Then when we get into the mental health system we get more forced treatment, more seclusion and bigger doses of drugs than white people do. That's like a double dose of colonisation.'

'Do you think the Maori services will fix all that?' I ask.

'Yeah, they can be excellent but jeez, some of them get really bossy. You know, Maori culture has this thing about the group being more important than the individual, which is fine but the elders think they can tell survivors what to do. They call the shots, even down at the Maori ward. I don't like it a lot of the time.'

I asked her what other Maori survivors thought about being told what to do. Rua said they would rather choose for themselves. She wanted to see Maori survivors develop their own peer-run initiatives, run by them, for them, instead of relying on services provided by 'normal' people, whether they were Maori or white.

I could see Rua was caught in the cross-currents created by the individualistic mad movement and the collective Maori world view. When Rua advocated for Maori survivors to Maori, she did not always get a good reception. Some of the elders in the community supported peer-run initiatives but others told her it went against the principles of Maoridom. They said Rua was doing what white people do, by dividing people up, going the separatist way, instead of keeping them together. Some of the elders humiliated her in big meetings for questioning them and subverting the Maori way of doing things. She returned from these meetings shaken and demoralised, finding more acceptance from survivors than from her own people.

In the meantime things started going wrong in the Maori ward and the hospital authorities didn't keep away as Titewhai had warned them to. One morning, very early, the hospital authorities raided the ward and took some files away. Titewhai retaliated on the news and pulled up the drawbridge to her castle. There was a long stand-off. Then one day a terrible thing happened. The staff beat up a patient who nearly died as the ambulance sped him off to hospital. Titewhai and some staff members were arrested. Titewhai was convicted of threatening to kill and jailed for nine months. The judge called the offence, 'an arrogant and frightening abuse of authority and power.'

We were deeply shocked and disappointed. What had happened down there to the friendly family atmosphere? How could the staff treat anyone like that? They almost killed him. We heard through the grapevine that some of the staff at Titewhai's service said it was culturally appropriate to give badly behaved people, 'a good hiding'. We could never, ever agree with them.

Maori services in other places continued to develop without the scandal that plagued Titewhai's service. Many Maori survivors chose them because they saw themselves in the faces of their helpers, and they could be themselves in the open family atmosphere of the service. These services often did more for their recovery than the ones in the white system.

———

Rua and I were walking around one of the wards in Carrington. Rua wore her shades, and trackpants and 'Why Be Normal?' badge. I wore my 'I Survived Carrington' badge. We'd come to visit Tom, who had spun out with the stress of trying to get out of his garage into a proper house.

Tom paced up and down the dim corridor, shaking so much that he was having trouble getting his cigarette into his mouth. He waved us down to a doorway. 'Have a look at this,' he said, pointing to a door.

There was a big homemade sign on the wired glass window: 'Patient Free Area'.

We stood in front of the door, swearing in indignation. 'That'd make a good photo for the newsletter,' Rua said. 'Tom, can you distract the staff while I take a photo?'

Tom went down to a couple of nurses standing at the other end of the corridor and started yelling that he needed a pill for his side-effects. They calmed him down and took him to the drug room while Rua got her camera out.

Before we left the ward we went up to see the charge nurse. 'Come on, guys,' says Rua. 'Get real – imagine if we put a sign up at the Psychiatric Survivors office with "Nurse Free Area" on it. Wouldn't make you very happy, would it?'

The nurse went red and her face hardened. 'If you talk like that you're not welcome here.'

'Doesn't look like the patients are welcome either,' we said, turning to walk out the door.

The photo went into the next edition of our newsletter. The 'Patient Free Area' sign came down the next day. Two weeks later it was up again.

←———×

There were a few decent psychiatrists at Carrington but some of them were just plain arrogant. No matter how much you challenged them, they still acted like the lords of the manor who knew things we peasants couldn't possibly understand. One thing they didn't know was their own privilege. Privilege is a bit like oxygen: you don't know it exists until you're starved of it. If you've never been starved of privilege, you can't understand how powerful it is.

The nurses didn't have the same privilege as the psychiatrists. They didn't possess the naive arrogance that deflects criticism like it's just a fly that needs to be shooed away. So they got defensive and moaned a lot.

I was standing in front of twenty nurses at Carrington facilitating a training day about advocacy. I talked to them about how they could provide services that put power back in the hands of the people who use them. It was a totally new concept to them and one that was unlikely to ever take root in the stony ground of the institution. It's all about being an equal partner with people, I said, limiting coercion, finding people's strengths, asking them what they need and respecting their decisions.

The nurses slouched in their chairs. Some were chewing gum; one rolled her eyes to the ceiling.

'We're too disempowered by management to make any of those sorts of changes,' one of them said. The group murmured in agreement. They all looked miserable.

I felt a flash of anger but subdued it quickly. 'You may feel powerless in your jobs but you can go home at night to a family, a warm house and good food. Think of your lives in comparison to the people living in Carrington. Your powerlessness is minor compared to theirs.'

The nurses persisted in complaining so I asked them, 'Are you powerless when you make people stay in pyjamas, when you ration their cigarettes or when you put them in seclusion? I don't think so.'

Some of them started to rouse. 'Come on, if they didn't wear pyjamas they'd wander and we get in the shit if we can't find them.'

'If we don't ration the cigarettes the patients just fight over them and the ward would be in chaos.'

By now I was boiling inside but I kept the lid on tight. 'You hold the power in those situations and you hold the key to passing on that power to the patients. But there's a paradox. As long as you view yourselves as powerless, you will not empower one patient.'

They were unimpressed with my flash of insight and continued to grumble until the end of the workshop.

Afterwards it dawned on me that the managers and psychiatrists at Carrington probably treated the nurses with the same kind of authoritarianism and contempt that the nurses treated the patients with. It seemed to reverberate down the hierarchy but it was always the patients who got kicked the hardest. And the patients did get kicked. It was such an everyday event at Carrington that some of the nurses freely owned up to doing it.

———×

Vince was a research psychologist who was interviewing staff and patients at Carrington about the Psychiatric Survivors advocacy project.

He was an intellectual hippie with a beard and long bushy hair in a ponytail. He had never been tainted by working in places like Carrington.

'I want to show you this,' he said, one day walking into the Psychiatric Survivors office. He handed me a typed piece of paper. 'This is an example of what we're up against.'

It was a transcript of his interview with 'Nurse 7'.

Nurse 7: It runs pretty good here. Things are just about as good as they could be. I don't think you'll get it running any better. Money is no object. Each ward is like a family. Better looked after than I am at home. There's very few patients that shouldn't be here.

Vince: How much do the staff talk to the patients?

Nurse 7: When I first got here I was told not to talk to the patients. But sometimes I feel sorry for them. Sometimes a patient will talk to me about their problems but I know the nurses will be angry if they hear me.

Vince: What do you think of the advocacy service here?

Nurse 7: The patients come back from the advocate all steamed up. Stirring up patients like that just gives them false hope. The main advocates are the nurses. They're the ones that see the patient's rights are adhered to – within reason. I mean, how much rights can a patient have when they're psychotic?

Vince: What sort of issues do you think require advocacy support?

Nurse 7: The medication is excessive – even I know that. And the treatment plans should be reviewed every six months but I know some who've been on the same treatment plan for thirty years. It's too late for them.

Vince: What about hitting?

Nurse 7: Yeah, even though I smack them now and again, I've seen some staff really hit them. I say to myself if I see it again I'll report it, but I don't want to be a troublemaker or a stirrer. I don't want to get involved with that. I like it here. Everything is all right here.

I put the paper on my desk. 'Shit, that's awful.'

'You know,' said Vince, throwing his big hands into the air, 'two staff have been convicted of assaulting a patient here over the last two years and that'll be the tip of the iceberg. There's a Commission of Inquiry being held into the death of a patient who allegedly died from over-medication in this hospital. Forty per cent of the complaints to the advocacy service are about being wrongly medicated, compulsorily treated or detained, being locked in seclusion, or being hit or abused by staff or other patients. No one could accuse me of exaggerating when I say that people's rights are being violated on a daily basis at this hospital. And yet no one seems to care!'

←——————→

The Psychiatric Survivors office was next to an empty old dormitory. Cracked pale-green paint covered the walls like murals of neglect. The lino floor was grubby and worn, and a cluster of wooden chairs occupied one corner. This was where we held our support groups twice a week for any of the patients who wanted to come along.

Some of them came to every group. Elizabeth had a minor learning disability and a major sense of injustice about how the hospital had treated her since she was admitted a quarter of a century before. She was in her sixties, thin and scrawny, and she talked incessantly between shallow puffs of her cigarettes about how she should never have been admitted to the hospital in the first place. She paced a lot and her tongue rolled uncontrollably, the legacy of years of anti-psychotics. 'I can't get out. My family don't want me back. They put me in here, you know. Don't even visit me. Rod, please tell boss nurse I don't feel well. They don't listen to me. Had a pain in my gut for months.'

Rod agreed to talk to boss nurse and reassured Elizabeth she was not the only patient the staff didn't listen to.

Another regular was manic Paul who was a well-known book illustrator. He was a large swarthy man with an over-loud laugh. 'You know they carted me here in a police limo. For setting fire to some old pictures on the floor of my studio. "Shouldn't a man be the king of his own castle?" I said to them when they came to the door, "I banish you from my kingdom. One more step over this threshold and my knights will slay you for your treachery and treason," I yelled.'

We all laughed as Paul stood up and made extravagant warlike gestures followed by a deep Shakespearean bow.

'And here we are, my friends, in the Tower of London, awaiting our slow execution to be administered by Sir Halo Peridol with the injection in the dungeon.'

Paul made another big bow and we laughed and clapped.

'There is a dungeon here beneath this very building with chains and manacles from years past. My fellow sirs, we must plot an uprising.'

'Hey, what about the ladies?' Lynette called.

Paul suddenly changed the subject to sex then swerved his rollercoaster conversation through Dante's *Inferno*, his Triumph motorcycles and cigar-shaped UFOs.

Lynette was a middle-aged ex-nurse who used to work in places like Carrington. She was angry and helpless. 'The drugs are killing me,' she fumed. 'They've stolen my energy. They've damaged my brain. Look at me. I'm overweight, my hair's all stringy, my voice is slurring and I blob all day. They shouldn't get away with it. The doctors and nurses didn't listen so I went to a lawyer and he stopped listening. Then I went to the hospital inspector. He refuses to see me now. He's supposed to be looking after my rights, for God's sake.'

It turned out that Elizabeth had terminal bowel cancer. She died a few months later. Paul bounced in and out of hospital for the next two years, then killed himself. I lost touch with Lynette until she rang me several years later. The hospital had closed down by then and she was on a community treatment order. 'The drugs are killing me,' she said. And I believed her.

←——————→

Carrington was scheduled for closure in two or three years. One by one the Victorian mental hospitals were being emptied of their damaged goods and bright happy faces would soon walk into them as the buildings were converted into design schools, luxury apartments and horror theme parks.

A lot of people didn't want Carrington to close. The public were suspicious and fearful. Families didn't want to take responsibility for their cast-offs or feared how their loved ones would cope. Even some of the patients were scared of life on the outside. Of course, the nursing staff resisted and they had the power of their unions behind them.

I was invited to a meeting by the local health board to plan the new community based services that would replace Carrington. The chief executive and the mental health managers were there. So were union representatives and a large collection of mental health professionals. I was the only mad person there.

The chief executive was a benign, well-dressed Englishman, a forward-thinking man who had closed down a large mental hospital in England. He had recently taken up his position and there were great hopes that he would rescue the local mental health services from their longstanding troubles. 'We must base our planning on the needs of the clients,' he started.

For the rest of the day the clients were barely mentioned. There was a lot of talk about the risks of closing down Carrington, the transition to community based services, funding shortages, poor working conditions, management structures and services not cooperating with each other. The nurses' union representative argued bitterly against the closure of Carrington because, he said, it would reduce the nurses' pay and conditions. I was starting to see the people who were the biggest threat to the closure were not the public or the politicians but the people who should care the most.

I sat feeling more and more alone and alienated in the middle of the rampant professional self-interest and the fog of management jargon. I knew if I didn't say something I would leave the meeting with the feeling that my reality had been suffocated by the weight of opinion in the room. So I got up to speak.

All day you have been talking about services without referring once to client needs. I came here after lunch from the Psychiatric Survivors drop-in. They know what their needs are. But what you're talking about here doesn't connect with what they're saying. Until you start talking about getting rid of poverty, unemployment, loneliness, neglect, exploitative boarding houses, professional self-interest and community prejudice, your words and your services will not help the lives of the people you are supposed to serve. Instead it will just perpetuate institutionalised thinking, your professional comfort zones, your distancing discourse, and the vast power structures that exclude us.

There was a ten-second silence, though it was more than just silence – it was the held breaths of over fifty people who'd been pushed to the edge of another reality.

A social worker with a five o'clock shadow stood up in his leather jacket and jeans and addressed the CEO. 'You have all the power. Everyone listens to you and turns to you for the answers. Could you give that power away? Could you empower the people by giving them the resources to find the answers for themselves? Because I don't see that happening. I see a consultation process that has been developed and delivered on your terms. Can you give away your power?'

I nodded in agreement with the social worker though I wasn't sure who he meant by 'the people'. Did he just mean the staff and the local community? Did he also mean the people who use services?

The CEO responded by saying he often didn't feel very powerful and that the only pleasure his power gave him was to see others develop. He was genuine but I thought there was some denial in his comments. Did he recognise the structural power he had relative to the other people in the room, and the power of his reputation that propelled others to believe he had the answers? Did he understand the huge power he had to determine the planning process, who came to meetings, and what went into the final plan? And whose reality most informed his power? Certainly not the people sitting in the Psychiatric Survivors drop-in.

After the meeting, I told the CEO that if he wanted to meet the needs of clients, he should come and talk to us and involve us in the drafting of the plan instead of just asking us to comment on it. He agreed that clients should be involved from the start but didn't show any intention of changing the process.

I left the meeting feeling unsettled and alone. When people don't share power, others often ascribe greedy or sinister motives to them. But the CEO was not driven by these kinds of motives. He wanted to share his power but he didn't understand the full force of it well enough to know how. And maybe if he did understand his power better he wouldn't want to share it anyway.

←——————→

Rod in his advocacy role supported some patients who'd requested their hospital notes under new freedom of information legislation. 'This woman was so upset at the things they wrote about her in her notes. She gave me a look at them. It was insulting. Things like calling her immature and manipulative and a hopeless case. It stinks.'

Rod, Corinne and I were having our weekly catch-up at Carrington. 'Yeah,' said Corinne, 'everyone I know who's read their notes has felt the same. My advice is, if you want to keep your self-respect, don't read them.'

'True,' I said, 'but it's a good way to understand what the professionals really think. Most of them never imagined that one day there'd be a law that allowed their patients to read them.'

Rod and I decided to request our own notes. We went to see Peter, the superintendent, who issued the request on our behalf. A couple of weeks later our files arrived at Carrington. Mine were about two inches thick.

I read through my notes from beginning to end and I was shocked. I knew that the psychiatrists' main interest in me was my psychopathology. I knew they found me frustrating, because their treatments didn't work and I kept coming back. I knew they were irritated when I questioned their expertise. But what I didn't know until I read my notes was how little regard they had for me as a human being in a desperate struggle. They wrote that I was 'lost and directionless', 'inappropriate', 'emotionally inhibited', 'colourless', 'aloof', 'schizoid', 'overdramatic' and 'non-compliant'. Only one psychologist wrote a sentence that could be interpreted as a description of my strength: 'Mary gave an insightful account of her illness.' Even that sentence has a double edge to it, given the colonisation of the word 'insight' by mental health professionals who confer it on people who see their 'illness' the same way as the professionals do.

Inside the big folder, no one wrote about my suffering or despair. No one described me as competent or strong, or even as an ordinary human being who was a conglomerate of good, bad and indifferent qualities.

I turned to Rod who was also in our office reading his notes. 'How are you doing?' I asked.

'Fuck, this is awful. I keep checking to see if they've got the right name on the cover.'

'Yeah, that's exactly what I've been doing.'

We squeal with laughter.

'I knew they didn't think much of me but these notes are so hostile,' said Rod.

'Well, what do you expect? I think we need to diagnose these professionals. They demonstrate lack of empathy, self-aggrandisement and excessive pessimism. That's got to be some kind of personality disorder with depressive features.'

We squeal even louder this time.

'It's quite hurtful, though,' said Rod.

'Yeah I know,' I replied, slapping my file on the desk, 'and this is a reminder of why we're doing our work.'

Later, I took my files to the photocopy room at the hospital. 'Can you photocopy these files, please.'

A large grumpy woman with thick legs and swept back grey hair glared at the files and looked up, 'The whole thing?'

'Yes please.'

'That'll be ten days, you know,' she said, hoping I would go elsewhere with my request.

'I can wait.'

She sighed and tossed my files into an empty tray marked 'Non Urgent'.

I walked to the car park thinking 'the customer is always wrong' culture at Carrington was like a chamber of mirrors that just reflected off each other, from the wards to the nurses' union, back to the management group and down to the photocopy room.

Three weeks later I stuffed my photocopied files in a supermarket bag and took them home. I leafed through the photocopies feeling more and more alienated. The files were all about me but I couldn't see me in them. Worse still, there was no process that gave me a right of reply or allowed me to add my version to them.

Then it occurred to me that my right of reply was sitting in my box of journals under my bed. While the hospital staff had written their

181

version of my madness, I had written mine crouched on my bed or hiding in the toilets. I dragged the box into the daylight, grabbed a pair of scissors and started to match my journal entries with the hospital notes by date. Over the next few hours I created a linear collage of my journals interspersed with their notes that wound from one end of the room to the other.

I was astonished at what I saw; two parallel accounts of my madness that could never meet, just like the sun and the moon that never shine in the same sky. When the staff wrote about me they did it in the course of an ordinary day's work. They wrote about what they saw on the outside through the thick lens of psychopathology. I wrote about what I felt on the inside, unfiltered by professionalism or pretensions of objectivity.

With some deletions, a little bit of editing and a lot of typing, the collage was transformed into words on clean paper. I called it 'Two Accounts of Mental Distress' and it spanned my time in hospital for an episode of depression. Later, at conferences and training sessions I read it out loud, with someone else reading out the clinical notes. It became a chapter in a British book called *Speaking Our Minds* about people's experiences of mental health services, published in 1996. Here is an extract from it. The writing in normal font is the notes. The writing in italics is mine:

Today I wanted to die. Everything was hurting. My body was screaming. I saw the doctor. I wanted to collapse against the wall and cry out and show him how I feel about things but I said nothing. Now I feel terrible. Nothing seems good and nothing good seems possible.

I am stuck in this twilight mood
where I go down
like the setting sun
into a lonely black hole
where there is room for only one.

Flat, lacking motivation, sleep and appetite good. Discussed aetiology Cont. Li Carb. 250 mg qid. Levels next time.

I am a long piercing scream
All screaming on the inside of me
and out of the pores of my skin.

My screaming and myself are one.
This is pure pain.

On arriving on the ward – could not talk. I have admitted her for a period of two weeks in order to consolidate her working relationship with us.

My world has been emptied out.
as if burglars broke into my mind
and stole all my power.
On their way out
they pulled down my blinds.
Now, I cannot see the world
and the world cannot see me.

Poor eye contact, slow speech and movements. Stated her head felt empty and fuzzy; vision disordered, things appearing very ugly. Mentioned need to find meaning in her depression – not just a wasteful experience.

A nurse came to me and said, 'Go to supper.' I said, 'No.' She growled at me for not making an effort, but all my effort is going into making these thoughts and writing them down. The nurse punished me saying, 'Well, I'm not bringing you any supper you know.'

Sitting in Ladies' Lounge with her head in her hands. Very difficult to involve in conversation. Not responding to activity around her.

Is attending the dining room with firm encouragement and eating small meals. Remains very withdrawn but occasionally gives vent to an incongruous sustained laugh – although says she isn't happy. Rx Chlorpromazine BD & Nocte as appears to be preoccupied with thoughts – hopefully medication will break the chain.

Last night they came to me
with chlorpromazine.
I refused it.
I am afraid medication will dull my mind
and the meanings in there will escape forever.

Refusing medication. States she hasn't been taking it because it doesn't do her any good. Not persuaded by explanations or reassurance.

During the night

between sleeps
I felt bad.
I was on the rack.
Every thought
set off a shrieking alarm in my head.
My body would jerk and go rigid
As if electric shocks went through me
every few seconds.
I nearly didn't make it through the night.
I nearly asked for chlorpromazine.

Awake at frequent intervals during the night. Found whimpering and thrashing around on her bed at 2.15 am saying, 'No, leave me alone.' Said she was frightened. Kept holding and massaging her head.

Every morning the night nurses
pull off my blankets.
They are rough.
I can't fight back.
Even their softest touches bruise me.
A nurse said to me
'Face the world.'
But I am facing all the pain inside me.
I cannot face both ways at once.

Mary is not to hide away in her bed. She is to be encouraged to get up for breakfast and engage in ward activities.

My back is hard like a shell.
My front is soft like jelly.
I hate to stand
because I cannot shield my front
from the jabbing gaze of the world.
I must lie
curled up or front down.

Lying in bed under blanket. Face covered by hands. Wouldn't leave bed to talk – 'not safe.' Brief whispered conversation from under her hands. Sleep worse than usual – can't eat – too frightened – body aching all over.

Everything hurts.
I am burning.
All the life in me
blazing out from the core of me
is getting stuck.
I can feel it
trying to burn through my skin.
I am almost on fire.

Experiencing frightening hallucinations, burning sensations, also seeing brightly coloured shapes when eyes shut. Request Everglade notes for EEG. Repeat EEG to exclude Temporal Lobe Epilepsy.

I have lost my self
What is my name?
I have no name.
All I am
is shape and weight
rapid shallow breathing
and a black space inside my head.

Misinterpreting at times. Obsessed with the feeling of not wanting to be in her body – wanted to be a speck of dust. Also concerned as to her purpose of being alive. Describing feelings of 'emptiness'. Sleep poor, appetite poor.

My mind is a pile
of broken up smudgy thoughts.
I am searching for one
that is clear enough to have meaning.
But as soon as I find a thought
it gets sucked into the blackness.

Remains psychotically depressed. Reported hearing voices but no other bizarre symptoms noted. Thoughts still coming in 'fragments'. Unable to complete them. Still spending most of time on bed. On 150mg Doxepin nocte.

Sometimes a speck of light gets into my black hole
The speck is a thought that has come back into focus.
I am coming up a bit but I feel all weak and wobbly from being on my

bed for days. Before I looked up. This took courage. It was like coming out of a cocoon; the light was strong, it was strange. The next thing I did was walk around and say hello to people. It feels good to be halfway back and looking up.

Is beginning to interact. Says she is feeling much better. Asked permission to go out which was refused. Accepted this well. Enjoyed a game of Scrabble, giggling at times but this was mostly appropriate e.g. at mildly humorous antics of other patients.

←——————→

Several years after 'Two Accounts' was published in *Speaking Our Minds*, two sociologists wrote a paper in a journal comparing *Speaking Our Minds* with another book of patients' experiences, written forty years earlier in 1957. The earlier book, *The Plea for the Silent*, was about people's stories of mistreatment in mental hospitals. It was edited by some British MPs, based on letters the patients had written to them. The patients were all anonymous and the MPs verified the credibility of the stories in their introduction. In *Speaking our Minds* all the authors were named and they asserted their own credibility without the need for others to do it for them. Even the titles of the two books illustrate the enormous changes that took place in the identities of people with lived experience over the forty years that fell between them.

The sociologists wrote that the patients in *The Plea for the Silent* did not show solidarity with other patients and some believed they shouldn't be in hospital, because they weren't as insane as the others. In contrast, the writers in *Speaking our Minds* also wrote about mistreatment, but many of them were active in the British mad movement and had a strong collective identity that transformed them from victims to survivors. No one would be considered too insane to be part of this movement.

Why such a difference? Against the forty-year backdrop of huge changes in the construction of social and personal identity, the patients in *The Plea for the Silent* saw the causes of their mental distress as personal problems, whereas the survivors in *Speaking our Minds* wrote of the social and economic determinants of mental distress, like sexual abuse, racism, sexism and social inequality. They wanted a wide range of therapies and options but the patients in 1957 only wanted 'someone to talk to'. The 1996 stories viewed the sources of their injustice as mainly systemic; they wrote about discrimination, compulsory treatment and unresponsive mental health services. The patients in 1957 talked about bad individuals as the source of their injustice.

The one thing the two books had in common was also the most important: everyone felt a sense of injustice. This has fuelled the public stories of mental patients since the seventeenth century. It's the one universal theme that spans not forty but four hundred years of recorded narratives, up to the present day.

I thought of all the cruel and desperate remedies inflicted on mad people throughout European history. I could almost understand the vigilante witch burnings, the chains and the exiling that predated psychiatry. Closed, superstitious communities that endured famines, wars and plagues were unlikely to be tolerant of people who acted strangely. What I couldn't understand was how a profession established to help, or at least 'do no harm', could administer or collude with solitary confinement, mechanical restraints, twirling chairs, ice baths, sterilisation, mass lobotomies, life-shortening drugs, routine compulsion and mental hospitals that remained overcrowded for up to a hundred years. It is not enough for them to point out the kindnesses and assistance their forebears and colleagues offered their patients. It is not enough to say that most psychiatrists have had good intentions.

The fact remains that psychiatry has done considerable harm, and as a profession it has not faced up to this. Until it does, psychiatry will continue to do harm – not out of malice, but out of an earnest grandiosity that monopolises the discourse, views itself as the most potent of all the mental health professions and colludes with social expectations to control the lives of mad people.

The closing of the old institutions has prevented some of the harm done by psychiatry and improved some people's quality of life. But on its own the impact of their closure was always going to be limited, without a new philosophy to underpin community based services.

The mad movement led the way in developing a new philosophy that promoted human rights, equal participation, recovery and well-being. Twenty years later, many mental health professionals still do not fully subscribe to this philosophy.

10.

GLOBAL MADNESS

I grew up hearing my mother tell us that New Zealand is a funny little country. We're the village at the end of the world, first settled by humans less than a thousand years ago. New Zealand doesn't even make it onto some maps of the world. No one else in the world is interested in our short parochial history, no one celebrates our plain flimsy buildings or envies our flat accents. And we feel something close to gratitude when our country is mentioned in the newspapers or TV screens of the northern hemisphere. We're the runt of the western world and we know it. This is why New Zealanders are among the world's greatest travellers.

So it was inevitable that I would want to learn from what I thought would be the more sophisticated, innovative work my mad colleagues must be doing in other countries. I applied for a Winston Churchill travelling fellowship in 1987 and didn't get one. I applied in 1988 and didn't get one. With youthful determination I applied again in 1989.

Sitting in front of my new Apple Macintosh Plus computer at the Psychiatric Survivors office, I wrote a proposal to visit consumer-run organisations and consumer participation projects in the USA, Britain and the Netherlands. My friend and colleague Lynette, a volunteer at

Psychiatric Survivors – large, intelligent and gentle – was in the next room wailing into someone's lap. I wrote about Lynette in the 'other comments' section of my application – about her lobotomy, her lost potential, her powerlessness and her suffering, about how I did my work because of people like Lynette, because if our movement didn't stand up for ourselves and people like her, no one else would.

The reply arrived four months later in an encouragingly thick envelope and informed me that I was one of two New Zealand applicants who had been granted a UK Winston Churchill Fellowship, gifted to New Zealand to mark the twenty-fifth anniversary of Winston Churchill's death. This meant I would receive more than double the funds I applied for, and collect a medal from the Queen in London.

I stayed at a friend's squat in Hackney. A week before the medal ceremony I received a letter there from a major at the Winston Churchill Fellowship, instructing ladies to wear a dress to it. The next day I visited the major at the fellowship's London office in a grand building in Belgravia. As I entered the foyer full of statues and brass plates, I smirked about the fellowship's New Zealand office: an open-plan work station in one of our plain, flimsy buildings, occupied by a solitary Internal Affairs clerk.

The major was a trim man who was terribly jolly and eager to help. 'I don't own a dress,' I told him, 'but I do have a very nice trouser suit.' He looked at me with the benevolence of someone who never worries about his place in the world. 'Oh, I think the Queen would be delighted to see you in a trouser suit.' I laughed all the way back to the squat.

The morning of the ceremony I put on my trouser suit, which I had bought second-hand in an outdoor market in Auckland, and reached for my only accessory – a clean pair of Doc Marten shoes.

Guildhall is a beautifully crafted stone building, six hundred years old. It was packed with people. The major came onto the stage and demonstrated how the male fellows should bow to the Queen. He called in his secretary to demonstrate the curtsey. I didn't want to curtsey and wondered if I could get away without doing it. I'd never felt any deference for the Queen. She was a perfect target for my anti-establishment leanings and as a teenager I had refused to stand when they played 'God Save the Queen' before the movies.

After a long wait trumpeters in yellow-and-red Elizabethan costumes, lining the galleries above, announced the Queen's arrival. As she walked down the aisle everyone stood for 'God Save the Queen' – even me. She wore a powder-blue coat and pillbox hat, with white gloves and that handbag. After several worthy, unmemorable speeches the ceremony began. The British fellows got their medals first and the small contingent of Commonwealth fellows waited until the end.

The major called out my name. Would I curtsey or not? I walked up to the Queen and sank my knees ever so slightly. She gave me a genteel handshake and passed me the medal. 'Oh, what's a consumer?' she asked. As I explained it to her she looked slightly surprised, even amused, as if I was describing a strange new species. I moved away and forgot to curtsey, thinking she's just an ordinary woman in extraordinary circumstances. Take the plum out of her mouth, bin that handbag, get her some clothes from a Marks and Spencer sale, and yeah, I could see her on *Coronation Street*.

←——————→

During the trip I talked to many survivors in the USA, Britain and the Netherlands and found that their experiences of the mental health system were similar to those we'd had in New Zealand. Virtually all the survivors I talked to had been hospital patients and this was generally where they felt most powerless and devalued. However, they did not see community based services as the great liberator. Usually 'community care' just rearranged the old fortresses of paternalism and neglect into mini-institutions, inadequate community services and restricted opportunities.

Ingrid in the Netherlands was tied up naked on a bed by her wrists and feet in hospital. Later she called a lawyer about it but after the lawyer talked to her doctor he said he couldn't advocate for her. Suzy from the USA woke up one day and didn't know who she was. She was locked in a security room in a private psychiatric hospital for two months in her underwear, and was beaten and sexually abused. Brendan from the USA checked himself into a private psychiatric hospital and was horrified at how the staff expectations generated such hopelessness and passivity among the patients. Virginia from England talked about taking on the role of a mad person when she was admitted to hospital, by breaking crockery and eating flowers because that is what she thought was expected of her. Steve, an African-Caribbean man, talked about being taken into hospital by the police to be greeted by a white psychiatrist in a pinstripe suit who asked superficial questions and sectioned him. There was nothing around him in the ward that spoke of his culture or reality. He learned not to say what he thought or felt.

Unlike many of the people I interviewed for my original research, these people were part of the international mad movement and they put their experiences of being devalued to political analysis. This analysis focused on the tripartite drivers of the traditional mental health system – the medical model, the use of biological sledgehammers such as drugs and electric shock treatment, and forced treatment.

The medical model claims that 'mental illnesses' are biological illnesses that need to be treated by biological means such as drugs. This is the dominant model in the mental health systems in all the countries I visited. Survivors criticised the medical model for placing a lot of power at the hands of experts, for being too deterministic, and for putting survivors in passive, disempowered roles. Suzy from the USA summed it up:

I get scared at people who believe in the medical model because it leads to programmes that are totally hopeless. If you are told that you are going to be sick for the rest of your life, there is no getting out of the mental health system because the assumption is you are going to need support and monitoring for the rest of your life. It's a very pessimistic model. I am against the medical model not so much because it is true or false, but because it is so pessimistic and not very practical. It doesn't help people.

Most of the survivors I talked to didn't support the use of drugs in psychiatry and were even more opposed to electric shock treatment. The people I talked to complained that drugs were an internal straitjacket, that they obscured an important learning experience and that some had debilitating side-effects. In some cases psychotherapy was also seen as a medical-model-type response, because an expert had the authority to label any feelings or actions as pathological. Many believed psychotherapy could be as oppressive as physical treatments. As one survivor put it:

Our minds have a way of helping us grow. Things that look crazy to other people can be growth experiences if they are not interfered with, which they are of course with drugs. We don't know how to get to the other side because we are never allowed to go there.

Many survivors who were somewhat suspicious of the voluntary use of drugs and electric shock treatment were totally opposed to forced treatment. During my travels I came across a quote by a survivor which said, 'The mental health business is the only business in the world where the customer is always wrong.' In most industries customers are generally considered to be right because they have choices and the capacity to exercise them. Forced treatment rests on a premise that some people diagnosed with mental illness do not have the capacity to exercise choices and if left to do so could cause serious harm to themselves or others. The mad movement has, in varying degrees, opposed forced treatment because it violates human rights, it corrupts the helping relationship, it is ineffective, it causes harm and it is based on over-generalised assumptions about madness and free will. Henry from the USA explained:

Forced treatment is one of the parts of the system that is still really entrenched. The majority of the mental health systems still have a long way to go with this. The problem is one of power and people giving up power voluntarily, which rarely happens. Getting the system to give up the power to forcibly treat people is probably going to be the hardest nut to crack of all. Some of the people in the part of the movement that is not so strongly against forced treatment are beginning to come around. I always like to say people tend to adopt liberating viewpoints eventually, if they are exposed to them. The thing that convinces people to adopt the viewpoint that forced treatment is wrong is simply that involuntary treatment doesn't work; it doesn't help people. Programmes that are voluntary do work; they are more life-affirming.

In New York I went to the American Psychiatric Association conference where survivors were protesting outside about compulsory electric shock treatment. The most creative effort was a head costume of broken eggshells worn by a woman who held a placard saying, 'I'd rather be cracked than fried.' The protesters chanted, 'Stop Shock' to the psychiatrists walking by. Then they joined hands in a circle and gave personal shock testimonies through a megaphone. Inside the conference, Kate Millet, psychiatric survivor and feminist author, spoke with eloquence about forced treatment in a debate between psychiatric survivors and psychiatrists:

When a psychiatrist is employed for a fee as an enforcer, capable of summoning the awesome powers of the State – locked buildings, bars, drugs, statutory arrest and re-arrest – we have in fact arrived at a point of large-scale surveillance and interference in private life – employing millions, operating through thousands of clinics and offices, accepted now in every institution in our society, and even unquestioned in our intellectual frame of reference, congratulated everywhere as a humane form of health.

Mystification and reverence for expertise has replaced proof, scepticism, advocacy, accountability and a sacred obligation to protect. Mental illness is argued not from scientific proof but from the assessment of behaviour, the way people act, the things they do and say. Of course this is not acceptable legal evidence of unreason, neither is it acceptable scientific evidence. Scarcely anything is as impressionistic and various as the manner in which human behaviour is assessed. What is crazy to one of us, is just funny or silly or cantankerous to another. The thought of losing one's liberty over one's deportment is a terrifying prospect. Yet the person committed stands to lose his or her freedom and every right.

After Kate Millet, a tiny psychiatrist named Nancy Andreasen spoke next and and made reference to her new book, *The Broken Brain*. Mark, a vocal protest leader with a ponytail, asked her:

'I'm standing here in one piece. I'm doing fine. So are most of the people in this room who you say have broken brains. You insult us. You have no evidence for your theory that mental illness is an irreversible disease of the brain.'

The other survivors cheered. Nancy opened her mouth but nothing came out. Mark continued: 'Your broken brain theories have led to the most inhumane treatments – drugs that damage our brains, shock that wipes out our memories, institutions that deprive us of our dignity and involuntary treatment that takes away our freedom. Don't you say an oath that says, "First do no harm"?'

Other survivors added to Mark's commentary on the harm that psychiatry had done to them.

Then one of Nancy's elderly colleagues said, 'We know there's a lot wrong with our services. We worry about it too. There are a lot of people out there who never get into treatment—.'

'Well, we're the ones who *did* get into treatment and it sucks!' one of the survivors yelled.

A professorial-looking psychiatrist stood up and said, 'My colleague Nancy has dedicated her life to understanding and treating mental illnesses which devastate so many people's lives. We psychiatrists only want the best for our patients. We know bad things go on in our systems of care—.'

'Yeah, you run these systems of care, so why don't you stop the bad things happening?' asked Mark.

'If only if were that simple,' replied the psychiatrist.

'It's not your intentions that are the problem,' Mark retorted, 'it's your whole "broken brain" model and you guys are clinging to it like a life raft so you can call yourselves scientists and doctors.'

There was an uproar of cheering and objections. Nancy stood at the podium looking like a startled sparrow. The psychiatrists and the survivors continued to talk past each other for another hour.

←———✳

Before my trip I had believed that forced treatment is done too often, for too long, for dubious reasons and without effective legal advocacy. But many of the survivor activists I came across claimed that forced treatment is inherently wrong. I hadn't yet come to this conclusion. I struggled to clarify if the state should have a role in forcibly preventing a suicidal person from jumping to their death or a manic person from spending themselves into financial ruin. Should agents of the state restrain these people, lock them up and even forcibly treat them? Can the state ever exercise genuine therapeutic benevolence while removing someone's freedom? I doubted it more and more.

I'd seen and heard about too much cruel and degrading treatment in the mental health system delivered by people in the name of benevolence and therapy. Take the punishment of solitary confinement, for instance. Re-label it as 'seclusion' and call it a treatment, with the implication that it is good for you, and you could be sure that mental health workers would struggle to see its underlying brutality. I decided at the time that a good standard to judge the actions of mental health workers would be that if an action, such as locking people up or forcibly injecting them, caused distress in non-therapeutic circumstances, we could not justify it in a therapeutic setting, without the full consent of the person involved. This standard would leave little, if any, justification for forced treatment.

✕————✕

My interest went much further than just critiquing the knowledge that drives our mental health systems. I wanted to find a new knowledge base to replace the knowledge that harmed our bodies, our freedom and our status in the world. The new knowledge needed to help us put value back into our experience. On my trip I hoped to find other survivors who were also trying to unlearn society's stereotype of madness. In Utrecht I talked with Ed who gave me his vision of the culture of madness in slightly halting English:

We should explore a total other direction. My fancy is that it could be a cultural movement where we defend the right to be mad and give some positive attribution to it instead of nurturing the idea that somebody should actually get well again. People have the right to be who they are; they have the right to be mad. If being mad is put on the same level as being black or being a homosexual or being a woman, I think that would be a far better approach; to bring madness out of the back rooms and into the open. Therefore you have to create a culture of mad people. That means that you have to write about it and make films about it and so on.

The thing about being mad is that a lot of mad people don't get well. They are not prepared to or able to act in a normal way. But instead of accepting that fact, people keep going to doctors and believe in all that therapeutic blah-blah, in modern pills and technology. I am sure that in a thousand years there will still be people who are mad, in spite of all the pills and genetic manipulation. I think the biological approach is like a big elephant that comes out of the bush and gives birth to a little mouse.

Psychiatry is wrong in itself, it uses the wrong concepts. The medicine kills people, and people should not be electroshocked. But at the moment our client organisation cannot generate a culture of madness. Most people in our organisation believe in normalisation or in fighting psychiatry. They are prisoners of the medical definition of them, and even when they don't believe in psychiatry, they see themselves only as patients who are labelled by psychiatrists – nothing more.

After this interview I wrote in my journal:

Today while I listened to Ed I discovered a point of reference that I've been seeking for a long time – the idea of a culture of madness. I think Ed was trying to say a culture of madness can take us beyond the reformist-abolitionist split that has created rifts in the mad movement in the Netherlands and elsewhere. A culture of madness gives us the opportunity to create alternatives rather than just repair or abolish the present order.

When he was talking I realised that I'm not deeply interested in psychiatry even though it has impacted on my life enormously and left me powerless and humiliated on occasions. My overwhelming experience of psychiatry has been its inadequacy and its total denial that madness has value and that mad people have the right to determine what that value is. After several years in the psychiatric system I decided it had very little to offer me and started to look elsewhere for answers. Peer-run alternatives now interest me far more than psychiatry does. It feels far more creative and effective to generate a culture of madness than to tinker with or destroy the culture of sanity and its guardian – psychiatry.

What is a culture of madness? It's anything that places value on madness and raises the status of being mad. Survivor-run alternatives do not necessarily do this but I think they always should. Otherwise these alternatives just parody the culture of sanity and defeat their purpose.

There are a lot of issues to explore about how to create genuine culture of madness alternatives. One is the issue of responsibility, paternalism and neglect. Psychiatry has been given the responsibility by society to get rid of madness and hide mad people. For them this responsibility is heavy enough to justify paternalism and the use of force. Another well-known historical trend in the treatment of madness has been neglect. Both neglect and paternalism continue because people fear and devalue madness. How then do peer-run services, particularly crisis ones, totally avoid being paternalistic and neglectful? Would there be a concept of diminished responsibility in a culture of madness? Could other people assume some responsibility for the mad person without risking paternalism in a crisis? The other question we need to ask is – could others leave all responsibility with the mad person without risking neglect?

Another problem with the claim that madness is OK is that unlike being black or gay, being mad is almost universally perceived to interfere quite drastically with a person's productivity and relationships. It is often a very unpleasant experience even before psychiatry has got hold of it. A culture of madness could be in danger of romanticising madness. It interests me that even the most radical anti-psychiatry people only go so far to say that madness is an OK response, albeit to bad life experiences. So even if madness itself is acceptable its causes are seen as negative and to be avoided. If someone told me my lesbianism was OK but I'm really just a lesbian because of negative life experiences I would feel insulted and invalidated. Yet the most radical analyses of madness that I know of do not go so far as to say madness is totally OK. I think this is difficult to do when madness is so closely linked to our concepts of disability and distress.

Later, in California, I interviewed Howie the Harp, one of the early leaders of the mad movement in the USA. Howie was incarcerated in a mental hospital as a teenager. He ran off to live on the streets where he joined the movement and helped others get out of mental hospitals. He was a founder of the Mental Patients Liberation Front in 1971 in New York. He was a larger-than-life person with a big belly, greying frizzy hair and a long beard. He offered me a light-hearted vision of a culture of madness:

We played at a conference of the Northern California Psychiatric Society. Little did they know that we would play one song I wrote while in the State Hospital called 'Crazy and Proud'. It talks about hating people who read psychology books and the last verse goes:

I won't be a nine to five robot,
well oiled and made of chrome.
I will never have your ulcers
or a split-level home.
You tried so hard to change me,
you bullied and you sneered.
But I will always remain just like I am,
loony, crazy and weird.

We invited two psychiatrists to come on stage with us and sing it along with us, without telling them what the song was about. When we got to 'you bullied and you sneered' I pointed at them and they couldn't handle that.

We in fact sang that song once at a demonstration in front of the American Psychiatric Association. And we heard that in one of the plenary sessions of that conference, a psychiatrist got up and, referring to our song, said, 'How are we going to deal with people who are proud of it?' They couldn't figure it out. They thought everybody would want to be cured of it, not proud of it.

←————→

I was surprised that many of the other survivors I visited did not think in terms of a culture of madness but saw themselves very much in relation to the psychiatric system, even those who were very opposed to it. I could see that repairing or abolishing the system alone would not generate better alternatives. Some utopian vision, however impractical, was needed to guide us beyond the present order. This was especially important for survivors who ran peer-run alternatives – and the main purpose of my fellowship was to visit these organisations so I could help to improve the ones like them, such as Psychiatric Survivors, that were being established in New Zealand. Peer-run alternatives are services run by and for people who had used or survived the mental health system. They could be support groups, crisis houses, drop-ins, residential services, information clearing houses and a lot more. They were most developed in the USA, and many people I talked to there remarked on how life changing it had been. One woman said:

Peer support made a huge difference to my life because I was really entrenched in the mental health system. I sat around for years in board and care watching TV and doing nothing. Self-help was a positive alternative for me. It gave me another way of dealing with my problems and it helped me get out of the system.

Peer-run alternatives were based upon a philosophy that was the antithesis of the traditional mental health system. First, they needed to honour the freedom of people to participate as they wish – to take part or not to take part, to choose how to take part, and to be involved in the collective decision-making. Unlike the mental health system, they also were able to provide roles for people to give as well as take. Those in peer-run alternatives who had put some distance between themselves and their distress could become positive role models for people still in the midst of their distress. Peer-run alternatives provided an environment where people could construct a more affirming story about themselves and to see hope in their futures. I knew all this could be difficult to achieve through my experience at Psychiatric Survivors but I didn't expect to see so many peer-run alternatives fall short of this philosophy on my travels.

The most impressive one I visited was a drop-in centre in New England in a gloomy suburban basement. It was led by Judi Chamberlin who wrote the book that had introduced me to the mad movement some years earlier. I interviewed Judi in a cheap Asian restaurant in Boston where she gave a fascinating account of the history of the movement. Judi then invited me to the drop-in's weekly business meeting.

There were around sixty members, defined as people who regularly called in. Fifteen or so of the members worked half a day per week for pay. The paid members were chosen by the membership for their history of involvement and commitment to the centre. All policy and expenditure decisions were made at the weekly business meeting, which all members were entitled to attend. The paid members had no more formal decision-making powers than other members but were likely to have a lot of influence. The centre had no co-ordinator, though Judi most closely approximated this role. Her presence at the centre was very part-time. She went to the weekly business meeting and was an obvious leader at the one I sat in on. However, she told me some of her ideas had not been taken up by the group. She was very committed to this kind of democratic decision-making but she lamented to me that some members wanted a more closed approach.

The paid members usually worked in shifts of three. They unlocked, made the coffee, emptied ashtrays, cleaned up and so on. They were also expected to ensure that the centre's rules were adhered to and to deal with arguments and other crises. All members were encouraged to initiate new activities at the centre such as meditation, outings, finding cheap tickets for movies, crafts and so on. Some were politically active though Judi recognised that people had to have their basic needs met before they could think about getting politically active. Apart from the duties of the paid members, no one was pressured to do anything.

The business meeting I sat in on was fairly chaotic. The chairperson wandered off and there was a lot of unstructured discussion. A lot of negative and positive feelings were expressed, from feelings of threat and anger at someone's comments, to appreciation of the work some members had done. The number of members was small enough to have almost total democracy and I was convinced it was the best way to run a peer-run alternative. From the moment a new survivor walked in the door they could use and develop their initiative and decision-making powers which were likely to have been stripped by the mental health system, and urgently needed to be built up again.

I then visited a peer-run support centre in California. As I arrived the door was open and a tall, good-looking man called Victor appeared to be preaching to a dingy roomful of seated people, mostly African-Americans like him. He welcomed me warmly and asked me to take a seat. He introduced me as an honoured guest from Australia until I corrected him. I felt a bit too honoured for my own comfort so I got up and said a few words about my psychiatric experience, the one thing I knew that equalised us. Apart from that I must have come across as very privileged and important to them.

While I was settling in, the immaculately dressed Victor continued to give his moral perspective on concerns raised by the clients. To one he explained that as people go through the programme at the support centre, they learn that making love in the back seats of cars is not the thing for them; they learn that making love in relationships is morally better. Soon after, a man began to walk out the door. Victor stopped him and said in a strict fatherly way, 'Stay here or don't come back. We've made an agreement that you won't wander in and out.' I had assumed that this kind of talk would always be avoided in any organisation that calls itself peer-run as this one did.

The people who used the support centre had urgent needs. As well as their homelessness and mental distress, which were the two criteria for membership, many of them were addicted to alcohol or street drugs. The centre provided a drop-in and living skills programmes for the homeless ex-mental patients in a poor urban area. Upstairs, on the first floor there was temporary accommodation for more than twenty people. The floor above this, called the Penthouse, was where a few made it to relative luxury and spaciousness on their way to completely independent accommodation. It felt as though the floors were arranged to make a metaphorical statement about going up in the world: people who were good in the eyes of the support centre deserved more space and comfort than the others. They even had a view. Down below, people were packed into dormitories which they were not allowed into during the day. 'Why?' I asked. The supervisor said there wasn't enough staff to look after them; they were too busy doing the paperwork.

Victor and another man, an accommodation supervisor, showed us around upstairs. As they talked about the support centre I noticed their pessimism about the clients, an attitude I had always assumed ate away only at the workers in mainstream mental health services. These two men, at least one of them an ex-client, shook their heads saying that hardly anyone made it up to the Penthouse. This attitude disturbed me. The accommodation supervisor said that he had made it up to live in the Penthouse and that the centre liked to employ ex-patients. Victor wasn't so clear about his own background. First he said he hadn't used mental health services, then he said he had. Perhaps he picked up my curiosity about whether staff were ex-patients or not. I believed strongly that they should be.

Something in me continued to feel unhappy about the centre. Perhaps Victor's preachy style was OK with African-Americans but I would have felt condescended to if he talked to me like that. I cringed when he pronounced his one true sexual morality to a roomful of grown adults and left no doubt that clients should not have more than one partner; otherwise they could not be making progress with the centre's 'Relationships Program'. Victor was a warm man and he did say to us, 'Talk to the clients – they're the real experts.' But I was unhappy about the way he pressured the man who was coming and going to stay in the room.

My own philosophy was that a true peer-run alternative was one which recognised and encouraged people's abilities and didn't take too much notice of their disabilities. In the mental health system it's the other way around, which is what is so destructive about it. I came away from my brief glimpse of the support centre feeling that the clients' abilities could be given more room to grow.

Soon after this, I spent several days in a large survivor organisation on the east coast of the United States. The first thing I noticed about the organisation was its enormous size. It employed about sixty survivors who operated several programmes ranging from residential services, advocacy, job training, support groups, drop-ins and consumer case management to technical support for survivors at state and national level. Its offices took up most of two floors in a large building.

The workers made me feel really welcome. Several of us had lunch with their leader. He was a very likeable and direct person, but as we talked I could tell things were a bit shaky with him. We found out later that he put himself in hospital that evening. His wife told me he wanted 'shock', which distressed her as he had always been anti-shock. Others wondered why he put himself into a hospital when he came from such an alternative perspective.

I had problems with this one, too. To me, peer-run alternatives and conventional mental health services had to be slightly allergic to each other. I wondered what effect a leader had on peer-run organisation if they demonstrated a high dependency on the services. Would this make for a confusing, contradictory role model? What would have happened to the tone of Psychiatric Survivors if I had been heavily into the services? Apart from my absence, would my heavy dependence on services subvert the peer-run basis of the group?

I wanted to know more about the leadership and the distribution of power within this peer-run service. Did everyone have enough of a say? How autonomous were the different programmes? How far would a programme have to stray from the organisation's philosophy to be brought into line? Was there room for more than one leader? Was recognition fairly distributed? I didn't get satisfactory answers to these questions. Sometimes I felt that people were a little defensive about the organisation. They might not have thought a lot about these issues, which indicated to me that their decision-making and group dynamics followed traditional patterns more than alternative ones. The workers were very dedicated but the office had a slightly bureaucratic feel about it. Political analysis wasn't high on the agendas of the people I talked to. These things may have been the result of being in a large organisation which kept its workers stretched to the limit.

I visited several programmes within this organisation, including a residential home for up to eighteen ex-patients, most of whom had been homeless. It was a comfortable, well-equipped place with three stereos, nice furniture and new paint and carpets. The manager showed us around. First we went into the kitchen. I spotted a notice by the door which said something like, 'Clients are not allowed in the kitchen unless accompanied by a staff member.' This statement did not come from a peer-run perspective. Even if there was a good reason for the clients not to use the kitchen, in a truly peer-run environment the notice wouldn't include the expression 'not allowed'. Instead it would indicate a collective decision rather than one that was imposed by staff on clients. Because the distinction between staff and clients is necessarily blurred in a true peer-run alternative, everyone is expected to take more or less equal responsibility for what goes on, rather than the less responsible clients being 'accompanied' to the kitchen by the more responsible staff. The notice could have read something like, 'The people in this household have agreed to use the kitchen as follows. . .'. You could even question the use of a notice at all – notices are an institutional form of communication not found in many ordinary households.

We left the kitchen and walked down the hallway. Next to the office I saw a door with a notice saying, 'Staff lavatory – keep out'. If there is one single gesture that can immediately separate conventional services from genuine peer-run initiatives, it is whether workers share the toilet with clients or not. Separate toilets indicate a perception that there is and ought to be a hierarchical and hygienic distance between worker and client.

In the office I spotted another notice: 'Barry is to be given one cigarette at a time because he was caught smoking in his room.' This notice speaks for itself. Peers don't 'catch' each other doing 'bad' things. They don't put confidential notices inside a closed office with a prescription for a staff response to non-conforming behaviour. If they do, it's because they have been so thoroughly soaked in the traditional service model they don't know any other way of interacting.

Upstairs, the women's and men's bedrooms contained two or three beds per room. Each door was labelled with a number and each bed was labelled with a letter of the alphabet. The manager knocked on the doors. If someone answered she asked their permission to show us the room. If no one answered she showed us the room anyway. My heart sank when I saw the numbers and the letters – I felt as though I was in a hospital again. And I felt really uncomfortable going into people's rooms without their permission.

I asked the house manager what part the residents had in the household decision-making. She said they had a weekly meeting with the residents to discuss things and all complaints were followed up. The residents also met regularly with a 'peer advocate' away from the staff so they could discuss things openly without feeling intimidated by the staff. This comment interested me. When I first heard it, it sounded good. Then I thought back to the way we organised feedback in Psychiatric Survivors. It never occurred to me that the people who use Psychiatric Survivors might feel too intimidated to give feedback in front of the workers. The manager's acknowledgement that the residents could feel intimidated in the presence of staff was an unintended admission that she was running more of a conventional service and less of a peer-run programme.

I didn't think much of this residence. But considering the abuse and homelessness many of the residents were taking refuge from, it was a haven and light years ahead of homeless shelters. In this context my criticisms might have been nit-picking. But the residence was part of a large peer-run organisation and in some ways it was defying its ideological roots.

There were no funded peer-run alternatives in Britain but I did go to an Alcoholics Anonymous meeting at the invitation of a survivor advocate who was a member. The hour-long meeting was started off by a member who talked for about thirty minutes. Then other members responded briefly with their own experiences. At the start there was a reading and a few quotes were stuck on the wall. The AA prayer concluded the meeting.

The people who spoke got straight to the heart of their shared problem. I wanted to look more closely at AA and other Twelve Step fellowships to see what we could use. There was some criticism of the AA approach, which focused almost entirely on the faults of the individual and ignored outside stressors such as poor relationships, poverty, unemployment and so on. In Twelve Step fellowships people are encouraged to see the source of their distress as within their own moral compass. This enabled people to 'reform' themselves but it ignored the determinants of their addiction that lay outside their control, such as social or even genetic factors. Some of the participants talked themselves down with comments about being self-centred or having over-large egos. I felt uncomfortable with this and I recalled another Twelve Step group, GROW, for people diagnosed with mental illness. GROW's starting statement is, 'I admit that I am inadequate and maladjusted'. I couldn't see how real peer-run initiatives could begin with such a self-damning statement.

Overall, the trip did more to arouse my anxiety about survivors assuming the role of hands-on providers than it did to expose me to the more sophisticated and innovative approaches I was seeking. Of all the survivor-run services I visited, only one appeared to be free of the destructive elements found in conventional services. Of course, these services were preferable to most conventional ones but I was perturbed to see elements of conventional service provider behaviour creep into them. On reflection, I could see that this was not surprising. As survivors we did not just absorb the oppressive mental health service model. We had absorbed authoritarian, hierarchical patterns all our lives: in the family, the education system, as employees, as oppressed minorities. No wonder they were so difficult to shake off.

I felt that the risks survivors take when they become service providers had not been explored enough by people in the mad movement. I asked people, 'How do survivors ensure they provide a true alternative and don't end up like their oppressors?' The usual answer went something like this: 'Because we've been through the same experience, we know what it's like to be oppressed and we wouldn't make it happen to others.' This type of reply ignored all the other experiences survivors have had which made them into what they are today. Even if we didn't have any power in society's authoritarian structures, those structures taught us particular ways to relate to other people, unless we made a conscious effort not to relate that way.

←———×

The year after my Winston Churchill Fellowship trip I was asked to organise and facilitate some meetings to establish an international network of consumers and survivors at an international mental health congress. I flew into Mexico City and checked into a glossy hotel room. The congress organisers had set aside a room for us to meet in the convention centre. Around a hundred came, mainly from Mexico but also from the USA, England, Europe, Japan and several other countries.

We met for two hours a day for five days to plan the new international survivors network. The meetings did not get off to a good start. The American consumers dominated, insisting that the meetings be run their way with observance to formal meeting rules few of us were familiar with. Conservative consumers from the South refused to support use of the term 'mental distress' in the new network's mission statement and insisted on us using 'mental illness' instead. I found them pushy and obnoxious, just like their political masters were on the international stage. The European survivors politely disagreed with them but got nowhere. The Mexican survivors seethed in silence and whispered 'Gringos' to each other. I stood in the middle trying to navigate the meetings towards a united plan. It was a nightmare and by the end of the week I was exhausted. On the final day the meeting was scheduled to elect a chair. One of the Mexican leaders, Leonora, suggested I put my name forward. I explained that I felt too burnt by the week to feel any enthusiasm for chairing the new network. They were worried that the Americans would put forward one of their more disruptive people, so I relented. With the help of the massive Mexican presence I was elected as the first chair of the World Network of Users and Survivors of Psychiatry.

After the congress I went to stay with Leonora, who lived in a Richmond Fellowship house for mad women in Mexico City. She was about my age, born in Venezuela, a lesbian with short black hair and a serious face. As we sat in her room she told me about her experiences:

My family don't want me no more, so they take me to the hospital. They say, 'You stay here, they look after you.' Then my family gone. The attendants tie my hands and feet to the bed. One of them rape me many times. It is terrible. I get pregnant. My family say, 'You must give your child to someone else to look after.' Oh it is so painful. I want to see my child but I don't know where he is.

As she talked Leonora held a naked doll with a small inoffensive penis. Her room was stuffed full of toys and ornaments. On the wall behind her was a glass case of dead butterflies, pinned down like Leonora in the hospital. On another there was a poster of Leonora's heroine, Frida Kahlo. Sometimes, she said, she saw Frida sitting on the end of her bed.

Leonora and her friends arranged for me to go to visit a local psychiatric hospital. They told me it was one of the best hospitals in Mexico because the patients could get dressed, keep some of their belongings and were given activities to do during the day.

We drove away from Mexico City through a dry dusty valley. A stout balding psychiatrist in a white coat greeted us outside the hospital. 'Come in my friends,' he crooned. 'We are very proud of this hospital. It is an honour to show it to you.'

The hospital was a one-storey building with several wings going off a small dusty courtyard. Leonora giggled into my ear, 'Oh, they make it so nice for foreign visitor.' We both laughed but I couldn't see anything nice in front of me at all.

Several patients dressed in rags lay curled up in the dry dirt where grass once grew. Others wandered slowly up and down the covered walkways between the courtyard and the hospital wings. A small group of women were huddled in a corner of the courtyard. The director smiled and pointed us in their direction. An attendant was helping them take battered old musical instruments out of a box and set them up to play. They sounded pitiful – too full of drugs and despair to care about music and rhythm. One of them, a middle-aged woman in a sacking veil, shook a broken tambourine at random intervals. With her other arm she held a wrapped-up doll to her breast as though it was the most precious thing in the world to her. When the first piece of music was finished she raised the doll up from her breast. What I saw shook me to the core. The doll had no face. There was just a jagged black grimy hole in the front of its head, like a half-eaten hollow Easter egg. I started to cry, not just because the woman clung so tenderly to her doll, not just because the doll was so grotesque, and not just because of the undeniable tragedy of her lost life. I cried because the doll with no face was such a powerful symbol of millions of lives that have been broken by trauma, despair and institutions.

←———→

As chairperson of the World Network of Users and Survivors of Psychiatry I was invited to many international meetings and conferences. On my first visit to Japan I spoke in a plain beige room in Osaka as part of an international survivor panel. Beside me sat Li from Shanghai. She was in her thirties with slightly buck teeth and a rounded figure by Chinese standards. She dressed in old-fashioned western clothes, wore brogues and talked with an earnest intelligence:

I am chronic schizophrenic. Many years in mental hospital in Shanghai. They look after me well. Give me insulin shock treatment so I get better. Now I live in apartment but psychiatrist say I am too sick to get work.

I come to this conference with my psychiatrist. He look after me in Shanghai too. He give me drug to correct broken brain. He tell me when I must go to hospital.

Li's testimony astonished me. Was she so grateful and unquestioning because she was raised in austere communism where powerful authorities obliterated all individual expression in the name of the collective good, where peaceful protesters were shot and the only safety was in conformity? Perhaps it was not surprising that Li expressed genuine thanks to the mental health system because the story it had given her was the only one she knew. How different it was for me, raised in an atmosphere where I was free to question, educated in the liberal arts and influenced by social movements such as feminism and indigenous rights.

Li accelerated my desire to get information on the mad movement translated into as many languages as possible so people could see there was more than one story. I would be much happier if Li and others like her could read the diverse literature out there, then decide to adhere to the original story they've been given. At least they would have had a choice.

Next I was up. I started my talk with a fairy tale I had written while working at Carrington:

Once, on an island surrounded by a deep unknown sea, a family lived in a large old house. The family lived and worked together harmoniously, until one of the daughters who was a painter went off on her own and started to paint strange pictures she and the others could not understand. Everyone felt frightened and helpless.

After a while her family said to her, 'You have got to go – your paintings don't belong to this house any more. We no longer feel safe.' They told the caretaker to lock the woman in the junk shed at the bottom of the property, on the slippery margin between the land and the sea. In the junk shed the woman suffered more terribly than ever, until she made friends with the sea who told her the meaning of her art. Then she started to long for her paints and brushes again. So she asked the caretaker to tell her family that she wanted to come home.

But her family still did not trust her to keep their house in order. They sent a message to the woman saying she could live on the back porch where they would provide her with food and blankets, but she could only come into the house if they invited her. Life on the back porch wasn't much better than in the junk shed. The woman still was not allowed her paints and brushes, and the loss of her art set off a terrible screaming inside her. The caretaker saw her pain and finally convinced her family to let her live inside the house again.

The woman was overjoyed to be in these warm and safe surroundings again. She seized her paints and brushes and painted while the others looked on. At first the family still couldn't understand the woman's paintings but after a while they saw the power of her work. 'Where did you learn to paint like this?' they asked her. She replied, 'When I was in the junk shed I made friends with the sea who told me the meaning of my art. But I didn't know I could paint like this until I picked up the tools you have denied me for so long.' Her family realised their mistake and from that time on they all lived together in the house, happily ever after.

I went on to say that mad people all over the world were locked in the junk shed at the bottom of the garden, while the rest of the community lived in comfort in the big homestead. In some countries our caretakers had let us out of the junk shed but we were still locked out of the house, forced to live on the back porch in community care ghettos. I then got specific about some of the conditions people had to endure:

In Mexico, my friend Leonora was locked up in a psychiatric hospital for years, where an attendant raped her in her straitjacket.

In the United States, Laura lived in a board-and-care home where she rotted her life away with no spare cash, support or meaningful activity.

In New Zealand, a young Maori man called Mikaere, whose only sickness was the loss of his culture died alone in solitary confinement after receiving electric shock treatment.

In Japan, Hiroto was locked up to hide his family's shame. He was trapped there with no legal means to get himself out.

In Canada, Vicki was forced to have treatment to cure her lesbianism.

In Zambia, David, who is now on the board of the World Network of Users and Survivors of Psychiatry, was charged with treason for expressing a political opinion and sent to a psychiatric hospital.

In many countries, people with mental distress have no human rights. In every country, they are prescribed psychiatric drugs, often without information about their toxic effects. Survivors are forcibly treated with electric shock treatment and frequently suffer distressing memory loss from it. Generally, they have little or no power to determine their own lives or the services they use. Many are condemned to the intolerable multiple stresses of poverty, inactivity, low self-esteem, inadequate housing, isolation and exploitation.

This is the appalling situation that has generated the mad movement into existence.

I don't know what the Japanese audience thought of Li's talk and mine. How two people with similar experiences could view them through such different lenses is one of the great mysteries of human diversity.

✦————✦

Japan has one of the most institutionalised mental health systems in the world. In the early 1990s more than 300,000 people were incarcerated in Japan's one thousand mental hospitals. The average length of stay in the hospitals was nearly a year; one in six patients stayed for twenty or more years. Most of the hospitals are privately owned and run under contract to the government. Some people worked hard in Japan to persuade the government to downsize the hospital system but the owners, fearing loss of business, habitually bribed government ministers to keep the hospitals open. At one point the government announced that 70,000 people currently in hospitals would be provided for in the community. Many of the hospital owners responded by building hostels to house these people just outside the hospital grounds.

Many of the survivors I met in Japan were not as grateful as Li was for the years they had spent languishing and drugged in hospitals. There was a small movement of survivors in Japan. One of their leaders Mari Yamamoto talked about her own experiences:

I was hospitalised when I was seventeen years old. One day the doctor told me there was a good injection for me. The injection was an anaesthetic for shock treatment. My family gave their consent for shock treatment but the doctor lied to me. Only later I found out it was shock treatment. My parents, the teachers and my psychiatrist judged me to be lazy, dependent, immature and spoilt. Every message was negative. The mental health system robbed me of my self-esteem and denied my real feelings. My feelings were just symptoms.

Ten years after her first hospitalisation Mari went to a local survivor group:

One member got angry and did not hesitate to express her emotion. I was surprised. I believed survivors should not express their feeling in the society. I believed all my feelings were symptoms, especially negative feelings. If I expressed my feeling, I might be punished by the mental health system and society. Then I started to think – I can speak out, I can express my feeling, even my feeling of anger. It was a revolution for me. It was my first step toward recovery. When I was a newcomer to survivor activities I would never have believed I could travel alone by intercity train or speak in a meeting. I am now editor of the newsletter and I travel to other countries by myself. I have also published my own book and translated two others into Japanese.

In the early years of my work in the mad movement I spent the summer of 1988 in Western Samoa. I flew into the airport at Samoa at 2am. The hot air hit me as I walked onto the tarmac like an open-air sauna.

The first morning as I walked the streets of Apia I saw a poor but vital nation at work. The Samoan police paraded down the main street in their blue lavalavas. The Bank of Western Samoa stood solid and proud among the shops. I walked past the undeniably Samoan parliament and government departments. And it struck me how colonised Maori were in comparison to their Polynesian relatives in these tropical islands. Maori had no institutions of law, finance or government. In temperate New Zealand they were too far outnumbered by white people.

Samoa was a place of lush beauty. Everything shimmered under the steaming hot sun: the fat, bright, wide-open hibiscus flowers, the round leafy trees sagging with breadfruit, the tidy rows of bougainvillea hedges, the long palms with their swaying fronds. The Samoans had also graced the landscape with their rustic thatched fales, well-tended gardens, their woven fine mats, their open-throated singing, their love of bright colours. Children teased each other on the streets, tossed back Coca-Cola and played reggae and Latino pop music on their ghetto-blasters. Multi-coloured wooden buses careered around the island. Children and dogs packed the backs of the utes coming to town. Brown bare-backed men in bright lavalavas fished on the turquoise reef. The Apia market overflowed with kava bowls, Samoan brooms, woven fans, fresh fish and taro. This was where Paul Gauguin and Robert Louis Stevenson had come to find paradise.

But Samoa was no paradise. Its people and culture were too complex, too deeply frayed by outside influences, to be the happy-go-lucky dwellers of the South Seas that many westerners painted them as. Samoa had the highest suicide rate in the world and its fair share of heavy drinking and domestic violence. Families were under stress as the old Samoan way broke down and migration halved its population in a generation. I visited the only two counsellors in Samoa – one a white nun, the other a Samoan health professional who had returned from New Zealand. They spoke of the low self-esteem of Samoans, how difficult it was for them to show anger or question authority, how the poor gave nearly all their money to the chiefs and the pastors and then couldn't provide for their own children.

The only doctor at Samoa's psychiatric service was an elderly man of German and Samoan descent, with moles on his face and thick grandfatherly glasses. He said that Samoans avoid showing their mentally ill or handicapped people – they tended to get hidden in the families, which took responsibility for them. Families usually brought their relatives into the psychiatric service when they got violent. Those who were put under a 'medical custody order' for being of unsound mind, mentally infirm, idiot, imbecile, feebleminded, or epileptic were sent to the prison because the psychiatric unit did not have 'security rooms'. The unit was mainly a day service staffed by one nurse. When she was sick or on holiday the unit closed down. At the time Samoa had no trained psychiatrist. There were plenty of traditional healers but the doctor didn't like them. He acknowledged they had some success but sometimes they made the patient worse, he said. He regretted that Samoans did not always accept psychiatric explanations for disorders.

Fiafia, the charge nurse in the psychiatric unit, did not entirely agree with the doctor. I went to see her at the unit in the hospital grounds, a basic one-storey building with a concrete floor. She told me that schizophrenia and affective disorders in Samoa were not like the ones she had seen in New Zealand. Usually people created the disorder when they got tired of the Samoan lifestyle. Most of the psychiatric patients she saw had received tertiary education in New Zealand or elsewhere. Perhaps it was the stress of being in a strange country, or sitting exams that caused their problems. Perhaps it was the food they ate, she said.

Fiafia talked about another prominent category in her diagnostic nomenclature – Samoan sickness. This sickness looked a bit like mania and depression but it was caused by spirits, usually of dead ancestors who spoke through the afflicted person to say what the family had done wrong. After the spirit had spoken, the person recovered. Some of the people who came to the unit were treated with a combination of western medicine and traditional healing. When Fiafia first arrived to work at the unit, people had been living there for years. She sent them all home. She tried to visit the patients but she didn't have transport. So she persuaded the public health nurses to visit the patients at home. And she educated the village women's committees and the village councils not to tease the patients but to support them.

On the face of it, Samoa's mental health service was woefully inadequate and violated the human rights of the people who were sent to prison on medical custody orders. It would probably have been ranked by western psychiatry as one of the worst in the world. But so were the services of many other poor countries where, a World Health Organisation study found, people diagnosed with schizophrenia recovered better than people in rich western countries. Western psychiatrists and others puzzled over these research results so much that they repeated the study and got the same results. They couldn't see how their well-funded services run by experts squeezed the resourcefulness out of mad people, their families and communities.

That is not to say that Samoa did any better than the west in providing for its vulnerable citizens. Sometimes they did worse. I visited a family in a village soon after I got there. The family's ancestors were buried in the front garden – they took great care with the gravestones and decorated them with flowers and other ornaments. Inside the fale, a modern bungalow, the children played while their gentle mother sat on the floor and talked to us in laboured English. We laughed about our different ways while she fanned her face. Outside I heard some long deep groans and I wondered if an animal was trapped or lost. Later, as I walked around the back of the house, I saw a wooden cage a few paces long and wide, with a dirt floor and a bowl of water in one corner. Prowling around inside it was a bony, bent boy of about fifteen. It was an unforgettable, sickening sight.

That night his mother, in a more serious mood, said he had an intellectual handicap and they prayed that one day they could send him to the big hospital in New Zealand, where he could be properly looked after. I told her that the big hospitals were all closing down because the people in them weren't being properly looked after. She looked confused. But I had to agree that her son in the cage could be better off in the big hospital. She smiled with gratitude while I struggled to hide my discomfort.

11.

THE UNFINISHED REVOLUTION

It took around fifteen years for me to make the transition from being a chronic psychiatric patient to becoming one of New Zealand's three Mental Health Commissioners. It wasn't so much the achievement I enjoyed but the irony of it.

Sometimes I imagined saying to Dr L'Estrange or Dr Lackland, who had pronounced career death on me, 'You're wrong. I'm going to be a national and international mental health leader one day.' They would have told me I had grandiose delusions and doubled my anti-psychotics. But truly, I would have been just as gobsmacked at this prediction coming true as they.

If I look through the lens of power it's hard to find the thread that connects me – the psychiatric patient – with me the commissioner. How did the wilted sapling that slouched through the doors of the Canary Ward become one of the big trees in the forest? How did a role subject to so much discrimination, disadvantage and distress lead to a role of international influence?

There are many possible answers. The most obvious one is that power is an uneven and invisible resource, like oxygen. Often people only notice power when they don't have it. They are like people exiled to the mountain tops who gasp because they don't have enough oxygen, while the privileged people at sea level breathe so comfortably they never think about their supply of oxygen. It wasn't until around 1970 that mad people began to organise and claim our oxygen. A few tribes of mad people rushed down from the mountains towards the sea brandishing our experiences of oppression and our vision for a better life. Over the next few decades more and more of us made the same journey.

It's an inner journey as much as an outer one. As I entered the Canary Ward for the first time I was ritually stripped of my credibility, my status and my dreams. But I was lucky enough to have started with a good supply of personal power – a socially and emotionally privileged background, an indifference to convention, a critical mind and good friends. Over time these forces gathered to fill the power deficit left by admission, diagnosis, treatment and prognosis.

I learned that mad people in other parts of the world were organising into a movement which was challenging the medical and coercive foundations of psychiatry. I learnt that I could transfer the logic and the language of oppression and liberation from the women's movement and indigenous movements to the situation mad people were in. I found a new discourse in which to place my experience of madness. I started to ask the psychiatrists and nurses tricky questions, to disagree with their unflattering assessments of me, and to voice doubt about their ability to help me. Of course, they didn't like it – and the fact that they didn't like it helped to prove my point.

After I stabilised I went looking for other mad people who, like me, no longer believed in the world according to psychiatry. We organised and challenged mental health professionals to change and gradually, many of them did. The discourse of the mad movement trickled into the discourse of the mental health system and drop by drop its logic and language began to change.

But it didn't change nearly enough.

<hr/>

The Mental Health Commission was established by the government in 1996 to monitor the mental health system and to take a lead in improving the workforce and reducing discrimination. It was led by three commissioners, one of whom was to be Maori, and another to be a person with lived experience of mental distress. I joined as a commissioner in 2000 and took responsibility for the Commission's work in the areas of recovery, discrimination and human rights. Before then I had drafted the recovery content for a Commission publication called *The Blueprint*. It was the first official document in New Zealand to indicate that mental health services needed to use a recovery approach, and New Zealand was one of the first countries in the world to do so.

We defined recovery as living well in the presence or absence of our mental distress. This was a simple sentence with revolutionary implications. It acknowledged that we can live well with our distress and that we need not wait until the symptoms have been eliminated. It downgraded the centrality of diagnosis and treatment and suggested that the primary role of services should be to support us to live well rather than to just treat symptoms. We went on to say that 'living well' could only be defined by the persons themselves.

One of the problems with the word 'recovery' is that it has a medical meaning. Often people confuse recovery as defined in mental health with recovery in medicine. We need to make a distinction between personal and clinical recovery to really get to grips with the philosophy of the recovery movement in mental health. Clinical recovery in medicine is a cure or a reduction of symptoms as a result of treatment by experts. Personal recovery in mental health, on the other hand, is a renewed sense of self and a restoration of valued roles as part of a process of personal growth led by the person themselves.

The recovery movement in mental health began to take root in the 1980s. At that time some major long-term outcome studies of people diagnosed with schizophrenia challenged psychiatric pessimism by showing that many people with major mental distress who were considered 'chronic' went on to live full lives in the community. Some leaders in the mad movement and in the psychosocial rehabilitation movement began to call for a new philosophy in mental health services with a greater emphasis on equal rights, an end to deficit-based approaches and a questioning of compulsory interventions. There has been much variation in the way recovery has been interpreted in practice. Recovery has become a very broad church, with some people on one side who think we just need to tweak the system, and people on the other side who believe we need a radical change. Some mad people who led the recovery movement no longer sign up to recovery because they believe it has been colonised by the mental health system.

Why do we need radical change in mental health services in the direction of a genuine recovery approach, especially as understood by the mad movement? First, we need to get beyond psychiatric pessimism and services that exist to contain and maintain people in their chronicity. The dominant story of people with major mental distress needs to change from the 'fading life chances' story that plots out a predetermined path that people have no control over to a 'hero's journey' story that shows that we can grow through and beyond life's crises. The second reason we need radical change is that the current system contributes to poor outcomes for people who use services. Most are unemployed, many are single and do not have children, and they die up to twenty-five years younger than their fellow citizens. Recovery is not easy or quick, but if mental health services were commercial enterprises that gave money-back guarantees to customers who did not regain their social and material opportunities, they would have all gone broke.

By the time I joined the Commission, the New Zealand mental health system was in a better position to take up recovery than its counterparts in similar countries. All the psychiatric hospitals had been closed down and close to thirty per cent of funded services were delivered by community based non-government organisations. The mad movement was relatively strong in New Zealand at the time and a well funded national anti-discrimination project had begun. Psychiatry and the pharmaceutical companies were less powerful in New Zealand than in North America and Europe. And in response to *The Blueprint* the government committed additional funding to community based mental health services.

Research shows clearly that hope and the belief others have in people is fundamental to recovery. People also said regaining their self-belief, learning how to manage their lives, being in loving and supportive relationships, having enough income to live on, and having a job or other way of making a contribution were all important to their recovery. Studies that ask people how they find conventional services, compulsory treatment and medication, on the other hand, show that people have very mixed experiences of them at best.

Recovery promotes our self-determination, connection to our communities and social justice. Traditional mental health services have routinely ignored these principles. Many people who worked in services found it hard to grasp what recovery principles might mean in their day-to-day work. I found one of the best ways to communicate recovery was to tell two stories about one person – the first about what happens to them in traditional services and the second about their passage through recovery based services. Take the story of Janet, for instance.

Janet started to experience severe distress at nineteen. Her life had been difficult for years. She was sexually abused between the ages of ten to fifteen by an uncle but she hid it from her family. As a teenager Janet got into some self-harm and heavy drinking to deal with her shame and alienation. Then she started to hear voices that reinforced the bad feelings she had about herself. Janet just managed to get her school qualifications and was accepted for nursing school.

Take a look at how life turned out for her in a 'pills and pillows' traditional service that didn't respond to her needs, stole her freedom and stripped her of her dreams:

Janet's story, version one

During her second year at nursing school, Janet's voices and feelings got so bad she decided to jump off a motorway bridge. Her best friend, Emma, took her to the GP who asked her about her voices, mood, sleep, appetite, libido and concentration. Janet was having a lot of trouble with all of them and the GP said she needed to see a specialist. He put a call through to the mental health service and told Janet, 'Sorry, they can't see you for three weeks but please ring the mental health crisis team if you feel unsafe.' The GP said the number was in the front of the phone book. Janet went away feeling as though there wasn't much help out there.

The next day things got so bad that Janet rang the crisis team and told them she wanted to kill herself. 'Make yourself a cup of tea,' they said. She felt totally humiliated and took a big overdose instead. Just then Emma came around and rang the crisis team. They told her to ring an ambulance.

'We've got another OD,' the nurse sighed to the doctor in the emergency department.

'That was a silly thing to do,' the doctor muttered. He asked Janet lots of questions about the drugs she'd taken and said she needed to stay overnight.

Emma came to get her the next morning and asked the nurse if the mental health people had seen her. 'No, you need to go through your GP,' the nurse answered.

A few weeks later Janet ended up in the psychiatric ward after another overdose. She told the psychiatrist about her problems and her sexual abuse but he said there was no evidence that sexual abuse causes psychosis. He said, 'Wait until the medication kicks in – you'll feel better about things then.' A lot of the nurses stayed in the nurses' office and didn't talk much to the patients.

One night Janet woke up feeling really paranoid and tapped on the window of the nurses' office. 'I'm under attack, I'm going to die,' she called out. One of the nurses raised her eyes to the ceiling, put down her hand of cards, opened the window and told Janet to go back to bed.

Some of the staff were nice but they weren't really interested in how Janet felt or how she would cope when she got out of hospital.

Janet got on with some of the other patients but they seemed like career psychiatric patients to her, which made her feel gloomy about her own future. Janet went to Occupational Therapy some mornings but she found it patronising. She slept about fifteen hours a day because the drugs made her dopey and listless. When she was up and about she felt crazy with boredom. Janet hated being locked up in the ward. Some of the experienced patients told her how to lie so she could get out of there quickly.

Two weeks later Janet was discharged with a prescription and an appointment with a psychiatrist at the community mental health centre. At the first appointment the psychiatrist asked Janet a few questions then told her she had psychosis as a result of a chemical imbalance in her brain. He said she needed the drugs like a diabetic needs insulin, wrote out a new prescription and said he'd see her in a month.

Janet had lost her place in her flat and was now living with her mother who was worried and didn't know how to respond. Janet's mother rang the psychiatrist to get his advice but she found him evasive and he didn't have any practical advice for her beyond ensuring Janet took her medication.

Janet returned to nursing school after a month. The head of the school called her into her office and said she was concerned that Janet's psychosis could interfere with her nursing career: 'We will have to monitor you closely when you're on placement. Your tutors will give you the information you missed out on while you were in hospital.' Janet noticed the other students were avoiding her.

She felt helpless, as though there was nothing she could do to make things better. Everyone seemed to treat her as though she was incompetent and unreliable. She felt lonely and useless. She told the mental health team how bad she felt every month when she saw them. They said, 'Take your medication and avoid stress.'

After a few months of struggle Janet left nursing school and went on a sickness benefit. At first she was relieved but after a while she realised she had nothing to get up for in the morning. The voices got worse and dark feelings closed in on her.

Then one morning she woke up in bright light and the voices told her she was an angel. She felt transformed, put on a see-through gown, walked into the city and blessed everyone she saw to save them from evil. It was going well until the police arrived. They yelled at Janet to freeze, threw her to the ground and handcuffed her. Her euphoria flipped into intense pain and panic. She tried to fight the police off all the way to the hospital while they mocked her for being a nutter.

The nurses put her straight into a locked cell with only a plastic mattress and a blanket. They held her down, injected her and left the room. Janet screamed to be let out but the nurse opened the flap on her door and told her to be quiet. Janet felt terrified and abandoned. After several hours she just curled up and went blank. She was in the locked room alone for several days.

When they let her out Janet said she wanted to go home but staff said she couldn't because she was under the Mental Health Act. Janet felt frightened and powerless – drugged out and unable to leave the building. She rang a lawyer but he told her the ward was the best place for her. The psychiatrist refused to reduce her drugs when she told him how horrible they were. After two months the staff organised for Janet to go into staffed accommodation with four other people.

Janet was driven to the house and left there. She had to sign a contract agreeing that she wouldn't drink or take drugs in the house or have sex there. She wasn't even allowed to go to the fridge to get food between meals. Janet had nothing in common with the other residents and they really irritated her. The staff had organised a programme but Janet didn't want to go out in the van with the others to do ten-pin bowling or eat out at Burger King. She sat around most days doing nothing and sleeping a lot.

Janet wanted to move out but whenever she mentioned this to the staff they told her she was too unwell to cope on her own. Her confidence plummeted and she couldn't see any future for herself. Janet was also desperately lonely; the staff discouraged family visits because they sometimes upset the residents.

Janet was on a community treatment order and a compulsory three-weekly injection. The drugs really slowed her down and she felt like a zombie most of the time. Her psychiatrist refused to reduce the drugs, telling Janet she could not survive without them.

How is Janet doing today? She is now twenty-five. She is estranged from her family who don't understand her or know how to help. She has lost most of her friends. She is on the invalid's benefit and has not worked for five years. She sits in the living room of her staffed accommodation most days smoking, drinking coffee and watching soaps. Her weight has doubled in that time. She continues to be on a community treatment order and to get injections that sap all her vitality.

Janet has no hope and sees no future. She lives with a death wish most of the time.

The mental health system is largely responsible for the terrible state Janet is in but it didn't have to be this way. Let's rewind her story and start it again as she starts to use recovery oriented services that give her hope, freedom and choices.

Janet's story, version two

During her second year at nursing school, Janet's voices and the feelings got so bad she decided to jump off a motorway bridge. Her best friend Emma had seen a place advertised on the internet where young people could go if they were feeling distressed or suicidal. So they went online, found rockup.com and Janet answered some questions. The results said, 'You're really depressed. Your local Rock Up would like to contact you to see if we can help.' Janet selected the 'phone me' option and got a call ten minutes later.

The next day Janet went to an appointment at the local Rock Up with Emma. You could go there for lots of stuff – health information, contraceptives, support groups, student loans, job search and info on the best gigs in town. Someone she knew from school was on reception. 'Welcome to Rock Up,' she said, and showed Janet and Emma the coffee machine.

A young woman came over. 'Hi. My name's Lisa. I'm a peer support worker and you'll be meeting with me and a clinical worker here.'

'What's a peer support worker?' Janet asked.

'Someone who was sitting right where you were a few years ago.'

Lisa and the clinical worker listened while Janet talked and cried; it was a relief to talk to people who seemed to understand. Lisa set up weekly appointments and gave Janet a number to ring at any time if she felt desperate or unsafe.

A few weeks later Janet started feeling suicidal again and rang Lisa who organised for her to go to a peer-run crisis house. It was a warm, homely place and Janet immediately felt welcome and safe. A woman called Helen introduced herself to Janet as her peer mentor. Helen explained that people develop problems for many different reasons and mentioned sexual abuse as one of them. Janet told Helen about her sexual abuse. Helen said they could organise free counselling for her. Then a psychiatrist came and offered Janet some medication to help with her sleep and the voices.

One night Janet woke up feeling really paranoid and went downstairs to see the peer worker on night shift. 'I'm under attack, I'm going to die,' she called out. The peer worker rubbed her back and reassured her that the feeling would pass.

A few days later Janet and Helen started to talk about what Janet needed when she got out so she could cope and get on with her life.

Janet got on with some of the other guests but Helen was an inspiration to her. It was amazing to share with someone who had been through similar experiences, who had come out the other side and learnt from her psychosis. Janet felt much less isolated and started to feel hope for the first time in ages. She also joined in the art sessions and a creative writing group and started to feel almost whole again. And she signed up for a peer-developed online recovery education course.

When Janet left the crisis house she went back to Rock Up to see Lisa, who reminded Janet that she was strong and could recover. Lisa went through the plan Janet had created with Helen and organised her sexual abuse counselling. Janet also saw the psychiatrist at Rock Up who went through the pros and cons of medication with her. Janet decided to stay on a very small dose of anti-psychotics.

Lisa went with Janet to discuss with her flatmates what had been happening to her. They decided to have Janet back. A family support worker from Rock Up also contacted Janet's mother, gave her some books and online references and invited her to a family recovery group with other parents, which she attended for over two years.

Rock Up contacted the student support service at Janet's nursing school. They liaised with Janet's tutors, invited her on a course called, 'Studying when life sucks' and helped her catch up with her studies. The support service also introduced Janet to a campus 'hearing voices' group where she discovered she could take charge of her voices. One of her classmates was a member of the group and they became good friends.

Janet felt she could make it a lot of the time. It was incredibly helpful meeting people who believed in her and understood what she was going through. She had some terrible days when the voices really got to her. The psychiatrist at Rock Up increased her anti-psychotics slightly to take the edge of the voices and that helped a bit.

Janet found nursing school a real struggle but the student support services did whatever it took to keep her there – helping her organise her assignments and finding strategies to deal with the stresses of being on placement.

But the stress of her first placement was too much and one morning she woke up in bright light and the voices told her she was an angel. She felt transformed, put on a see-through gown, walked into the city and blessed everyone she saw to save them from evil. Two people in uniforms came up to Janet and asked her some questions. They said they'd like to help Janet get her strength back, because having sole responsibility for saving people was very hard work.

Janet agreed and went with them to a house where a psychiatrist said, 'We want you to stay here for a while because we think you need a complete break from saving people or you will collapse. We also want to give you some drugs to calm you and help you sleep.' A nurse showed Janet to her room and sat with her while she paced and raved.

The next day Janet felt full of energy and wanted to go and give blessings to the people in the city again. A staff member took her to a quiet place in the park and stayed close to her while she did an angel ritual. Janet often went for walks with a staff member to let off some steam. No one ever stopped her leaving the building but someone always went out with her. The psychiatrist was happy to reduce the drugs after ten days when Janet told her how horrible they were. After two weeks the staff asked Janet if she wanted to go to a five-bedroom recovery house for an intensive three-month stay.

The staff and the other residents welcomed Janet to the house and told her what went on there. The residents made their own house rules and chose what they got involved in. Over the next few weeks the staff sat down with Janet and discussed every area of her life. She had to think hard about what she wanted and they helped her come up with a plan for going back to nursing school, linking up with her friends, finding a flat and going back to her sexual abuse counselling. She also went to a local photography course.

Over the three months Janet really started to believe that she could recover and have a good life. She learnt not to be ashamed, to keep herself healthy and to rebuild her life. She got the confidence to look for a summer job and go to parties again. She also made some great friends.

Janet stayed on a small dose of anti-psychotics but she didn't like the effect they had on her. Her psychiatrist explained that she may not need them if she continued with the sexual abuse counselling and the other things she was doing with her life. It took her two years to get completely off them.

How is Janet doing today? She is now twenty-five. Things are better with her family since they went to a family recovery group. They are proud of the way she is overcoming adversity. Some of Janet's old friends drifted away but she has made many new ones. She is working as a mental health nurse in a place similar to Rock Up, where she is open about her experience. The sexual abuse counselling helped her deal with her trauma. She still hears voices sometimes but has learnt ways of putting them in their place so they don't intrude too much. Life is good most of the time.

←——————→

Most people would have no trouble choosing to go with recovery based services but like any system the mental health system excels at resisting change. For a start, people usually don't like change and the people with the most power feel they have the most to lose. Add to that the gargantuan nature of human systems, which change with as much speed and grace as a tanker doing a U-turn in a canal. Then consider the level of discrimination against mad people by our communities and their knee-jerk demands to ensure public safety, and you'll see that the transition from traditional to recovery based services was never going to be easy.

Why do the Janets of this world experience the first story far more often than the second? There's a profoundly simple answer to this –

madness has zero status as a human experience, and this taints most human responses to it. It doesn't matter if the response shows itself as fear, hostility, control, incomprehension or pity – they all trace back to the ancient taproot of stigma.

The biggest barrier to recovery is stigma and discrimination, whether it comes from ordinary people, community leaders, mental health workers, families or mad people themselves. There is a naive and simplistic community consensus that mad people cannot be responsible for their unpredictable or violent behaviour, therefore someone else needs to take control. For the last two hundred years or more, communities have abdicated their responsibility for people with serious mental distress to mental health experts and services. These experts and services are expected to take total responsibility for people with mental distress, particularly those in crisis, who should be contained and tightly controlled. So when something goes wrong, the services are held fully to blame for not containing and controlling the person.

There are some implicit assumptions in this consensus that are unsustainable. Firstly, that people with mental distress are not capable of taking any responsibility for their actions; in many cases people, even when in crisis, have capacity for personal responsibility. Secondly, that mental health services can avert every disaster; clearly human beings, no matter how skilled, are fallible in their predictions. The third assumption is that coercive practices are required to keep the community safe from violent, unpredictable people. The truth is only a small percentage of people with mental distress fit this category.

Unfortunately, this unrealistically demanding consensus has led to risk-averse practices in mental health services, such as compulsory treatment, locked doors and other restrictions on liberty. Sometimes these responses are driven more by possible risk to the reputation of the organisation or professionals than to what is optimal for the person experiencing mental distress. In addition to this, mental health practitioners and spokespeople in the public arena, who are understandably on the defensive, tend to publicly collude with this consensus instead of questioning it.

One of the worst examples of community discrimination I encountered during my years at the Mental Health Commission came from a former historian who went on to become a minister of health during the period of deinstitutionalisation in New Zealand. Since resigning from politics Michael Bassett had become a newspaper columnist. After a person in contact with mental health services, who had no history of violence, killed a stranger on the street, he wrote a column in a daily newspaper:

What most worries the public is why so many clearly insane people aren't in secure care [and] that in practice, 'community care' puts patients' rights ahead of public safety [. . .] There have been many horrendous rapes, sexual assaults and stabbings by patients playing hide and seek with their caregivers. The cause is always the same: someone who in former times would have been locked up has been let out. It's another crusade where the balance has tipped too far. There must be higher levels of detention. When in doubt, detain. Never rely on unsupervised self-medication. It's time politicians enforced these simple rules. [We] would all sleep more easily if the pendulum that swung against psychiatric hospitals returned nearer to equilibrium. There's a problem however: hospitals will have to be rebuilt. Earlier crusaders sold most of them in the hope of making their new orthodoxy irrevocable. Another high price for listening to the politically correct with no pause button.

The column was not the worst piece of ignorant gutter press I have read on the issue but the writer, who should have known better, was perilously uninformed and had not thought at all deeply about the issues.

The first thing he should have known is that 'mental illness' is not a significant driver of crime: youth, gender and substance abuse are as significant or more so. He should have known that recent studies in England and in New Zealand had shown that the proportion of homicides committed by people with a diagnosis of mental illness declined during the era of deinstitutionalisation, from 1970 to 2000. He should have reminded the reader that the vast majority of homicides are committed by people who have no 'mental illness' and that people with 'mental illness' are much more likely to be the victims of such crimes than to be the perpetrators.

The second thing he should have questioned is the simplistic assumption that an increase in patients' rights is correlated with a decrease in public safety. The implication is that 'insane people' are a dangerous class of people, when the evidence doesn't support this. Would he have ever thought to warn that an increase in young men's rights is a threat to public safety and 'if in doubt, detain' them?

The third thing this educated man should have known is that rare events such as homicide are notoriously hard to predict, and even harder to predict when a person has no history of violence. According to some experts an 'if in doubt, detain' policy would require the detention of many thousands of people with a diagnosis of mental illness to possibly prevent one homicide. Any politician should know that such a policy would be a moral and fiscal failure.

He could have also questioned why he described a man walking down the street without a health professional in sight as a 'patient'. Why did he not refer to him as a person or a citizen? Perhaps it was because a primary identification as a psychiatric patient disqualifies a person from full citizenship and equal rights. Once this disqualification has been achieved, a lower status in the world is justified and he can now dismiss attempts to raise the status of mad people as 'politically correct' or as 'crusades'. The columnist did not even know at the time if the 'psychiatric patient' part of the man was a factor in his crime; he lazily assumed, like most other media commentators, that if he was a psychiatric patient his mental illness was responsible. It was almost as though the man was a psychiatric patient and nothing else – not a son, not a father, not an angry disappointed man, not a stressed beneficiary, just a walking 'mental illness'.

The writer could have touched on some even deeper issues. Why do we set psychiatric patients apart from other citizens? Why are we so afraid of the infrequent threat that a small minority of them pose to public safety? If he had got inside the experience of madness he would have found that it does not make us less human. It does not turn us into automatons locked into a pre-determined pathway to destruction, who play devious games to avoid help and who need constant supervision. He would have found that like any overwhelming experience, such as extreme grief, chronic anger, severe trauma or falling in love, madness hurls us into a world of altered perceptions which can lead to judgments and decisions we would not otherwise make; these experiences do not so much remove free will but change the perceptual and cognitive foundations upon which we make decisions. If he had got inside the experience of madness he also might have discovered respect for people who survive the massive rigours of madness, the states of siege, the existential disintegration, the chasms of despair and the terrifying isolation. He might even have seen that these states are bolder expressions of common human dilemmas and that madness is embedded in our humanity.

Perhaps he had never questioned or even noticed his bedrock beliefs about the nature of madness. If he had, he would have seen that our culture does not ascribe any value or meaning to madness and this opens the floodgates to fear, pity, discrimination, exclusion, coercion and to the type of column he felt justified in writing. He might then have tried to imagine a world where our culture did ascribe meaning and value to madness. He would have come to an inescapable conclusion that mad people would be in a far better social position than they are now and that columns like his would be considered absurd and offensive.

The mental health system colludes most powerfully with community stigma and discrimination through the use of forced treatment and detention. Many professionals see right through this collusion but they keep doing it and seldom challenge it in public. Others believe that force is clinically necessary.

The Mental Health Commission embarked on work to reduce and eliminate the use of solitary confinement and to raise questions about the use of compulsory treatment. We were not prepared for the massive backlash we got from families, psychiatrists and the legal fraternity who were rattled by the Commission asking such fundamental questions.

It started when I spoke about forced treatment from the perspective of people subjected to it at an international mental health conference in Wellington. I claimed that forced treatment was a barrier to recovery and that mental health services resorted to it too often, for too long and often for the wrong reasons.

The use of force can be more traumatising than the experience of the mental health problem itself. Being restrained, held down and injected, put in seclusion, locked in wards, told where to live and told what drug to take, can understandably create intense anger and humiliation, and even aggravate past memories of abuse.

Force can also undermine people's trust in mental health services. In an American study of over 300 service users, 55% of those service users who had been involuntarily hospitalised responded that their fear of force caused them to avoid mental health services. In addition to this, the potential or threat to use force undermines the voluntary use of mental health services. In a British survey of 500 service users, 44% of so called voluntary patients did not regard their status as genuinely voluntary.

Compulsory service users experience more discrimination than voluntary ones. People subject to force cannot always vote, hold public office, or enter other countries. The existence of force also gives the message to the wider community that mad people are either helpless victims or deranged perpetrators, and are unable to take responsibility for themselves.

I went on to talk about how services could become more recovery oriented and reduce the use of force through crisis prevention, advance directives, more varied and humane crisis options, and advocacy.

A few weeks later the psychiatrist who oversaw New Zealand's compulsory treatment legislation called me to his office. Eric was a benign gentleman with a World War Two moustache but his younger colleague Larry was cold and suspicious.

'We heard you speak against compulsory treatment,' Eric said. 'We're a little bit concerned and we'd like to have a chat about it with you.' Larry sat beside him, looking dark with his arms folded.

Eric told me stories about people he knew whose lives had been transformed through compulsory treatment – people with no insight into their condition who blossomed once they got into treatment. I told Eric stories about people who had been violated by force. Larry said nothing.

We discussed the research on people's experiences of compulsory treatment. It says they are often ambivalent, with complaints about loss of freedom on one hand but acceptance that there may be some benefits on the other.

'Yes,' I said, 'but the benefits they experience may have less to do with the compulsion to take medication and more to do with getting into the priority queue for services. I know people with full-time jobs and bringing up children who want to stay on their compulsory order because they get free drugs. These studies are often conducted by the same people who administer compulsory treatment. I don't think that's a great way to get people to tell the truth about what they feel.'

'But some people do feel grateful,' said Eric.

'I've thought about this a lot. When I was young I read a lot of literature that was critical of psychiatry. It gave me another reference point. But a lot of people who use services have never come across these ideas – they just accept the world according to psychiatry, like a medieval peasant accepted the word according to the Vatican.'

Eric laughed and Larry darkened.

'Have you ever wondered if there is a bit of the Stockholm syndrome happening, feeling positive regard towards the people who take away your freedom?' I asked. 'The strange thing is, people who have had their freedom taken away don't always try to take it back. Uncle Tom was loyal to his slave masters, and at the height of the suffragette movement in England most women didn't agree they should have the vote. So the gratitude argument doesn't wash with me much.'

Larry placed his hands palms down on the table in front of us. 'We use our powers with the best of intentions,' he said.

'I'm sure you do, but what did they say about the road to hell?'

'There's a lot of pressure on psychiatrists to keep people safe. Failure to use compulsory powers can have devastating consequences, not only for the patient but for our careers as well,' said Larry.

I thought about an acronym for CARE in mental health services invented by one of my mad colleagues – Cover Arse, Retain Employment. We ended our meeting no closer to any agreement than when we started.

Later, someone told me that Larry thought my views were danger-ous. A generation earlier a priest had said the same thing about my mother when she questioned the authority of the Catholic Church. It isn't the lack of agreement that worries me most about being called dangerous. It's that priests and psychiatrists, for all the good they set out to do, seem to be in denial about how dangerous they can be to the people they have the power to coerce, persuade, treat or absolve. Surely, the act of questioning this power is far less dangerous than exercising it.

My resolve to create a debate about compulsory treatment didn't waver but I knew the argument wouldn't be won by exchanging conflicting anecdotes or drawing on the inconclusive evidence on the effectiveness of compulsory interventions. In a modern democracy most arguments for freedom are won when we make an appeal for equality. Special compulsory treatment legislation for people diagnosed with mental illness is rooted in inequality. Here's why.

In most countries the legal criteria for compulsory interventions include danger to self or others. These criteria create double standards for justifying the loss of liberty – one for people diagnosed with mental illness and one for the rest of the population. When it comes to danger to self, general health service users have the right to refuse treatment with dangerous consequences to themselves, but mental health service users do not. When it comes to danger to others, the criminal justice system has no power to take a person's liberty away before they have committed a crime, but the mental health system can remove someone's liberty on suspicion they *might* commit a crime.

To get around these discriminatory double standards, some people have proposed that incapacity should be the major criterion for compulsory treatment and that there should be generic incapacity legislation to regulate compulsory interventions for general health service users as well as mental health service users. This makes sense not only from an equality point of view but also because in some studies psychiatric and general hospital inpatients have similar rates of incapacity.

I liked the idea of a generic incapacity law. If mad people were subjected to compulsory treatment under a generic law on an equal basis with other members of the community, it is unlikely that the community would tolerate an increase in use of coercion; it is far more likely that its use among mental health service users would drastically decrease.

So far so good, until I discovered that some of these advocates for a generic law proposed a different threshold for incapacity in mental health than in general health. A psychiatrist who argued for the incapacity criterion defined capacity as 'agreeing that one has an illness and might benefit from treatment'. I couldn't imagine a person in a physical health setting putting up with being told they had to take treatment because their denial that they had a disease indicated they lacked capacity. And a mental health legal expert advocated a special capacity test for people with a diagnosis of mental illness to capture the 'complex and subtle' loss of capacity thought to be peculiar to this group. This statement smells of what Australian mad academic Flick Grey calls 'benevolent othering' and is deeply discriminatory.

The only way to achieve equality with other citizens is to scrap special mental health legislation altogether. It is inherently discriminatory. But there is a danger that special provisions for mad people could creep into generic legislation, which would be equally discriminatory.

←———→

The Mental Health Review Tribunal invited me to talk to them on user and survivor views on compulsory treatment. People on long-term compulsory treatment orders go to the Mental Health Review Tribunal when they want to get off their order and their psychiatrist won't oblige. Most of them probably wouldn't bother if they knew that in a good year only one in twenty-five applicants gets off their order.

I went to see the tribunal at the Royal Society. The corridor was lined with photographs of dead scientists, staring through the glass, who had made great discoveries about rocks, insects, atoms and infections. I walked into a room full of psychiatrists and lawyers sitting around the Royal Society board table, looking important.

I talked about force to them – people feel violated by it, it doesn't work, it erodes trust, the legal protections are a farce. They didn't agree with most of it. They leaned forward, their counter-attack spiked with words like 'lack of insight', 'non-compliance' and 'risk'. We played ping-pong, our words bouncing back and forth until the chair said time was up.

One of the psychiatrists then stood to speak about insight. He was an expert on it. Dressed in an outdated suit and glasses, he stood in front of us looking awkward, but his composure grew as he started to recite some of the mantras of his profession. 'The Oxford dictionary defines insight as the capacity to understand hidden truths,' he said.

That means insight is a struggle for everyone, I thought.

He quoted some dead psychiatrists: 'Sir Aubrey Lewis of the Maudsley Hospital wrote in 1934 that insight is a "correct attitude to morbid change in oneself".' He then told us that Dr Anthony Someone, also from the Maudsley, elaborated on Lewis's work and wrote that 'a patient has insight when he accepts the morbid changes as illness, he labels these changes as abnormal, and he accepts the need for treatment.'

Stripped of all the fancy words, Sir Aubrey, Dr Anthony Someone and their loyal followers were really saying that insight is agreeing with your psychiatrist who knows the truth. I closed my eyes, exasperated at their arrogance.

'The problem is only forty per cent of schizophrenics have full insight,' he continued. 'The rest are partially or completely unaware. This makes it particularly difficult for us to treat some of them. Insight is usually linked with compliance, though some patients accept treatment and still believe there is nothing wrong with them. They have partial insight.'

He paused, with an earnest frown. 'Why do patients so often lack insight? Is it a core symptom? Or is it a defence mechanism? After all, lack of insight protects the patient against the distress created by his illness. And we know that people who develop insight can be more prone to suicide.'

I was tempted to ask him if insight should be discouraged as part of our country's suicide prevention strategy.

'Lack of insight is often a predictor of chronicity. But of course insight can also lead some patients to become chronic.'

So if insight doesn't kill you, it can hinder your recovery. I started to wonder what was so good about it.

He finished and the others clapped. I shuffled in my seat. Part of me enjoyed the irony of witnessing an expert saying stupid things; part of me was plain angry.

'Aren't you applying an unsophisticated theory of knowledge to your understanding of insight?' I asked politely. 'How can you believe that psychiatrists are inevitably right and the patients, as you call them, must be wrong if they disagree? Philosophers have been trying to solve the question of what humans can really know for centuries. They haven't agreed yet. How can you be so sure your profession has a monopoly on insight?'

He responded with big words about cognitive deficits and the nature of mental illness and then restated his position that psychiatrists are right and patients who disagree with them are wrong. Instead of answering the question, he simply underlined it.

I left the meeting and walked past the dead scientists again. I smiled at them and asked under my breath, 'How was that for science, fellas?' I wondered if the dead men would ever be joined by someone who made great discoveries about 'psychiatric brain disease'. I couldn't see it, somehow.

A while later the Commission published a discussion paper by an American survivor activist called Tina Minkowitz that argued vehemently against force, followed by commentaries from lawyers and psychiatrists. On the morning of publication I talked on national radio about how we need a major rethink on compulsory treatment, how it happens too often, for too long and sometimes for the wrong reasons. People don't get adequate legal advocacy. Psychiatrists and lawyers need to reflect on their practice. The government should amend the law. And the public needs to stop over-estimating the violence of people with mental illness and under-estimating their competence to make decisions about their treatment.

I'd just put dinner on the table that night when the phone rang. A tight, angry voice said, 'I heard you on the radio this morning and I just want to say I completely disagree with everything you said.'

It was Norman, a member of a family organisation and the father of a young man diagnosed with mental illness who was 'treatment resistant' and on twenty-eight pills a day. I had come across parents like Norman before. They ulcerated with a grief that had turned to fury at a mental health system that had failed their children and left them to pick up the pieces. Their children were young or middle-aged adults, but to their parents they would always be fifteen.

'What kind of a testimony is it to free speech when people like you can get up and say such idiotic things? It's absolutely disgraceful to think you are getting paid taxpayers' dollars to spout such rubbish.'

I thought of thanking him for his opinion then putting the phone down but I was curious. 'Can you tell me what you objected to?'

He yelled, 'A person in your position saying things like that. You ought to be sacked.'

'Saying things like what?'

'You haven't got a shred of evidence.'

'That's not really true. We have lots of evidence that at the very least raise questions about compulsory treatment. And it's not just about evidence, it's mostly about values.'

'Well, your values are stuffed,' he barked. 'I went to a meeting of sixty of our members today and not one of them agreed with anything you had to say. They're furious.'

'What exactly are they furious about?'

'I'm going to ring the health minister to ask him to sack you.'

I tried my best to be polite to Norman, even telling him a joke or two to disarm his hatred. Nothing worked. The abuse kept coming.

'What I said was controversial but we want to stimulate debate on the issue. I don't have a monopoly on the truth, but nobody else does either. And this has always been a one-sided debate in the past. The views of the people this issue most affects have been silent.'

Norman didn't respond and I started to wind up the conversation. I told him I was coming to a conference in his city later in the week. 'I hope I don't get hung, drawn and quartered there,' I laughed. He didn't.

Two days later I met Norman at the conference. I shook his hand and smiled. He smiled back sheepishly. I found myself surrounded by a group of aging mothers of adults with mental illness. One, Isabel, pleaded with me, 'You don't understand how terrible it is for families.' Her old eyes watered and her friend Ngaire laid a hand on her arm.

Ngaire wagged her free forefinger at me, 'If it weren't for compulsory treatment my son would be dead. He gets sick as soon as he goes off his medication. Do you know he had a knife at my throat once because he thought I was going to poison him?'

Norman tapped me on the shoulder, 'My son will never recover. Never.'

'I know there are people who continue to experience mental health problems, but surely your sons and daughters can learn from their experience and live a worthwhile life. That's what I mean by recovery. It's not necessarily a cure.'

Isabel wiped her eyes with a used tissue. 'My son can't learn from his experience.'

'Neither can mine,' said Norman.

'I find that really hard to believe.'

'Your problem is that you don't meet the really bad ones,' said Isabel.

'Look, I've met plenty of people like your sons and daughters.'

Ngaire started getting angry. 'But you don't speak for them. We're the only ones that speak for them. You exclude them with all that recovery talk. You're doing very nicely, thank you very much, but you don't speak for my son. He likes being on his compulsory treatment order – it makes him feel safe.'

'Why does he need compulsory treatment to feel safe?'

'Because that's the only way we can get a decent service for him. As soon as he comes off the order, the services just fall away.'

I was starting to see that compulsion was Ngaire's lever for forcing the mental health system to provide an adequate service for her son. It wasn't necessarily about forcing her son to take medication at all. A compulsory treatment order was the ticket that allowed her son to jump the queue to get treatment. No wonder they liked it so much.

'But people should have the same access to services whether they're voluntary or not,' I said. 'It's a travesty to use compulsion as a means of getting an adequate service.'

Ngaire looked confused.

Norman leaned towards me. 'What you're saying is dangerous. My son's compulsory treatment order has been renewed this week. He always objects and if he starts hearing people like you on the radio, he'll just object even more.' He started to yell. 'And if he comes off his order, he'll probably die, and it'll be because of people like you!'

There were several of them now standing in front of me, their haunted faces glowing with anger. Part of me was still curious, part of me enjoyed the clash of ideas, but deep down I was starting to feel pummelled. 'It's time for me to go. We can continue this conversation another time if you want,' I said.

Ngaire invited me to a meeting to meet their sons and daughters. 'I'd really like to do that,' I said.

She said, 'We'll round them up for you.'

'I only want to meet them if they want to meet me, so please don't make it compulsory,' I laughed.

I returned to my hotel, put my feet up and turned on the radio in search of some distraction from compulsory treatment and the family lobby – music, light-hearted banter, even world poverty and impending ecological disaster would have been welcome. But instead I got Gwen, one of the family network members I had never met, who was being interviewed about compulsory treatment, in response to my statements on the radio.

She said in a cool controlled voice that there was too much reluctance to use compulsory treatment: 'Just last week a woman went to a psychiatric hospital. She told them she would kill herself if she didn't get help from them. They didn't admit her and she went on to commit suicide.'

Gwen didn't seem to understand that the woman who killed herself wanted a service. She didn't need a compulsory treatment order. If anything, the service needed a compulsory responsiveness order to ensure that the woman in distress at the door got the help she deserved.

Gwen started talking about me. 'She comes from the consumers' lobby which gives her a prejudiced view in the first place. She was a very surprising appointment.'

Interviewer: 'But don't you think consumers know what is best for them?'

Gwen: 'No, I don't. I think the families' voices are the ones that should be heard, and I say this for three reasons. One, the families do most of nursing. Two, they are the most in danger. And three, the families are not unbalanced; they have a record of having a good mind – they can be advocates, they can understand the system, read psychiatric papers and books, and keep on top of things. I think it's the families that are likely to know better than someone who has a history of recurring mental disorder and whose views are highly coloured by just their personal experience.'

Later I wondered why I didn't feel infuriated by Gwen's infantilising caricature of mad people, or Norman's accusations, or the way Isabel and Ngaire had written off their sons. I guess it's because I didn't give their opinions much credibility, but more than that, I could also see the unresolved pain they were in. They reminded me of fish trapped in a net, flapping so much they couldn't see the hole they could release themselves through.

←———→

Several weeks later a work acquaintance rang me. She'd had an unnerving phone call from Norman, who told her he wanted to string me up and crucify me the way Jesus was two thousand years ago. I joked that Norman must be worried I'm right because most people think Jesus was, but I was a little spooked. A few months later I went with a group of other Mental Health Commission people to a conference in Norman's home city. At the opening reception Norman told one of my fellow commissioners that he would like to load stones in my pockets and throw me off a wharf – the world would be better off without me. Later that evening he told a staff member he would like to pour oil at my feet and set light to me. To another colleague he said he would like me to be burnt at the stake. By now I was starting to feel very spooked.

The other commissioners called the police, who said they couldn't do anything because Norman hadn't made the threats directly to me. They then complained to the chairs of two voluntary committees he sat on. Norman was stood down from those committees and sent the Commission a short grudging apology. I knew that his threatening talk came from distress so deep he couldn't reach the bottom of it. I didn't want to add to his distress but he needed a clear message to keep his violent fantasies to himself.

Someone once told me that the family movement in mental health is more psychiatric than the psychiatrists. They are changing but some still want more hospitals, more drugs and more compulsory treatment. They are full of pessimism and paternalism and believe the recovery approach gives false hope. But the problem is not false hope – it is far more pernicious than that. In the words of one mad activist, these families are suffering from false hopelessness.

Norman illustrated this well when he published an opinion piece around the time he was openly fantasising about my death. After mentioning the sadness of being a parent of adult an son who could not look after himself, he quoted from the start of a book, *Surviving Schizophrenia*, by an American psychiatrist called E Fuller Torrey, who has just told a woman that her daughter has schizophrenia. 'Oh my God, anything but that,' she replied. 'Why couldn't she have had leukaemia or some other disease instead?'

'But if she had leukaemia, she might die,' Torrey pointed out.

The woman looked sadly down at the floor and said softly, 'I would still prefer that my daughter had leukaemia.'

Torrey went on to say: 'Schizophrenia is a cruel disease. The lives of those affected are often chronicles of restricted experiences, muted emotions and unfulfilled expectations. It leads to a twilight existence.' According to Torrey and the mother who wished her daughter had leukaemia, people with schizophrenia are deeply diminished human beings. Some of the worst stigma comes not from hostile strangers but from grieving families and deficits-based psychiatrists.

←——————→

In my role as a Commissioner I joined the New Zealand delegation to the United Nations in New York to negotiate the drafting of a new convention on the rights of people with disabilities, which included people with 'psychiatric disabilities'. This was an opportunity among other things to change the international position on force. No previous

UN human rights conventions had dealt specifically with this issue for people with mental illness. The UN had come up with a less binding set of principles on the treatment of people with mental illness in 1991 which endorsed the use of compulsory treatment, seclusion and mechanical restraints if it was done in accordance with the law of the country. We were not happy with these principles.

We met in a curved amphitheatre of a room in the United Nations building to consider the first draft of the convention. The delegates from the member states sat in alphabetical order and the representatives from non-government organisations sat at one side. Among them were a vocal handful of survivor activists determined to ensure that the convention banned the use of force. The assembled were essentially an editorial committee of two hundred. They spent several days picking through the draft convention clause by clause while someone typed and retyped, sometimes many times over, the proposed changes on an electronic screen. The member state representatives took turns to enunciate their positions; they delivered their jibes and insults according to the rules of international diplomacy, through fake flattery and other forms of elaborate double-speak. The real meetings took place to the side, in the UN corridors and embassy offices where people schemed, lobbied and traded deals to support each other on different articles of the convention.

One of the key articles, for the mad people among us and our supporters, was 'Liberty and Security of the Person'. The draft article stated that deprivation of liberty shall in no case be based on disability. Some member states argued that this must be altered because they feared their country's compulsory treatment and detention laws would contravene the convention. Of course, this was precisely what the survivor activists and our allies wanted. The survivor representatives staunchly defended the wording of the article in the main meeting while others of us spoke, lobbied and made deals in the side meetings.

Thanks to the dogged determination of the survivor activists and their ability to negotiate support for their position, the wording of Article 14 survived into the final document which was passed by the General Assembly at the end of 2006. Afterwards the office of the United Nations High Commissioner for Human Rights wrote a commentary on Article 14 and concluded that legislation that empowers the state to compulsorily detain people on the basis of disability must be abolished. The United Nations special rapporteur on torture wrote that the acceptance of involuntary treatment and involuntary confinement ran counter to the provisions of the UN Convention on the Rights of Persons with Disabilities. Member states so far appear to have been silent on this issue.

——————

The recovery philosophy's cornerstones of self-determination, connection to our communities and social justice is a direct challenge to the use of compulsory interventions, particularly if they are not applied on an equal basis with other citizens. It's also a direct challenge to the overwhelming dominance of medical interventions in mental health services today. People who use mental health services can virtually guarantee that they will be prescribed psychiatric drugs. A minority will be offered psychotherapy, support for education and employment, or housing of their choice. A tiny minority will have access to peer support and recovery education. Even those who feel helped by medication say that most of their problems are their loss of personhood as well as the loss of the social and economic opportunities which privileged citizens take for granted. But most of the resources for mental health systems in the western world still go into clinical services and drugs, and into hospital beds that cost more per night than the executive suite in a five-star hotel.

Over my years at the Commission I grew more concerned about the mental health system's over-reliance on psychiatric drugs, which is fed by a number of mutually reinforcing dynamics – a belief that the drugs are the most potent eradicator of symptoms, their quick and easy delivery, and the symbiotic power of the psychiatry and the drug companies. The trouble is that the drugs are like non-renewable energy: they are convenient, they pollute and they generate enormous wealth. The mental health system needs to develop and channel many more clean, renewable resources for recovery, such as human kindness, healing environments, peer support, and social and economic justice.

While doctors continue to prescribe psychiatric drugs at increasing rates, more and more experts and people who use these drugs have raised the alarm. I was in an interesting position, reading their critiques: although I had tossed out my anti-psychotics and mood stabilisers many years earlier, I was still taking anti-depressants. When I started taking the anti-depressants twenty years earlier, it felt as though a magician had appeared out of a puff of smoke and conjured the key to the door that got me out of mental health services. It turned out that much of this was probably the placebo effect and that the magician was in me more than in the pill. Nevertheless, from day one I had been ambivalent about the anti-depressants: the side-effects annoyed me, I worried about their long-term effects and I wondered if I'd still be on them if I'd been given the help I really needed twenty years earlier. In the early years my attempts to reduce or withdraw from them failed so I accepted their place in my life. Later I was reluctant to try life without them at a time when I was accumulating work and family responsibilities for my children Ruby, Felix and Rupert.

While I was at the Commission I went on a new type of anti-depressant. Every time life got rough over the next few years the psychiatrist suggested a dose increase until I reached the maximum dose without any extra benefits and with more side-effects. At the same time I started reading expert critiques of the use of drugs in psychiatry which claimed that the drugs were prescribed too often and for too long and that psychiatry was in denial about their weak benefits and the substantial harm they can do.

One psychiatrist analysed all the long-term studies that had been done on outcomes for people diagnosed with schizophrenia from the 1880s to the 1990s. He discovered that outcomes hadn't improved since psychiatric drugs became the mainstay of treatment in the 1950s. Over the century there were some fluctuations in recovery rates from schizophrenia and these were correlated with fluctuations in the labour market. His work suggested that having a job was more important for recovery than taking a pill. Other experts claimed that long-term studies showed that people diagnosed with schizophrenia on little or no anti-psychotics may do better than people on more sustained or higher doses. Others claimed that anti-depressants were barely more effective than a placebo, after including in their analysis the research the drug companies didn't publish because it didn't favour their products.

Reading about the outcomes was sobering but understanding more about what the drugs do to our bodies was scary. The old anti-psychotics that came on the market in the 1950s caused disfiguring involuntary muscle movements in many who had been on them for a long time. The new anti-psychotics, introduced in the 1990s, were marketed as the great solution to the plague of side-effects in the older drugs, though at least one drug company knew beforehand that they could cause life-shortening diabetes-related illnesses. These wonder drugs contribute to the mortality rate of mad people, who die up to twenty-five years younger than average. Of course, I didn't have to read about the damage the drugs do. I saw it all around me in some of my peers: the light had gone from their eyes, the spring had gone from their step, they were emotionally blunted, they were ill and overweight, and many died before their time.

I had always been told that the drugs I was on corrected a chemical imbalance, the way insulin does with diabetes. It turns out that this analogy is somewhere between disingenuous and naive. When scientists discovered that diabetes was caused by insulin deficiency they looked for a substitute. But it happened the other way around with psychiatric drugs. All of the main drug groups were discovered by serendipity and theories about the nature of the chemical imbalance they were correcting were inferred, often incorrectly, from the brain changes the drugs created. More than this, some experts wrote that the drugs do not correct a chemical imbalance at all but *create* a chemical imbalance instead, by sedating or stimulating the brain in non-specific ways that may reduce the experience of symptoms but also create cognitive impairments. They also suggested that over time the brain may 'overcompensate' for the drug-induced chemical imbalances, making it supersensitive to developing future depression or psychosis, and setting people up for relapse when they stop taking the drug.

Some of the critics' findings are speculative and many are controversial. When I raised these issues with psychiatrists I got a variety of responses. Most had not read the critical literature because they didn't graze far beyond their usual journals. Some had little more grasp of the science than I did. Some said things like, 'Yes, the drugs are horrible but what else have I got to offer desperate people?' and, 'Yes, some of the drugs are life-shortening but I have patients who swear by them after years in the wilderness.' Others just got prickly and gave me patronising advice on keeping my mouth shut.

Finally I decided to come off the last of my drugs, an anti-depressant with notorious withdrawal effects. With bold optimism, I reduced them over three weeks with no problems until I got down to the smallest dose, when things started to get uncomfortable. The psychiatrist prescribed me a small dose of a similar anti-depressant that didn't have withdrawal effects to help smooth out the transition. Over the next few days I paced. I roared. I threw things. My turmoil was so intense that I nearly bashed my head against the wall and began to have suicidal thoughts so I could end the hell I was in. I went back on a minimal dose of my usual anti-depressant, bought a microgram scale, emptied the granules from the capsules into a medicine jar, weighed them every morning and reduced the dosage slightly every three weeks. It took nearly two years.

Life without the drugs is just the same as life with them, minus the side-effects.

←———→

My role at the Mental Health Commission was the closest I'll ever get to the seat of state power. I was a reluctant bureaucrat so I lined my beige office with kitsch ornaments, bad-taste souvenirs and incriminating memorabilia from psychiatric hospitals to cast off the spell of public-sector sobriety. While I knew that in my role I needed to be mindful of all stakeholders, my big commitment was to advance the interests of people who experience madness. We were the only group, apart from families, who did not have a power base in professional associations, academic departments, the public service and mental health services. I believed that the Mental Health Commission was in a good position to help fill that gap, so I frequently nudged the boundaries and stuck my head out for mad people.

Many of my mad colleagues appreciated it but some professional groups, particularly the psychiatrists and nurses, did not. I sat at many meetings with leading managers and professionals in the mental health system. They talked constantly about tight budgets, risk management, lack of beds, staff complaints, critical incidents and unreasonable accountabilities. These things needed to be considered but I didn't once hear them talk about the impact of their decisions on the people who came to their services in distress. I didn't once hear them ask who were they really doing their jobs for – their bosses, their political masters or the people who come to their door? They never asked if the services they led helped or harmed people, or if the billions of dollars spent on mental health services would be better used in a different way. They were not bad people and their jobs were not easy, but they reminded me of mole-like creatures busily digging around in the undergrowth while a great forest of ethical, compassionate and transformative openings towered above them.

In one such meeting at the Mental Health Commission, a disgruntled psychiatrist issued a catalogue of complaints. 'As clinicians, we feel disenfranchised by the Commission. You've been captured by the service user lobby. In fact, you're a service user commission. You're not a Mental Health Commission any more.'

I sat there pondering one of the biggest back-handed compliments I have ever received. I was stunned that mad people had the power to make psychiatrists feel disenfranchised. In one way, we were making real progress – mental health professionals were conceding that their two-hundred-year power cartel was breaking down. In another way, I felt nervous about groups whose power has been challenged because they will do everything they can to claim their power back. And in a third way, I wasn't as sure as the psychiatrist that power is a finite resource that needs to be defended and pillaged, as land or food are when they are in short supply. With all this going through my mind, I didn't know how to respond to him. He was in no mood for reflective discussion so I remained silent.

The psychiatrist got his way in the end. After my time the Commission reverted to answering the call of the more powerful stakeholder groups and my mad colleagues once again felt disenfranchised. And I was left wondering if I had mishandled the politics of juggling different stakeholder interests, or if I had rightly stood my ground in asserting the interests of the most important and most powerless stakeholder of them all.

←——————→

The history of psychiatry is like a concerto. Every historical phase or movement differs but they are all variations on a theme. Psychiatry has always been both an agent of coercion and of freedom. The dark music of coercion has dominated its history, particularly in institutional and publicly funded psychiatry, but the tones of freedom break through now and then – when Philippe Pinel took the chains off the asylum inmates, when the early asylum superintendents promoted kindness and work, when social psychiatry developed community based services and when the mad movement advocated recovery, freedom and equality. The recovery revolution is unfinished. Janet and the millions of others in her position around the world still do not have reliable access to holistic services that treat them with respect, give them hope, value their freedom and promote their participation in society. Like all the other liberation efforts in the history of psychiatry there is a real risk that the recovery revolution will remain unfinished unless some fundamental shifts take place.

Imagine a world where discriminatory attitudes to madness are not tolerated, whether these attitudes come in the form of primitive fears about axe murderers or clever theories about brain disease. Instead, madness is seen as a profoundly disruptive crisis of being, from which value and meaning can be derived – an experience that adds to our humanity rather than diminishes it.

Imagine services that are run like democracies, with power coming from the bottom up. Mad people are the drivers of their own recovery and mental health workers support them from the passenger seat. Mad people also lead in the development and delivery of services – as politicians, bureaucrats, CEOs, psychiatrists, team leaders, peer workers and the rest. Madness is seen as a qualification, not something to be kept in the closet.

Imagine if all or most hospital services were replaced with community and home based services. People in crisis have easy access to small intimate places where safety is ensured by human contact rather than by locks and keys. Services are viewed as sets of relationships rather than sets of buildings.

Imagine a world where services heal the trauma that contributes to madness and strive to improve the whole of people's lives, without obsessing over their 'symptoms'. Biological treatments compete on the menu with peer support, recovery education, housing support, education and employment support, advocacy and talking therapies – which are all as available to people as the drugs are now.

Imagine the day when governments and the mental health system publicly acknowledge the harm psychiatry has done over the last two hundred years to mad people, their families and even to professionals. This liberates mental health services to become oases of healing rather than agents of control.

Imagine a world where discriminatory mental health legislation is replaced with generic legislation that authorises the conditions for interventions without consent on an equal basis for all health consumers. Compulsory interventions are as rare in mental health services as they are in other health services. The insanity defence has been abolished and mad people who commit crimes are dealt with in a humane, rehabilitation oriented criminal justice system that provides tailored responses to the multitude of factors that interfere with human responsibility.

Imagine governments running anti-discrimination and social inclusion programmes with the same urgency they put into smoking and road deaths. These programmes change attitudes, behaviour and structural discrimination using a human rights approach and the visible leadership of mad people.

Imagine a world where governments put as much effort into growing wellbeing as they do to growing wealth. They commit to long-term strategies for reducing childhood trauma, income inequality and other social ills that increase people's chances of landing in the mental health system in the first place.

There are many people who do not want all these changes or believe they are possible. They are afraid. Traditional professionals are afraid of losing power, being shown up or becoming less relevant. Communities are afraid of public disorder. Families are afraid of losing their loved one. Sometimes even mad people are afraid of freedom and the responsibilities of full citizenship. They all know in their own ways that something is profoundly awry with human responses to madness. But courage and imagination – the qualities we need most to make the world a better place – have deserted them.

←———→

As a young woman I looked back on my work after doing it for two years and felt impatient because nothing had changed. Later I thought we can only meaningfully assess change in ten-year blocks. I am now at a point where I doubt if many of these changes will happen in my lifetime. Sometimes I think I backed the wrong movement. If I had dedicated my life to gay rights, my efforts would have been rewarded by the decriminalisation of gay sex, marriage equality for gay people and a massive shift in people's attitudes. In comparison, the rights of mad people have made very modest gains over the last few decades. But as long as we live in societies that value freedom and equality there is hope.

Our time is yet to come.

EPILOGUE:

THE WAY IT COULD HAVE BEEN

I'm locked inside a black box.

I've hidden the blackness all my life hoping there is a purpose to everything. I've painted the walls with false windows and a view of a grand universe. I've drawn fake pictures of a life worth living. I've made a pretend door that leads into a promising future.

Now all the decorations are gone. The bare boards have closed in on me with the terrible truth that life is a sham. It started when I couldn't see the point in going to my university lectures. Then I couldn't bring myself to see my friends. Now I don't see the point in being alive.

I've been in bed for days with my door shut and the curtains drawn. My whole being is screaming at the terrible truth I've discovered. I struggle to put a thought or a sentence together. I can't talk. I can barely move. My chest burns and I rasp with shallow breathing. Sleep comes in broken snatches.

I wake. It must be daytime because light is seeping through the gap in the curtains. I stare at the clock and slowly realise the day and the time. With enormous effort I leave my bed and crawl down the road to my next appointment with Dr L'Estrange. I crouch in front of him like a snapped stem. He brings his chair next to mine, places his broad hand on my bent back and asks me to breathe deeply and slowly like him. 'We're here to help you find your way out of the dark place you are in.' He asks me if I want to stay at a crisis house run by people who have recovered from distressing experiences similar to mine. He could visit me there. I nod and he makes the phone call.

Dr L'Estrange goes to get Angela, the peer support worker at Student Health. She takes me home, helps me pack my belongings and drives me to an ordinary looking house called the Guesthouse. A large woman in a flowing dress called Cheryl answers the door. 'Welcome, Mary. Let me take your bag and I'll show you to your room.' It's a sunny room with a firm double bed, an armchair, a poster about recovery on the wall and a small ensuite bathroom. I crawl onto the bed. Cheryl puts the bag down beside me and covers me with a rug. 'What can we do to make you more comfortable?' she says. I can't think of a reply.

'You're safe here,' she says. 'Most of the people who work here have been where you are right now and we've all come through it.'

A flicker of light passes through my black box.

Cheryl tells me they are here to listen if I want to talk. I just need to ring the bell if I need anything. I can get snacks and drinks from the kitchen at any time. They will bring meals up to me if I can't get out of bed. I can join the others in the lounge. I can take part in the peer-led support and learning groups. There is a video and book library. They can organise a massage or a chaplain or a doctor's appointment. If I want to leave the house in the next few days, someone will come with me.

'Why do you bother? It's over for me,' I whisper.

'Because I thought it was over for me once. I thought I was in my own self-made grave but it turned out to be a cocoon instead.'

But I can't see any butterflies waiting to be born in my black box.

I wake in the middle of the night, filled with foreboding. I jerk with the feeling of electric shocks going through me every time I have a thought. Between jerks I feel smouldering inside my chest. I start to wail at the terror of my existence.

The person on the night shift comes in. 'Hey, what's happening for you?' she says.

'I'm freaking out.'

Alice turns on my bedside light and brings a chair up to my bed. 'Is it something you can talk about?' she asks. I keep wailing. My terror is too huge to contain in words; it occupies the whole landscape of my being. Alice puts a calming hand on my shoulder and gradually anchors me back to safety.

The next morning Dr L'Estrange comes to visit me. He asks me how did I sleep, have I eaten, do I still feel suicidal, can I reach out to people, do I need a letter from him for the university. Then he asks if I am able to talk about the pain I'm in. I tell him about the black box and my devastating discovery that life is a sham.

'Your pain is real,' he says. 'You're fighting for the survival of your being.' He tells me about the hero's journey archetype that reveals the pattern in all human lives and stories. The hero leaves the world they trust and enters an unknown world where they lose their way. They fall into a dark place where they fight their dragons and demons. 'You are in that dark place now,' he says. But then the hero finds a passage out of the dark place and, although scarred, has survived and learnt from the experience. The hero makes a long and challenging journey back to the world they know with new knowledge and insights.

'But there's no passage out for me.'

'The deeper you go into the dark place, the harder it is to find – but you will find it.'

Dr L'Estrange starts to talk to me about medications. He explains they could help lift my mood and energy levels but they also have a lot of side-effects, sometimes serious ones. He asks me to think about anti-depressants and suggests I take something to help my sleep for a week or two. He says even if the drugs do work well they just provide a platform for my recovery – the rest of it is dependent on me, having people around who believe in me, and the right support and opportunities to find my place in the world. But right now I just need to take shelter from the storm, he says.

I'm not so sure I believe Dr L'Estrange but I feel that he has stopped me falling and given me a ledge to cling on to.

Later I'm lying on my bed when a stylish middle-aged woman with blonde hair and buck teeth comes to see me. 'Hi, Mary, my name's Pat. I'm a peer worker here. Would you like to come to our peer support and learning group?'

She gently leads me down the stairs to one of the living rooms. Pat introduces me to Ruth, Joy, Darren and Monique and hands out some flip-chart paper and art materials. She shows us the group ground rules on the wall. We can take part as much or as little as we like, most of the wisdom and knowledge is within the group, we are all equals and we don't judge other people's realities. She then introduces an activity called 'Doom to Zoom' and asks us to fold our paper in three. On the left third she asks us to draw or write an expression of how we feel when life is really bad. On the right third she asks us to do the same for how we feel when life is really good again.

On the left side of my paper I draw a long tunnel. I've just been whooshed down the tunnel from the everyday world to my private hell. I'm lying at the end of the tunnel with a butcher's meat cleaver embedded in my heart; it has split me in half from top to bottom. On the right hand side my body is all stitched up and I'm throwing the meat cleaver over a cliff into the sea.

Pat calls us back to the circle and brings her own drawing with her. Ruth starts to talk about hers in a quiet voice. 'That's me when my thoughts get all jumbled;' she says, pointing to a pile of knotted string glued to her paper. Ruth is around my age with brown, shoulder-length hair and a frightened face. Then she points to a flower shape glued to the other side of the paper, made from the same kind of string.

'Wow – that's great,' says Pat. We all murmur in agreement. Ruth looks a little less scared.

Next in the circle is Joy. She is thin and pale with straight red hair clipped back at the temples. She wears blue plastic glasses and tidy conservative clothes, and clutches a blank sheet of paper. Joy doesn't respond – not even a flicker of a word or a movement. She's a breathing statue.

Pat asks Joy if she feels like talking or just saying silent. Joy says nothing. Ruth touches Joy above her elbow.

'I've lost my mind,' Joy whispers.

'Let me find it for you,' says a young man called Darren with a round face and curly hair. 'I lost my mind too and I found it under this sofa.' He sweeps his hands underneath. 'Here it is,' he says. He smiles as he gathers Joy's invisible mind in his palms and places it on her lap. People start laughing and a thin smile passes over Joy's lips.

'Mary, do you feel like talking about your pictures?' says Pat.

'That's me cut off and cut open here, and that's me stitched up and throwing away the meat cleaver over there,' I mumble, looking at the floor.

Monique says that my picture reminds her of hers. In the first one she's locked in a cage harming herself with a knife, but in the second picture she has used the knife to pick the lock. That starts a discussion about how the things that harm us can also heal us if we learn to use them differently.

At the end Pat talks about her own pictures – the first, a pile of jumbled jigsaw pieces with letters on them and the second, the completed jigsaw with 'A life worth living' written on it. 'For me a life worth living was always there but when I crashed the pieces all fell apart and I had to learn to put them back together again.' Pat asks if we want to work on the middle section tomorrow and share our ideas on what helps us to get from the first picture to the second one. Some people nod and Cheryl comes in to say lunch is ready.

I start to go up the stairs to my room. Darren and Monique ask me to come to lunch with them. Part of me wants to escape but I turn around and go with them to the dining room. It's a warm room with a long wooden table in it that seats about ten people. Cheryl and Pat sit down with us to eat chicken pie and salad. I gag on my food and leave it on the plate. Cheryl offers me a smoothie. I take it back to my room and sip it slowly through a straw.

Later Pat knocks on my door and comes into my room. I'm lying curled up on top of my bed. 'How are you getting on, Mary?'

'No good.'

'Is it hard to be with people at the moment?'

'Yeah. I'm like a stone. I'm heavy. I sink. No one can see into me. I can't express myself.'

Pat looks at me and says, 'It's hard to live with those sorts of feelings but they will ease.'

'I can't see it.'

'Is it better for you to be alone or with others?'

'Alone. I've got no skin.'

'Do you want the rug over you?'

'Yes please.'

Pat pulls the rug over my body and says she will come and say hi before she leaves for the day. I bury myself in under the rug thinking maybe Pat understands, maybe she can help me put my own jigsaw puzzle back together again.

The next morning Pat comes and asks me if I want to come to the peer support and learning group.

'I've got nothing to say.'

'You don't have to say anything.'

Pat leads me down the stairs again to the living room. She starts up a discussion about how we can help to shift ourselves from feeling really bad to feeling good again. Ruth says she doesn't know how to turn her tangle into a flower. Darren wants to stop using alcohol and drugs. Monique wants to find a job so she can pay off her debts.

I look at my picture of me and the meat cleaver and the blank bit in the middle looks like a chasm the size of Asia. 'I don't know how to get across the page,' I whisper.

'No one does at the start,' Pat says. 'If they did they would be there already. Think about one small step you can take today and don't try to map the whole journey.'

I write at the top of the middle section, 'I am the hero of my own journey looking for a pathway across this page' in small faint handwriting.

Pat tells me I've come a long way in two days.

The next day my parents drive two hundred miles to visit me. I see them walking up the path towards the Guesthouse. My father's hair is whiter than ever. He's wearing a leather zip-up jacket and beige trousers. My mother's big owly glasses flash in the light, her skirt swishes and she's wearing a patterned satin scarf. Cheryl opens the door and welcomes them. She tells them I am in a bad way but I am strong and will get through it. They look relieved. She brings them up to my room and we talk about what's happening to me.

Dr L'Estrange and Pat arrive to see us. My parents are worried raw; my mother gets loud and demanding and my father shelters in rationality and the occasional joke. Pat and Dr L'Estrange listen carefully to their worries and eventually share a joke about the occupational hazard of parental anxiety. Dr L'Estrange reassures us all that I will recover and goes through all the services and supports they are connecting me to. Pat says that the best my parents can do for me is to respect my struggle even when they don't understand it, to keep believing in me, and to hold the hope when I have lost it. She then gives them a sheet of paper with information for families and suggests they go to a family support service in their own town.

As Dr L'Estrange and Pat walk out of the room my mother is calm. 'I feel so much better – you're in good hands,' she says. My father nods and puts his arm around her shoulder.

I stay for two weeks at the Guesthouse. Every day I go to the peer support and learning group and every day I add another sentence to the page. We discuss the meaning of our experiences and learn to see them as breakthroughs rather than just breakdowns. Pat introduces us to mindfulness, ways to change our thinking patterns and ways to prevent going into crisis. Ruth, Monique and I become friends. Slowly, the lid to my black box opens.

Dr L'Estrange comes to see me the day I leave and Pat joins us.

'You're looking better,' he says. 'What helped you?'

'People believing in me, I guess, and seeing people who work here say they have been through similar experiences and are doing OK.'

Pat and Dr L'Estrange help me to sort out the assistance I need. They tell me about a supported education service at the university where I can get help with doing my study and negotiating with my lecturers and the university system. One of the peer support workers from Student Health will get in touch with me in the next two days. Pat hands me a PeerZone postcard and tells me they are peer-led workshops that support people to lead their own recovery.

Dr L'Estrange asks me if I have thought about the anti-depressants.

I tell him I want to do it without them.

'Are you ready to go home?' he asks.

Cheryl helps me pack my stuff and gives me some information on local services and community resources. We say our goodbyes. As I walk out the front door I start to feel lost and scared. Life stands over me like a Himalayan mountain but I know the Guesthouse has given me some equipment to continue the big climb.

The next day Angela the peer support worker at Student Health comes to see me at my flat. I tell her I feel weak and wobbly, like a foal with buckled legs. She tells me what other people in my situation have found useful – things like good sleep, staying away from drink and drugs, finding the balance between doing too little and too much, and being gentle on myself.

Angela takes me down to the Education Support office to see David. I've missed a whole lot of assignments. He takes all the details and says he will let my lecturers know and help me negotiate some extensions with them. He then tells me about their mentoring service where someone can help me organise my study.

The next week I go to my first PeerZone workshop for students who experience mental distress. Warren, one of the peer workers at Student Health, is the facilitator. I spot Ruth from the Guesthouse and go and sit with her. 'How are you?' she asks.

'Still pretty crap sometimes.'

'Yeah, same here.'

Warren welcomes us to the group and we introduce ourselves. He tells us about PeerZone and what we can expect to get out of it. 'It will help you in three ways,' he said. 'First, major mental distress like we've all had derails your identity and life narrative. Our lives feel like a train wreck. PeerZone is a place where we can start to build a new and more positive picture of ourselves and sort out how we can get back on the rails of life. Does that make sense to you?'

Everyone nods.

'The second thing that PeerZone does is that we introduce some practical tools to help you get on with the life you want – things like life planning, challenging negative thoughts, ways to make personal change easier, ways to manage money when you don't have much, that sort of thing. We all know how to do a lot of that practical stuff but mental distress takes us to a whole new level because it trumps the coping skills we have. So we need to learn new ones. It's a bit like me and my boat. I could sail it fine on nice calm days but the first time I sailed it in a storm the bloody thing capsized. I had to really learn how to sail in rough conditions. It's the same with us.'

'We've already done some of the stuff you're talking about at the Guesthouse,' I say.

'That's great,' said Warren. 'This is not a classroom where the teacher stands at the front and stuffs all the students with knowledge. I'm just here to provide a fun and safe structure to make sure we can all share the knowledge and wisdom we bring to this group. So if you know stuff that you think might work for others, tell us about it.'

'Maybe Ruth and I could tell you about the "Doom to Zoom" activity we did,' I say.

'Bring it as a well-being tool and we'll make some time at the beginning of the next workshop.'

Warren then explains the third way PeerZone can help. 'Distress totally isolates us. There's only room for one. And when we return to the ordinary world others don't always understand what we've been through. We need each other for the return journey and we're going to encourage you to make contact outside the workshops as well, if you want that.'

Over the weeks I make some good friends at the PeerZone workshops and I start to feel strong again. I pass all my exams and never use mental health services again.

ACKNOWLEDGEMENTS

Madness Made Me took me over ten years to write. The writing itself was fun but I struggled to find time and create a structure for the book. I went to several creative writing courses to kick-start another phase of writing. My tutors Norman Bilbrough, Renee, Harry Ricketts and my mentor Chris Else all encouraged me to keep going. Stephen Stratford edited the manuscript and gave some valuable advice. My mother Clare O'Hagan, my partner Sara McCook Weir, my daughter Ruby Porter and my friends Zoe Truell and Nicola Tod read and proofed drafts and offered their comments and corrections. Mary Egan Publishing prepared the manuscript for publication and George Connor designed the cover. I also want to acknowledge two song lyrics I quote: *Bright Eyes* written by Mike Batt and *Frenzy* written by Tim Finn and Eddie Rayner. All these people and more helped to shape this book but I want to make a special acknowledgement to my partner Sara for being such a tenacious midwife throughout the long gestation and birth of this book.